LEGAL PATH SERIES®

CRIMINAL PROCEDURE

Keyed To

Dressler
2nd Edition

ALSO AVAILABLE IN THIS SERIES:

Civil Procedure keyed to: Friedenthal, 9th Ed
Civil Procedure keyed to: Yeazell, 6th Ed
Civil Procedure keyed to: Hazard, 9th Ed
Contracts keyed to: Farnsworth, 6th Ed
Criminal Law keyed to: Kadish, 7th Ed
Criminal Law keyed to: Dressler, 3rd Ed
Criminal Procedure keyed to: Kamisar, 11th Ed
Criminal Procedure keyed to: Saltzburg, 7th
Criminal Procedure keyed to: Dressler, 2nd Ed
Constitutional Law keyed to: Chemerinsky, 2nd Ed
Constitutional Law keyed to: Stone, 5th Ed
Constitutional Law keyed to: Sullivan, 15th Ed
Corporations keyed to: Hamilton, 9th Ed
Corporations keyed to: Eisenberg, 9th Ed
Evidence keyed to: Mueller, 5th Ed
Evidence keyed to: Waltz & Park, 10th Ed
Property keyed to: Dukeminier, 5th Ed
Torts keyed to Epstein, 8th Ed
Torts keyed to Prosser, 11th Ed
Torts keyed to Vetri, 3rd Ed

LEGAL PATH SERIES®

CRIMINAL PROCEDURE

First Edition

David Rosenberg, Esq.

Harvard Law School

Mclaren Legal Publishers LLC

New York

ISBN 0-9779855-7-1

Published by
Mclaren Legal Publishers LLC
136 West 21 Street, 8th Floor
New York, NY 10011

www.mclarenpublishing.com
Email: contact@mclarenpublishing.com

Printed in the United States of America

HOW TO USE THIS BOOK

This law school study aid is a "keyed" book. It summarizes all of the major cases in the law text book to which it is linked and in the order those cases are printed in the casebook. Our cases are presented in the IRAC format (Issue, Rule, Analysis and Conclusion). Each case uses a text symbol preceding the Issue, Rule, Analysis and Conclusion of the case referenced. The material that follows provides additional detail.

"Repetition is the Mother of Learning"

Throughout each case, many of the key Black Letter law and/or Issues are repeated. You may see the same legal conclusion repeated in the Issue, Rule, Analysis and/or Conclusion. This was done intentionally. All too often, the most important concepts in law school are mentioned only once by a law professor in a lecture hall. However, more often than not, what is mentioned the least is what is tested the most. We feel the more you see (and read) exactly what is important, the more likely you will be to remember it. Recalling key legal points quickly is the key to the successful application of those same rules on an exam. This *is* the difference between an "A" and a "C" for the course.

"All of what you need, none of what you don't"

Our law school study guides give you exactly what you need to understand the key principles of the case, including the sometimes elusive Black Letter law. We are not a replacement for an in depth legal analysis of the subject matter covered; however, we do present what is absolutely critical in a very concise format.

"Do it right in the beginning; it'll be easier in the end"

You may notice that the issues for each case are very specific. They are presented to you as accurately as we can print them. However, be mindful that there may be slight variations in their interpretation from lecture hall to lecture hall. With that in mind, our experience has taught us that if you do the labor-intensive, hard work in the beginning of the course and parse out the specific issue(s), rule(s) and conclusion, the analysis will be easier to formulate and write. It is the analysis of a case that separates the A, B and C grades on an exam (trust me).

"Who's the Plaintiff, who's the Defendant?"

You may notice that in some cases, a case title lists the plaintiff v. defendant in one order but the facts list the parties in the opposite order or may refer to the plaintiff/defendant as the petitioner/respondent/appellant/appellee. This is usually seen, for example, when one party is appealing to a higher court or where various counterclaims and cross-claims are asserted by the parties. When you see the parties change in the facts, keep the procedural history (and the parties) of the case organized in your mind and don't get confused.

Abbreviations used in this book

I This symbol "I" stands for "Issue" using the IRAC method of case analysis. What follows is the issue of the case.

R This symbol "R" stands for "Rule" using the IRAC method of case analysis. What follows is the rule or black letter law of the case.

A This symbol "A" stands for "Analysis" using the IRAC method of case analysis. What follows is the Analysis of the case.

C This symbol "C" stands for "Conclusion" using the IRAC method of case analysis. What follows is the conclusion of the case.

* Use of the word "his" in this book is gender neutral and is meant to encompass both "his" and "her."

ALPHABETICAL TABLE OF CASES

Powell v. Alabama

287 U.S. 45 (1932)

FACTS

Three (3) cases were argued together and submitted for decision as one case. The petitioners, hereinafter referred to as defendants, are African Americans charged with the crime of rape, committed upon the persons of two white girls. The crime is said to have been committed on March 25, 1931. The record shows that on the day when the offense is said to have been committed, these defendants, together with a number of other African Americans, were upon a freight train on its way through Alabama. On the same train were seven white boys and the two white girls. A fight took place between the African Americans and the white boys, in the course of which the white boys, with the exception of one named Gilley, were thrown off the train. A message was sent ahead, reporting the fight and asking that every African American be gotten off the train. The participants in the fight, and the two girls, were in an open gondola car. The two girls testified that each of them was assaulted by six different African Americans in turn, and they identified the seven defendants as having been among the number. None of the white boys was called to testify, with the exception of Gilley, who was called in rebuttal. The indictment was returned in a state court of first instance on March 31, and the record recites that on the same day the defendants were arraigned and entered pleas of not guilty. There is a further recital to the effect that upon the arraignment they were represented by counsel. But no counsel had been employed, and aside from a statement made by the trial judge several days later during a colloquy immediately preceding the trial, the record does not disclose when, or under what circumstances, an appointment of counsel was made, or who was appointed. During the colloquy referred to, the trial judge, in response to a question, said that he had appointed all the members of the bar for the purpose of arraigning the defendants and then of course anticipated that the members of the bar would continue to help the defendants if no counsel appeared. Upon the argument here both sides accepted that as a correct statement of the facts concerning the matter. There was a severance upon the request of the state, and the defendants were tried in three several groups, as indicated above. As each of the three cases was called for trial, each defendant was arraigned, and, having the indictment read to him, entered a plea of not guilty. Whether the original arraignment and pleas were regarded as ineffective is not shown. Each of the three trials was completed within a single day. Under the Alabama statute the punishment for rape is to be fixed by the jury, and in its discretion may be from ten years imprisonment to death. The juries found defendants guilty and imposed the death penalty upon all. The trial court overruled motions for new trials and sentenced the defendants in accordance with the verdicts. The judgments were affirmed by the state supreme court. Chief Justice Anderson thought the defendants had not been accorded a fair trial and strongly dissented. In this court the judgments are assailed upon the grounds that the defendants, and each of them, were denied due process of law and the equal protection of the laws, in contravention of the Fourteenth Amendment, specifically as follows: (1) They were not given a fair, impartial, and deliberate trial; (2) they were denied the right of counsel, with the accustomed incidents of consultation and opportunity of preparation for trial; and (3) they were tried before juries from which qualified members of their own race were systematically excluded. These questions were properly raised and saved in the courts below. The only one of the assignments which we shall consider is the second, in respect of the denial of counsel; and it becomes unnecessary to discuss the facts of the case or the circumstances surrounding the prosecution except in so far as they reflect light upon that question.

Powell v. Alabama

287 U.S. 45 (1932)

I Does the denial of the assistance of counsel contravene the due process clause of the Fourteenth Amendment to the Federal Constitution?

R The Fourteenth Amendment Due Process Clause guarantees criminal defendants the right to use counsel they have retained and, in capital cases where the defendant is ignorant or feeble0minded, the right to have counsel appointed.

A The record shows that immediately upon the return of the indictment defendants were arraigned and pleaded not guilty. Apparently they were not asked whether they had, or were able to employ, counsel, or wished to have counsel appointed; or whether they had friends or relatives who might assist in that regard if communicated with. It is hardly necessary to say that the right to counsel being conceded, a defendant should be afforded a fair opportunity to secure counsel of his own choice. Not only was that not done here, but such designation of counsel as was attempted was either so indefinite or so close upon the trial as to amount to a denial of effective and substantial aid in that regard. That the action of the trial judge in respect of appointment of counsel was little more than an expansive gesture, imposing no substantial or definite obligation upon any one, is borne out by the fact that prior to the calling of the case for trial on April 6, a leading member of the local bar accepted employment on the side of the prosecution and actively participated in the trial. Nor do we think the situation was helped by what occurred on the morning of the trial. At that time, Mr. Roddy stated to the court that he did not appear as counsel, but that he would like to appear along with counsel that the court might appoint; that he had not been given an opportunity to prepare the case; that he was not familiar with the procedure in Alabama, but merely came down as a friend of the people who were interested; that he thought the boys would be better off if he should step entirely out of the case. Mr. Moody, a member of the local bar, expressed a willingness to help Mr. Roddy in anything he could do under the circumstances. It is not enough to assume that counsel thus precipitated into the case thought there was no defense, and exercised their best judgment in proceeding to trial without preparation. Neither they nor the court could say what a prompt and thorough-going investigation might disclose as to the facts. No attempt was made to investigate. No opportunity to do so was given. Defendants were immediately hurried to trial. An affirmation of the right to the aid of counsel in petty offenses, and its denial in the case of crimes of the gravest character, where such aid is most needed, is so outrageous and so obviously a perversion of all sense of proportion that the rule was constantly, vigorously and sometimes passionately assailed by English statesmen and lawyers. One test which has been applied to determine whether due process of law has been accorded in given instances is to ascertain what were the settled usages and modes of proceeding under the common and statute law of England before the Declaration of Independence, subject, however, to the qualification that they be shown not to have been unsuited to the civil and political conditions of our ancestors by having been followed in this country after it became a nation.

Powell v. Alabama

287 U.S. 45 (1932)

In the light of the facts outlined in the forepart of this opinion - the ignorance and illiteracy of the defendants, their youth, the circumstances of public hostility, the imprisonment and the close surveillance of the defendants by the military forces, the fact that their friends and families were all in other states and communication with them necessarily difficult, and above all that they stood in deadly peril of their lives - we think the failure of the trial court to give them reasonable time and opportunity to secure counsel was a clear denial of due process.

The United States by statute and every state in the Union by express provision of law, or by the determination of its courts, make it the duty of the trial judge, where the accused is unable to employ counsel, to appoint counsel for him. In most states the rule applies broadly to all criminal prosecutions, in others it is limited to the more serious crimes, and in a very limited number, to capital cases. A rule adopted with such unanimous accord reflects, if it does not establish the inherent right to have counsel appointed at least in cases like the present, and lends convincing support to the conclusion we have reached as to the fundamental nature of that right. The judgments must be reversed and the causes remanded for further proceedings not inconsistent with this opinion.

C

Judgments reversed.

Betts v. Brady

316 U.S. 455 (1942)

FACTS

Defendant Betts defendant, a Maryland indigent, was indicted for robbery. However, Maryland law only provides for the appointment of counsel for murder and rape charges. Thus, Betts's request for an attorney was denied. After representing himself without a jury, the defendant was convicted and sentenced to eight years imprisonment. This, despite the fact that he pled not guilty and called witnesses who testified he was somewhere else at the time. On appeal, the defendant argues that Maryland's refusal to appoint him a lawyer was a denial of his 14th Amendment due process rights

I Are state courts mandated to appoint counsel for all indigent criminal defendants?

R State courts do not need to appoint attorneys for all indigent criminal defendants; however, federal courts must appoint counsel for all federal crimes.

A State courts do not need to appoint attorneys for all impoverished criminal defendants; however, federal courts must appoint counsel for all federal crimes. The 14th Amendment Due Process Clause does not specifically incorporate the Sixth Amendment right to counsel. Thus, the denial of a due process claim is analyzed by considering the totality of the facts in each individual case. In most states, policy decisions dictate that appointed counsel is not fundamental to a fair trial, and we are reluctant to disturb those policy considerations. In the instant case, we find that Maryland's expedited trial procedure was reasonable and find the defendant was competent to defend himself, since he previously served time for larceny. (*Please note*: modern case law holds that for both state and federal courts, indigent defendants charged with felonies or misdemeanors punishable by more than 6 months in jail must be appointed counsel).

C No. Federal courts must appoint counsel for all federal crimes, but state courts need not appoint attorneys for all indigent criminal defendants. Judgment affirmed.

Brown v. Mississippi

297 U.S. 278 (1936)

FACTS

Petitioners were indicted for the murder of one Raymond Stewart, whose death occurred on March 30, 1934. They were indicted on April 4, 1934, and were then arraigned and pleaded not guilty. Counsel were appointed by the court to defend them. Trial was begun the next morning and was concluded on the following day, when they were found guilty and sentenced to death. Aside from the confessions, there was no evidence sufficient to warrant the submission of the case to the jury. After a preliminary inquiry, testimony as to the confessions was received over the objection of defendants' counsel. Defendants then testified that the confessions were false and had been procured by physical torture. The case went to the jury with instructions, upon the request of defendants' counsel, that if the jury had reasonable doubt as to the confessions having resulted from coercion, and that they were not they were not to be considered as evidence. On appeal to the Supreme Court of the State, the judgment was affirmed and their motion for a new trial was denied.

I

Do convictions, which rest solely upon confessions shown to have been extorted by officers of the state by brutality and violence, violate due process of law required by the Fourteenth Amendment of the U.S. Constitution?

R

Confessions supporting a conviction must not be obtained through coercion; and such interrogation must not violate the defendant's due process rights under the 14th Amendment.

A

Here, we are not concerned with a mere question of state practice, or whether counsel assigned to petitioners were competent or mistakenly assumed that their first objections were sufficient. In an earlier case the Supreme Court of the State had recognized the duty of the court to supply corrective process where due process of law had been denied. In *Fisher v. State*, the court said: "Coercing the supposed state's criminals into confessions and using such confessions so coerced from them against them in trials has been the curse of all countries. It was the chief iniquity, the crowning infamy of the Star Chamber, and the Inquisition, and other similar institutions. The Constitution recognized the evils that lay behind these practices and prohibited them in this country. ... The duty of maintaining constitutional rights of a person on trial for his life rises above mere rules of procedure, and wherever the court is clearly satisfied that such violations exist, it will refuse to sanction such violations and will apply the corrective." In the instant case, the trial court was fully advised by the undisputed evidence of the way in which the confessions had been procured. The trial court knew that there was no other evidence upon which conviction and sentence could be based. Yet it proceeded to permit conviction and to pronounce sentence. The conviction and sentence were void for want of the essential elements of due process, and the proceeding thus vitiated could be challenged in any appropriate manner. It was challenged before the Supreme Court of the State by the express invocation of the Fourteenth Amendment. That court entertained the challenge, considered the federal question thus presented, but declined to enforce petitioners' constitutional right. The court thus denied a federal right fully established and specially set up and claimed, and the judgment must be reversed.

C Judgment reversed.

Duncan v. Louisiana

391 U.S. 145 (1968)

FACTS

Appellant Gary Duncan was 19 years of age when tried. While driving on Highway 23 in Plaquemines Parish on October 18, 1966, he saw two younger cousins engaged in a conversation by the side of the road with four white boys. Knowing his cousins, Negroes who had recently transferred to a formerly all-white high school, had reported the occurrence of racial incidents at the school, Duncan stopped the car, got out, and approached the six boys. At trial the white boys and a white onlooker testified, as did appellant and his cousins. The testimony was in dispute on many points, but the witnesses agreed that appellant and the white boys spoke to each other, that appellant encouraged his cousins to break off the encounter and enter his car, and that appellant was about to enter the car himself for the purpose of driving away with his cousins. The whites testified that just before getting in the car appellant slapped Herman Landry, one of the white boys, on the elbow. The Negroes testified that appellant had not slapped Landry, but had merely touched him. The trial judge concluded that the State had proved beyond a reasonable doubt that Duncan had committed simple battery, and found him guilty. Appellant was convicted of simple battery in the Twenty-fifth Judicial District Court of Louisiana. Under Louisiana law simple battery is a misdemeanor, punishable by a maximum of two years' imprisonment and a $300 fine. Appellant sought trial by jury, but because the Louisiana Constitution grants jury trials only in cases in which capital punishment or imprisonment at hard labor may be imposed, the trial judge denied the request. Appellant was convicted and sentenced to serve 60 days in the parish prison and pay a fine of $150. Appellant sought review in the Supreme Court of Louisiana, asserting that the denial of jury trial violated rights guaranteed to him by the United States Constitution. The state Supreme Court, finding "[n]o error of law in the ruling complained of," denied appellant a writ of certiorari. Pursuant to 28 U.S.C. 1257 (2) appellant sought review in the U.S. Supreme Court, alleging that the Sixth and Fourteenth Amendments to the United States Constitution secure the right to jury trial in state criminal prosecutions where a sentence as long as two years may be imposed. We noted probable jurisdiction, and set the case for oral argument with No. 52, *Bloom v. Illinois*.

I

Does the Sixth Amendment right to a jury trial apply to the states through the Fourteenth Amendment?

R

The Sixth Amendment right to a jury trial applies to the states through the Fourteenth Amendment.

A

The U.S. Supreme Court held: (1) Since trial by jury in criminal cases is fundamental to the American scheme of justice, the Fourteenth Amendment guarantees a right of jury trial in all criminal cases which, were they tried in a federal court, would come within the Sixth Amendment's guarantee of trial by jury; and (2) The penalty authorized for a particular crime is of major relevance in determining whether it is a serious one subject to the mandates of the Sixth Amendment, and it is sufficient here, without defining the boundary between petty offenses and serious crimes, to hold that a crime punishable by two years in prison is a serious crime and that appellant was entitled to a jury trial.

C Reversed and remanded.

Wolf v. Colorado

338 U.S. 25 (1945)

FACTS

Facts omitted.

I

Does the federal exclusionary rule apply to the states?

R

The Fourth Amendment's prohibition against unreasonable searches does NOT require state courts to exclude evidence obtained in violation of the Fourth Amendment as it does in federal courts.

A

The protection of a person's privacy against arbitrary and unreasonable police intrusion is guaranteed by the Fourth Amendment and is enforceable against the states through the Due Process Clause of the Fourteen Amendment. However, while we acknowledge violations of the Fourth Amendment mandate sanctions against the violating party, the way in which these sanctions should work, however, is a problem that should be left up to the individual states to solve in whatever way they see fit. In *Weeks v. United States*, we held that the Fourth Amendment barred the use of evidence secured through an illegal search and seizure in a federal prosecution. This ruling was a matter of judicial implication and has subsequently been firmly applied. We continue to adhere to it today. However, the immediate question we must answer though is whether this exclusionary rule should be extended to the states. In considering this question, we realize that it is an issue which brings out different answers from different people. We hold, therefore, that in a prosecution in a State court for a State crime, the Fourteenth Amendment does not forbid the admission of evidence obtained by an unreasonable search and seizure. And though we have interpreted the Fourth Amendment to forbid the admission of such evidence, a different question would be presented if Congress, under its legislative powers, were to pass a statute purporting to negate the *Weeks* doctrine. We would then be faced with the problem of the respect to be accorded the legislative judgment on issues as to which, in default of that judgment, we have been forced to depend upon.

C

No. The Fourth Amendment's prohibition of unreasonable searches and seizures does apply to the states, but does not require state courts to exclude evidence obtained in violation of the Fourth Amendment as it does in federal court.

Weeks v. United States

232 U.S. 383 (1914)

FACTS

An indictment was returned against the plaintiff in error, defendant Weeks below, and herein so designated, in the district court of the United States for the western district of Missouri, containing nine counts. The seventh count, upon which a conviction was had, charged the use of the mails for the purpose of transporting certain coupons or tickets representing chances or shares in a lottery or gift enterprise, in violation of 213 of the Criminal Code. Sentence of fine and imprisonment was imposed. This writ of error is to review that judgment. The defendant was arrested by a police officer, so far as the record shows, without warrant, at the Union Station in Kansas City, Missouri, where he was employed by an express company. Other police officers had gone to the house of the defendant, and being told by a neighbor where the key was kept, found it and entered the house. They searched the defendant's room and took possession of various papers and articles found there, which were afterwards turned over to the United States marshal. Later in the same day police officers returned with the marshal, who thought he might find additional evidence, and, being admitted by someone in the house, probably a boarder, in response to a knock, the marshal searched the defendant's room and carried away certain letters and envelops found in the drawer of a chiffonier. Neither the marshal nor the police officer had a search warrant. An indictment was issued against Weeks which included a count of using the mail system to transport illegal lottery tickets in violation of federal law. Weeks objected to the search and petitioned for the return of the items taken. The petition was overruled and Weeks was thereafter convicted.

I Is the seizure of evidence found within a defendant's home by a federal marshal acting with a warrant a violation of the defendant's Fourth Amendment rights?

R The Fourth Amendment prohibits federal officers from obtaining evidence through unreasonable searches and seizures.

A It is thus apparent that the question presented involves the determination of the duty of the court with reference to the motion made by the defendant for the return of certain letters, as well as other papers, taken from his room by the United States marshal, who, without authority of process, if any such could have been legally issued, visited the room of the defendant for the declared purpose of obtaining additional testimony to support the charge against the accused, and, having gained admission to the house, took from the drawer of a chiffonier there found certain letters written to the defendant, tending to show his guilt. These letters were placed in the control of the district attorney, and were subsequently produced by him and offered in evidence against the accused at the trial. The defendant contends that such appropriation of his private correspondence was in violation of rights secured to him by the 4th and 5th Amendments to the Constitution of the United States. We shall deal with the 4th Amendment, which provides: 'The right of the people to be secure in their persons, houses, papers, and effects, against unreasonable searches and seizures, shall not be violated, and no warrants shall issue but upon probable cause, supported by oath or affirmation, and particularly describing the place to be searched, and the persons or things to be seized.'

The effect of the 4th Amendment is to put the courts of the United States and Federal officials, in the exercise of their power and authority, under limitations and restraints as to the exercise of such power and authority, and to forever secure the people, their persons, houses, papers, and effects, against all unreasonable searches and seizures under the guise of law. This protection reaches all alike, whether accused of crime or not, and the duty of giving to it force and effect is obligatory upon all entrusted under our Federal system with the enforcement of the laws. The tendency of those who execute the criminal laws of the country to obtain conviction by means of unlawful seizures and enforced confessions, the latter often obtained after subjecting accused persons to unwarranted practices destructive of rights secured by the Federal Constitution, should find no sanction in the judgments of the courts, which are charged at all times with the support of the Constitution, and to which people of all conditions have a right to appeal for the maintenance of such fundamental rights.

We therefore reach the conclusion that the letters in question were taken from the house of the accused by an official of the United States, acting under color of his office, in direct violation of the constitutional rights of the defendant; that having made a seasonable application for their return, which was heard and passed upon by the court, there was involved in the order refusing the application a denial of the constitutional rights of the accused, and that the court should have restored these letters to the accused. In holding them and permitting their use upon the trial, we think prejudicial error was committed. As to the papers and property seized by the police, it does not appear that they acted under any claim of Federal authority such as would make the amendment applicable to such unauthorized seizures. The record shows that what they did by way of arrest and search and seizure was done before the finding of the indictment in the Federal court; under what supposed right or authority does not appear. What remedies the defendant may have against them we need not inquire, as the 4th Amendment is not directed to individual misconduct of such officials. Its limitations reach the Federal government and its agencies. It results that the judgment of the court below must be reversed, and the case remanded for further proceedings in accordance with this opinion.

C

Reversed.

Mapp v. Ohio

367 U.S. 643 (1961)

FACTS

On May 23, 1957, three police officers arrived at the Defendant Mapp's residence armed with information that "a person was hiding out in the home was wanted for questioning in connection with a recent bombing, and that there was a large amount of policy paraphernalia being hidden in the home." Miss Mapp and her daughter by a former marriage lived on the top floor of the two-family dwelling. Upon their arrival at that house, the officers knocked on the door and demanded entrance but appellant, after telephoning her attorney, refused to admit them without a search warrant. They advised their headquarters of the situation and undertook a surveillance of the house. The officers again sought entrance some three hours later when four or more additional officers arrived on the scene. When Miss Mapp did not come to the door immediately, at least one of the several doors to the house was forcibly opened and the policemen gained admittance. The officers conducted a widespread search and found obscene materials. No search warrant was ever produced, nor was this failure explained it anyway. Defendant was convicted on the strength of the evidence seized. The Ohio Supreme Court, after acknowledging that no warrant was ever produced, affirmed the conviction.

I

Does the exclusionary rule apply to evidence used in state court proceedings as well?

R

The federal exclusionary rule applies equally to both the state and federal Governments.

A

The federal exclusionary rule requiring evidence gathered in violation of the Fourth Amendment to be excluded from criminal proceedings applies equally to both the state and federal Governments. Prior to *Wolf*, almost two thirds of the States were opposed to the use of the exclusionary rule. Now more than half of the states have wholly or partially adopted or adhered to the W*eeks* rule requiring exclusion of the evidence seized in violation of the Fourth Amendment. Thus, the rationale supporting the failure of the *Wolf* court to extend the exclusionary rule to the states can no longer be deemed controlling. We therefore hold that all evidence obtained by searches and seizures in violation of the Constitution is, by that same authority, inadmissible in state court. Our decision today gives to the individual no more than that which the Constitution guarantees him, to the police officer no less than that to which honest Law enforcement is entitled, and, to the courts, that judicial integrity so necessary in the true administration of justice.

C

Yes. The exclusionary rule applies equally to both the state and federal Governments.

Katz v. United States

389 U.S. 347 (1967)

FACTS

Acting on suspicion that Defendant Katz was transmitting gambling information over the phone to clients in other states, FBI agents (plaintiffs) attached a electronic listening device to the outside of a public telephone booth that Katz used to place what he assumed to be private calls. Over the defendant's objection, the trial court permitted the Government to introduce evidence of the defendant's end of the telephone conversations, and the defendant was convicted of transmitting wagering information by telephone.

I

Do Government actors need to obtain a search warrant in order to wiretap a public pay phone?

R

A search within the meaning of the Fourth Amendment has occurred where the Government conducts investigative activity that intrudes upon a justifiable expectation of privacy.

A

We decline to adopt the defendant's formulation of the issues: (1) Whether a public telephone booth is a constitutionally protected area so that evidence obtained by attaching an electronic listening recording device to the top of such a booth is obtained in violation of the right to privacy of the user of the booth and (2) Whether physical penetration of a constitutionally protected area is necessary before a search and seizure can be said to violate the Fourth Amendment of the United States Constitution. We conclude that *Olmstead* (surveillance without any trespass and without the seizure of any material object fell outside the ambit of the Constitution) and *Goldman* (Fourth Amendment was thought to limit only searches and seizures of tangible property) have been so eroded by our subsequent decisions that the "trespass" doctrine there enunciated can no longer be regarded as controlling. The Government's activities in electronically listening to and recording the petitioner's words violated the privacy upon which he justifiably relied while using the telephone booth and thus constituted a "search and seizure" within the meaning of the Fourth Amendment. The fact that the electronic device employed to achieve that end did not happen to penetrate the wall of the booth can have no constitutional significance. The question remaining for decision, then, is whether the search and seizure conducted in this case complied with constitutional standards. In that regard, the Government's position is that its agents acted in an entirely defensible manner: They did not begin their electronic surveillance until investigation of the petitioner's activities had established a strong probability that he was using the telephone in question to transmit gambling information to persons in other States, in violation of federal law.

C

Judgment reversed.

United States v. White

401 U.S. 745 (1971)

FACTS

In 1966, (defendant-respondent) James A. White was tried and convicted under two consolidated indictments charging various illegal transactions in narcotics. He was fined and sentenced as a second offender to 25-year concurrent sentences. The issue before us is whether the Fourth Amendment bars from evidence the testimony of Governmental agents who related certain conversations which had occurred between defendant White and a Government informant, Harvey Jackson, and which the agents overheard by monitoring the frequency of a radio transmitter carried by Jackson and concealed on his person. On four occasions the conversations took place in Jackson's home; each of these conversations was overheard by an agent concealed in a kitchen closet with Jackson's consent and by a second agent outside the house using a radio receiver. Four other conversations - one in respondent's home, one in a restaurant, and two in Jackson's car - were overheard by the use of radio equipment. The prosecution was unable to locate and produce Jackson at the trial and the trial court overruled objections to the testimony of the agents who conducted the electronic surveillance. The jury returned a guilty verdict and defendant appealed.

I

Are a defendant's Fourth Amendment rights violated by an electronic transmission of the conversation between himself and an agent of the Government who monitors the conversation?

R

Even when an agent of the Government electronically transmits his conversation with the Government, a defendant's expectation of privacy in not violated.

A

We hold that the defendant's expectation of privacy is not violated when an agent of the Government electronically transmits his conversation with the defendant. As such, the Fourth Amendment is inapplicable. In *Hoffa v. United States* (case where a Government informant whose testimony regarding conversations with the defendant was used to obtain a conviction), we held that a Government agent can conceal his true identity and engage in incriminating conversations with the defendant. Thereafter, the informant may write down the contents of that conversation. If the law provides no protection to the defendant whose trusted confidant is a police agent, neither should it protect him when that same agent records or transmits his conversations and later offers it into evidence to prove the prosecution's case. It seems illogical to hold the Government's conduct unreasonable when an informer uses a recorder, but reasonable when the same conduct occurs without the recorder.

C

Reversed.

Smith v. Maryland

442 U.S. 735 (1979)

FACTS

The telephone company, at the request of the police, installed at its central offices a pen register to record the numbers dialed from the telephone at petitioner's home. Prior to his robbery trial, petitioner moved to suppress "all fruits derived from" the pen register. The Maryland trial court denied this motion, holding that the warrantless installation of the pen register did not violate the Fourth Amendment. Petitioner was convicted, and the Maryland Court of Appeals affirmed.

I

Does the use of a pen register [a device that monitors the numbers that are dialed from a telephone – in this case a private telephone] constitute a search under the Fourth Amendment?

R

The installation and use of the pen register is not a "search" within the meaning of the Fourth Amendment, and hence no warrant is required.

A

The installation and use of the pen register was not a "search" within the meaning of the Fourth Amendment, and hence no warrant was required. Application of the Fourth Amendment depends on whether the person invoking its protection can claim a "legitimate expectation of privacy" that has been invaded by government action. This inquiry normally embraces two questions: first, whether the individual has exhibited an actual (subjective) expectation of privacy; and second, whether his expectation is one that society is prepared to recognize as "reasonable." *Katz v. United States*. Petitioner in all probability entertained no actual expectation of privacy in the phone numbers he dialed, and even if he did, his expectation was not "legitimate." First, it is doubtful that telephone users in general have any expectation of privacy regarding the numbers they dial, since they typically know that they must convey phone numbers to the telephone company and that the company has facilities for recording this information and does in fact record it for various legitimate business purposes. And petitioner did not demonstrate an expectation of privacy merely by using his home phone rather than some other phone, since his conduct, although perhaps calculated to keep the contents of his conversation private, was not calculated to preserve the privacy of the number he dialed. Second, even if petitioner did harbor some subjective expectation of privacy, this expectation was not one that society is prepared to recognize as "reasonable." When petitioner voluntarily conveyed numerical information to the phone company and "exposed" that information to its equipment in the normal course of business, he assumed the risk that the company would reveal the information to the police.

C

Affirmed.

Kyllo v. United States

533 U.S. 27 (2001)

FACTS

Suspicious that marijuana was being grown in petitioner Kyllo's home in a triplex, agents used a thermal imaging device to scan the triplex to determine if the amount of heat emanating from it was consistent with the high-intensity lamps typically used for indoor marijuana growth. The scan showed that Kyllo's garage roof and a side wall were relatively hot compared to the rest of his home and substantially warmer than the neighboring units. Based in part on the thermal imaging, a Federal Magistrate Judge issued a warrant to search Kyllo's home, where the agents found marijuana growing. After Kyllo was indicted on a federal drug charge, he unsuccessfully moved to suppress the evidence seized from his home and then entered a conditional guilty plea. The Ninth Circuit ultimately affirmed, upholding the thermal imaging on the ground that Kyllo had shown no subjective expectation of privacy because he had made no attempt to conceal the heat escaping from his home. Even if he had, ruled the court, there was no objectively reasonable expectation of privacy because the thermal imager did not expose any intimate details of Kyllo's life, only amorphous hot spots on his home's exterior.

I

Does the Government need a warrant when it uses a device that is not in general public use to explore details of a private home that would previously have been unknowable without physical intrusion?

R

Where the Government uses a device that is not in general public use to explore details of a private home that would previously have been unknowable without physical intrusion, the surveillance is a Fourth Amendment "search," and is presumptively unreasonable without a warrant.

A

The question whether a warrantless search of a home is reasonable and hence constitutional must be answered no in most instances, but the antecedent question whether a Fourth Amendment "search" has occurred is not so simple. This Court has approved warrantless visual surveillance of a home, see *California* v. *Ciraolo,* ruling that visual observation is no "search" at all. In assessing when a search is not a search, the Court has adapted a principle first enunciated in *Katz* v. *United States*: A "search" does not occur--even when its object is a house explicitly protected by the Fourth Amendment - unless the individual manifested a subjective expectation of privacy in the searched object, and society is willing to recognize that expectation as reasonable, see, *e.g., California* v. *Ciraolo*. While it may be difficult to refine the *Katz* test in some instances, in the case of the search of a home's interior--the prototypical and hence most commonly litigated area of protected privacy - there is a ready criterion, with roots deep in the common law, of the minimal expectation of privacy that *exists*, and that is acknowledged to be *reasonable*. To withdraw protection of this minimum expectation would be to permit police technology to erode the privacy guaranteed by the Fourth Amendment. Thus, obtaining by sense-enhancing technology any information regarding the home's interior that could not otherwise have been obtained without physical "intrusion into a constitutionally protected area," *Silverman* v. *United States* constitutes a search--at least where (as here) the technology in question is not in general public use. This assures preservation of that degree of privacy against government that existed when the Fourth Amendment was adopted. Based on this criterion, the information obtained by the thermal imager in this case was the product of a search. The Court rejects the Government's argument that the thermal imaging must be upheld because it detected only heat radiating from the home's external surface. Such a mechanical interpretation of the Fourth Amendment was rejected in *Katz*, where the eavesdropping device in question picked up only sound waves that reached the exterior of the phone booth to which it was attached. Reversing that approach would leave the homeowner at the mercy of advancing technology - including imaging technology that could discern all human activity in the home. Also rejected is the Government's contention that the thermal imaging was constitutional because it did not detect "intimate details." Such an approach would be wrong in principle because, in the sanctity of the home, *all* details are intimate details. It would also be impractical in application, failing to provide a workable accommodation between law enforcement needs and Fourth Amendment interests. Since the imaging in this case was an unlawful search, it will remain for the District Court to determine whether, without the evidence it provided, the search warrant was supported by probable cause - and if not, whether there is any other basis for supporting admission of that evidence.

C

Reversed and remanded.

United States v. Karo

468 U.S. 705 (1984)

FACTS

After a Drug Enforcement Administration (DEA) agent learned that respondents Karo, Horton, and Harley had ordered 50 gallons of ether from a Government informant, who had told the agent that the ether was to be used to extract cocaine from clothing that had been imported into the United States, the Government obtained a court order authorizing the installation and monitoring of a beeper in one of the cans of ether. With the informant's consent, DEA agents substituted their own can containing a beeper for one of the cans in the shipment. Thereafter, agents saw Karo pick up the ether from the informant, followed Karo to his house, and determined by using the beeper that the ether was inside the house where it was then monitored. The ether then moved in succession to two other houses, including Horton's, before it was moved first to a locker in one commercial storage facility and then to a locker in another such facility. Both lockers were rented jointly by Horton and Harley. Finally, the ether was removed from the second storage facility by respondent Rhodes and an unidentified woman and transported in Horton's truck, first to Rhodes' house and then to a house rented by Horton, Harley, and respondent Steele. Using the beeper monitor, agents determined that the beeper can was inside the house, and obtained a warrant to search the house based in part on information derived through use of the beeper. The warrant was executed and Horton, Harley, Steele, and respondent Roth were arrested, and cocaine was seized. Respondents were indicted for various offenses relating to the cocaine. The District Court granted respondent's pretrial motion to suppress the seized evidence on the grounds that the initial warrant to install the beeper was invalid and that the seizure was the tainted fruit of an unauthorized installation and monitoring of the beeper. The Government appealed but did not challenge the invalidation of the initial warrant. The Court of Appeals affirmed, except with respect to Rhodes, holding that a warrant was required to install the beeper in the can of ether and to monitor it in private dwellings and storage lockers, that the warrant for the search of the house rented by Horton, Harley, and Steele, and the resulting seizure were tainted by the Government's prior illegal conduct, and that therefore the evidence was properly suppressed as to Horton, Harley, Steele, Roth, and Karo.

I Does the installation of a beeper in a container with the consent of the original owner constitute a seizure under Fourth Amendment when the container is a delivered to a buyer with no knowledge of the presence of the beeper?

R The monitoring of a beeper in a private residence, a location not opened to visual surveillance, violates the Fourth Amendment rights of those who have a justifiable interest in the privacy of the residence; where there is no justifiable interest in the privacy of the residence, there is no violation.

A No Fourth Amendment interest of Karo or of any other respondent was infringed by the installation of the beeper. The informant's consent was sufficient to validate the installation. And the transfer of the beeper-laden can to Karo was neither a search nor a seizure, since it conveyed no information that Karo wished to keep private and did not interfere with anyone's possessory interest in a meaningful way. The monitoring of a beeper in a private residence, a location not opened to visual surveillance, violates the Fourth Amendment

---

rights of those who have a justifiable interest in the privacy of the residence. Here, if a DEA agent had entered the house in question without a warrant to verify that the ether was in the house, he would have engaged in an unreasonable search within the meaning of the Fourth Amendment. The result is the same where, without a warrant, the Government surreptitiously uses a beeper to obtain information that it could not have obtained from outside the curtilage of the house. There is no reason in this case to deviate from the general rule that a search of a house should be conducted pursuant to a warrant. The evidence seized in the house in question, however, should not have been suppressed with respect to any of the respondents. The information that the ether was in the house, verified by use of the beeper without a warrant, would be inadmissible against those respondents with privacy interests in the house and would invalidate the search warrant, if critical to establishing probable cause. But because locating, without prior monitoring, the ether in the second storage facility was not an illegal search (use of the beeper not identifying the specific locker in which the ether was located and the locker being identified only by the smell of ether emanating therefrom) and because the ether was seen being loaded into Horton's truck, which then traveled the highways, it is evident that there was no violation of the Fourth Amendment as to anyone with or without standing to complain about monitoring the beeper while it was located in the truck. Under the circumstances, the warrant affidavit, after striking the facts about monitoring the beeper while it was in the searched house, contained sufficient untainted information to furnish probable cause for issuance of the search warrant.

C Reversed.

Spinelli v. United States

393 U.S. 410 (1969)

FACTS

Defendant Spinelli was convicted of interstate travel with the intent of conducting illegal gambling activities. Petitioner was convicted of illegal interstate gambling activities despite his claim that the Commissioner's warrant authorizing the FBI search that uncovered evidence used at his trial violated the Fourth Amendment. He argued that the FBI agent's supporting affidavit did not afford probable cause for issuance of the warrant. The affidavit alleged that: the FBI had followed petitioner on five days, on four of which he had been seen crossing one of two bridges leading from Illinois to St. Louis, Missouri, and had been seen parking his car at a St. Louis apartment house parking lot; he was seen one day to enter a particular apartment; the apartment contained two telephones with specified numbers; petitioner was known to affiant as a gambler and associate of gamblers; and the FBI had "been informed by a confidential reliable informant" that petitioner was "operating a handbook and accepting wagers and disseminating wagering information by means of the telephones" which had been assigned the specified numbers. Viewing the information in the affidavit in its totality, the Court of Appeals deemed the principles of *Aguilar v. Texas* satisfied and upheld the conviction. The defendant challenged the search warrant at every stage of the proceedings, but failed.

I

Is a search warrant valid if it is issued without (1) facts and specifics that support the underlying circumstances from which the informant gained his knowledge; or (2) facts and specifics supporting the officer's belief that the informant is both reliable and credible?

R

An informant's tip does not provide probable cause for the issuance of a search warrant if the tip does not state the reasons why the informant is reliable and does not include specifics regarding the specific facts known by the informant.

A

An informant's tip does not provide probable cause for the issuance of a search warrant if the tip does not state the reasons why the informant is reliable and does not include specifics regarding the facts known by the informant in sufficient detail such that the magistrate may know he is relying on something more substantial than a casual rumor based on the accuser's genuine reputation. To that end, the *Aguilar* two part test is utilized. The first step is to apply the *Aguilar* standard in assessing the tip's probative value. A magistrate must ask: can it fairly be said that the tip, even when certain parts of it have been corroborated by independent sources, is as trustworthy as a tip which would pass *Aguilar's* test without independent corroboration? That is, is the information reliable? The second part of the test asks if the informant is reliable and trustworthy. Applying these principles to the instant case, we must first consider the weight given to the informant's tip independent from the rest of the affidavit. It is clearly inadequate. The affiant swore that this informant was "reliable" but offered the magistrate no reason for this conclusion. The tip did not have a sufficient statement of the underlying circumstances from which the informer concluded that Spinelli was running bookmaking operation. There is no statement of how the FBI source received this information. There is nothing indicating why the informant believed his sources to be reliable. Without a statement detailing the manner in which the informant was gathered, it is very important that the tip described

---

the accused's criminal activity in sufficient detail, so the magistrate may know that he is relying on more than a casual rumor or an accusation. We conclude, therefore, that the informer's tip, even when corroborated to the extent it was, is not sufficient to provide the basis for a finding of probable cause.

C

Judgment reversed.

Illinois v. Gates

462 U.S. 213 (1983)

FACTS

On May 3, 1978, the Police Department of Bloomingdale, Ill., received an anonymous letter which included statements that respondents, husband and wife, were engaged in selling drugs; that the wife would drive their car to Florida on May 3 to be loaded with drugs, and the husband would fly down in a few days to drive the car back; that the car's trunk would be loaded with drugs; and that respondents presently had over $100,000 worth of drugs in their basement. Acting on the tip, a police officer determined respondents' address and learned that the husband made a reservation on a May 5 flight to Florida. Arrangements for surveillance of the flight were made with an agent of the Drug Enforcement Administration (DEA), and the surveillance disclosed that the husband took the flight, stayed overnight in a motel room registered in the wife's name, and left the following morning with a woman in a car bearing an Illinois license plate issued to the husband, heading north on an interstate highway used by travelers to the Bloomingdale area. When Gates reached his residence the car and house were searched. The search revealed over 350 lbs. of marijuana, some weapons and other contraband. The trial court ordered this evidence suppressed because the warrant application was insufficient. The ruling was affirmed by both the Illinois Court of Appeals and the state Supreme Court.

I Can a search warrant be issued on an informant's tip when its predictions are corroborated by independent police work, even though there is nothing to indicate the veracity or reliability of the informant or the basis of his information?

R A search warrant founded on an informant's tip may be properly issued if, given (1) the totality of the circumstances set forth in the warrant application, including (2) the veracity and basis of knowledge of the informant and (3) any corroboration of the informant's information, there is a fair probability that contraband or evidence will be found in the place to be searched.

A As the Illinois Supreme Court correctly concluded, the informant's anonymous letter, standing alone, was an insufficient basis for issuing a warrant. It provides nothing from which one might conclude that the author is either honest or the information reliable. It gives no basis for the informant's predictions. We do not address the question whether the rule requiring the exclusion at a criminal trial of evidence obtained in violation of the Fourth Amendment should be modified since it was not presented to or decided by the Illinois courts. However, we hold that the rigid "two-pronged test" under *Aguilar-Spinelli* for determining whether an informant's tip establishes probable cause for issuance of a warrant is abandoned, and the "totality of the circumstances" approach that traditionally has informed probable cause determinations is substituted in its place. The elements under the "two-pronged test" concerning the informant's "veracity," "reliability," and "basis of knowledge" should be understood simply as closely intertwined issues that may usefully illuminate the common sense, practical question whether there is "probable cause" to believe that contraband or evidence is located in a particular place. The task of the issuing magistrate is simply to make a practical, common sense decision whether, given all the circumstances set forth in the affidavit before him, there is a fair probability that contraband or evidence of a crime will be found in a particular place. And the duty of a reviewing court is simply to ensure that the magistrate had a substantial basis for concluding that probable cause existed. This flexible, easily applied standard will better achieve the accommodation of public and private interests that the Fourth Amendment requires than does the approach that has developed from *Aguilar-Spinelli.* The judge issuing the warrant had a substantial basis for concluding that probable cause to search respondents' home and car existed. Under the "totality of the circumstances" analysis, corroboration of details of an informant's tip by independent police work is of significant value. Here even standing alone, the facts obtained through the independent investigation of the Bloomingdale police officer and the DEA at least suggested that respondents were involved in drug trafficking. In addition, the judge could rely on the anonymous letter, which had been corroborated in major part by the police officer's efforts.

C

The judgment of the Illinois Supreme Court therefore must be reversed.

Payton v. New York

445 U.S. 573 (1980)

FACTS

On January 14, 1970, after two days of intensive investigation, New York detectives had assembled evidence sufficient to establish probable cause to believe that Theodore Payton (defendant 1) had murdered the manager of a gas station two days earlier. At about 7:30 a.m. on January 15, six officers went to Payton's apartment in the Bronx, intending to arrest him. They had not obtained a warrant. Although light and music emanated from the apartment, there was no response to their knock on the metal door. They summoned emergency assistance and, about 30 minutes later, used crowbars to break open the door and enter the apartment. No one was there. In plain view, however, was a .30-caliber shell casing that was seized and later admitted into evidence at Payton's murder trial. Peyton was convicted. In the companion case, on March 14, 1974, Obie Riddick (defendant 2) was arrested for the commission of two armed robberies that had occurred in 1971. He had been identified by the victims in June 1973, and in January 1974 the police had learned his address. They did not obtain a warrant for his arrest. At about noon on March 14, a detective, accompanied by three other officers, knocked on the door of the Queens house where Riddick was living. When his young son opened the door, they could see Riddick sitting in bed covered by a sheet. They entered the house and placed him under arrest. Before permitting him to dress, they opened a chest of drawers two feet from the bed in search of weapons and found narcotics and related paraphernalia. Riddick was subsequently indicted on narcotics charges. At a suppression hearing, the trial judge held that the warrantless entry into his home was authorized by the revised New York statute, and that the search of the immediate area was reasonable under *Chimel v. California*. The Appellate Division affirmed the denial of the suppression motion.

I

While making a warrantless arrest, is evidence seized from a suspect's home absent exigent circumstances admissible against the suspect in criminal proceedings?

R

Police are required to have an arrest warrant before entering a suspect's home to make an arrest, otherwise any evidence seized therein is inadmissible against the suspect, absent exigent circumstances.

A

The Fourth Amendment, made applicable to the States by the Fourteenth Amendment, prohibits the police from making a warrantless and nonconsensual entry into a suspect's home in order to make a routine felony arrest. To be arrested in the home involves not only the invasion attendant to all arrests, but also an invasion of the sanctity of the home, which is too substantial an invasion to allow without a warrant, in the absence of exigent circumstances, even when it is accomplished under statutory authority and when probable cause is present. The reasons for upholding warrantless arrests in a public place, *United States v. Watson*, do not apply to warrantless invasions of the privacy of the home. However, for Fourth Amendment purposes, an arrest warrant founded on probable cause implicitly carries with it the limited authority to enter a dwelling in which the suspect lives when there is reason to believe the suspect is within. The state suggests that only a search warrant based on probable cause to believe the suspect is at home at a given time can adequately protect the privacy interest at stake, and since such a warrant is manifestly impractical, there need been no warrant of any kind. We disagree. An arrest warrant requirement may afford less protection than a search warrant requirement, but it will suffice to interpose the magistrate's determination of probable cause between the zealous officer and the citizen. Because no arrest warrant was obtained in either case, the judgments below must be reversed.

C

Judgment reversed.

Lo-Jo Sales Inc. v. New York

442 U.S. 319 (1979)

FACTS

A New York State Police investigator, after purchasing two films from petitioner's "adult" bookstore and after viewing them and concluding that they violated state obscenity laws, took the films to a Town Justice, who also viewed the films. Based on the investigator's affidavit, the justice issued a warrant authorizing the search of the store and the seizure of other copies of the two films. The investigator's affidavit also asserted that "similar" films and printed matter portraying similar activities could be found on the premises and requested that the justice accompany the investigator in executing the warrant so that the justice might determine independently if any other items at the store were possessed in violation of law and subject to seizure. The justice included in the warrant a recital that authorized the seizure of "[t]he following items which the Court independently [on examination] has determined to be possessed in violation" of law. However, at the time the justice signed the warrant no items were listed or described following this statement. The justice also signed a warrant for the arrest of the store clerk for having sold the two films to the investigator. Thereafter, the justice, the investigator, and nine other law enforcement officials entered the bookstore, arrested the clerk (the only employee present), and advised him of the search warrant; they conducted a search that lasted nearly six hours, covering various areas of the store, and examined and seized numerous films, projectors, and magazines. The seized items were inventoried at a State Police barracks and each item was then listed by the police on the search warrant. Petitioner was charged with obscenity in the second degree. The trial court denied petitioner's pretrial motion to suppress the evidence as having been searched for the seized in violation of the First, Fourth, and Fourteenth Amendments; petitioner then entered a guilty plea. As permitted by New York law, petitioner appealed the denial of the motion to suppress, and the convictions were affirmed.

I

Can the police seize items during a valid search with a valid warrant if those items seized are not listed in the warrant?

R

A warrant must particularly describe the things to be seized such that those items not particularly described therein are excluded from the search.

A

The Fourth Amendment does not permit the action taken here, where, except for the specification of copies of the two films previously purchased by the investigator, the warrant did not purport to particularly describe the things to be seized but, instead, left it entirely to the discretion of the officials conducting the search to decide what items were likely obscene and to accomplish their seizure. The Fourth Amendment does not countenance open-ended warrants to be completed while a search is being conducted and items seized or after the seizure has been carried out. The Town Justice's presence and participation in the search did not ensure that no items would be seized absent probable cause to believe that they were obscene; nor did his presence provide an immediate adversary hearing on the issue. The justice conducted a generalized search and was not acting as a neutral and detached judicial officer. This procedure is not authorized by *Heller v. New York*. Here, the Town Justice undertook to telescope the processes of the application for a warrant, the issuance of the warrant, and its execution. The actions involved here cannot be justified on the theory that because the items at issue were displayed in areas of the store open to the general public, petitioner had no legitimate expectation of privacy against governmental intrusion and warrantless search. Merely because a retail store invites the public to enter, it does not consent to wholesale searches and seizures that do not conform to Fourth Amendment guarantees. The actions involved cannot be sustained on the ground that petitioner's clerk consented to the sweeping search. After the clerk was under arrest and aware of the presumed authority of the search warrant, his conduct complying with official requests cannot, on this record, be considered voluntary.

C Reversed and remanded.

Richards v. Wisconsin

520 U.S. 385 (1997)

FACTS

Officers in Madison, Wisconsin obtained a warrant to search petitioner Richards' hotel room for drugs and related paraphernalia, but the magistrate refused to give advance authorization for a "no knock" entry. The officer who knocked on Richards' door was dressed, and identified himself, as a maintenance man. Upon opening the door, Richards also saw a uniformed officer and quickly closed the door. The officers kicked down the door, caught Richards trying to escape, and found cash and cocaine in the bathroom. In denying Richards' motion to suppress the evidence on the ground that the officers did not knock and announce their presence before forcing entry, the trial court found that they could gather from Richards' strange behavior that he might try to destroy evidence or escape and that the drugs' disposable nature further justified their decision not to knock and announce. The State Supreme Court affirmed, concluding that Wilson did not preclude the court's pre Wilson *per se* rule that police officers are never required to knock and announce when executing a search warrant in a felony drug investigation because of the special circumstances of today's drug culture.

I Is the doing away with the knock-and-announce requirement justified where there is a threat of physical violence or destruction of evidence with the dwelling to be entered?

R If the police can show reasonable suspicion that it would be futile, dangerous or that by following the knock-and-announce requirement the destruction of evidence would result, the knock-and-announce requirement may be dispensed with.

A In *Wilson v. Arkansas*, we held that the Fourth Amendment incorporates the common law requirement that police knock on a dwelling's door and announce their identity and purpose before attempting forcible entry, recognized that the flexible reasonableness requirement should not be read to mandate a rigid announcement rule that ignores countervailing law enforcement interests and left it to the lower courts to determine the circumstances under which an unannounced entry is reasonable. However, the Fourth Amendment does not permit a blanket exception to the knock and announce requirement for felony drug investigations. While the requirement can give way under circumstances presenting a threat of physical violence or where officers believe that evidence would be destroyed if advance notice were given, the fact that felony drug investigations may frequently present such circumstances cannot remove from the neutral scrutiny of a reviewing court the reasonableness of the police decision not to knock and announce in a particular case. Creating exceptions to the requirement based on the culture surrounding a general category of criminal behavior presents at least two serious concerns. First, the exception contains considerable overgeneralization that would impermissibly insulate from judicial review cases in which a drug investigation does not pose special risks. Second, creating an exception in one category can, relatively easily, be applied to others. If a per se exception were allowed for each criminal activity category that included a considerable risk of danger to officers or destruction of evidence, the knock and announce requirement would be meaningless. The court confronted with the question in each case has a duty to determine whether the facts and circumstances of the particular entry justified dispensing with the requirement. A "no knock" entry is justified when the police have a reasonable suspicion that knocking and announcing their presence, under the particular circumstances, would be dangerous or futile, or that it would inhibit the effective investigation of the crime. This standard strikes the appropriate balance between the legitimate law enforcement concerns at issue in the execution of search warrants and the individual privacy interests affected by no knock entries. Because the evidence in this case establishes that the decision not to knock and announce was a reasonable one under the circumstances, the officers' entry into the hotel room did not violate the Fourth Amendment. That the magistrate had originally refused to issue a no knock warrant means only that at the time the warrant was requested there was insufficient evidence for a no knock entry. However, the officers' decision to enter the room must be evaluated as of the time of entry.

C

Affirmed.

Warden v. Hayden

387 U.S. 294 (1967)

FACTS

The police were informed that an armed robbery had occurred and that the suspect, respondent, had thereafter entered a certain house. Minutes later they arrived there and were told by respondent's wife that she had no objection to their searching the house. Certain officers arrested respondent in an upstairs bedroom when it became clear he was the only man in the house. Others simultaneously searched the first floor and cellar. One found weapons in a flush tank; another, looking "for a man or the money," found in a washing machine clothing of the type the suspect was said to have worn. Ammunition was also found. These items were admitted into evidence without objection at respondent's trial which resulted in his conviction. After unsuccessful state court proceedings respondent sought and was denied habeas corpus relief in the District Court. The Court of Appeals found the search lawful, but reversed on the ground that the clothing seized during the search was immune from seizure, being of "evidential value only."

I

Does the Fourth Amendment permit the search and seizure of materials that are "merely evidentiary?"

R

In the Fourth Amendment permit the search and seizure of materials that are "merely evidentiary?" if there is probable cause to believe it was aid in the apprehension or conviction.

A

"The exigencies of the situation," in which the officers were in pursuit of a suspected armed felon in the house which he had entered only minutes before they arrived, permitted their warrantless entry and search. *McDonald v. United States*. The distinction prohibiting seizure of items of only evidential value and allowing seizure of instrumentalities, fruits, or contraband is no longer accepted as being required by the Fourth Amendment. There is no rational distinction between a search for "mere evidence" and one for an "instrumentality" in terms of the privacy which is safeguarded by the Fourth Amendment; nor does the language of the Amendment itself make such a distinction. The clothing items involved here are not "testimonial" or "communicative" and their introduction did not compel respondent to become a witness against himself in violation of the Fifth Amendment. *Schmerber v. California*. The premise that property interests control government's search and seizure rights, on which *Gouled v. United States*, partly rested, is no longer controlling as the Fourth Amendment's principal object is the protection of privacy, not property. The related premise of *Gouled* that government may not seize evidence for the purpose of proving crime has also been discredited. The Fourth Amendment does not bar a search for that purpose provided that there is probable cause, as there was here, for the belief that the evidence sought will aid in a particular apprehension or conviction. The remedy of suppression, with its limited, functional consequence, has made possible the rejection of both the related *Gouled* premises. Just as the suppression of evidence does not require the return of such items as contraband, the introduction of "mere evidence" does not entitle the State to its retention if it is being wrongfully withheld. The numerous and confusing exceptions to the "mere evidence" limitation make it questionable whether it affords any meaningful protection.

C

Reversed.

Welsh v. Wisconsin

466 U.S. 740 (1984)

FACTS

On the night of April 24, 1978, a witness observed a car that was being driven erratically and that eventually swerved off the road, coming to a stop in a field without causing damage to any person or property. Ignoring the witness' suggestion that he wait for assistance in removing his car, the driver walked away from the scene. The police arrived a few minutes later and were told by the witness that the driver was either very inebriated or very sick. After checking the car's registration, the police, without obtaining a warrant, proceeded to the petitioner's nearby home, arriving at about 9 p.m. They gained entry when petitioner's stepdaughter answered the door, and found petitioner lying naked in bed. Petitioner was then arrested for driving a motor vehicle while under the influence of an intoxicant in violation of a Wisconsin statute which provided that a first offense was a non-criminal violation subject to a civil forfeiture proceeding for a maximum fine of $200. Petitioner was taken to the police station, where he refused to submit to a breath-analysis test. Pursuant to Wisconsin statutes, which subjected an arrestee who refused to take the test to the risk of a 60-day revocation of driving privileges, petitioner requested a court hearing to determine whether his refusal was reasonable. Under Wisconsin law, a refusal to take a breath test was reasonable if the underlying arrest was not lawful. The trial court, ultimately concluding that petitioner's arrest was lawful and that his refusal to take the breath test was therefore unreasonable, issued an order suspending petitioner's license. The Wisconsin Court of Appeals vacated the order, concluding that the warrantless arrest of petitioner in his home violated the Fourth Amendment because the State, although demonstrating probable cause to arrest, had not established the existence of exigent circumstances. The Wisconsin Supreme Court reversed.

I Is the warrantless, nighttime entry of petitioner's home to arrest him for a civil, non-jailable traffic offense prohibited by the special protection afforded the individual in his home by the Fourth Amendment?

R The warrantless, nighttime entry of petitioner's home to arrest him for a civil, non-jailable traffic offense, is prohibited by the special protection afforded the individual in his home by the Fourth Amendment.

A The warrantless, nighttime entry of petitioner's home to arrest him for a civil, non-jailable traffic offense, was prohibited by the special protection afforded the individual in his home by the Fourth Amendment. Before government agents may invade the sanctity of the home, the government must demonstrate exigent circumstances that overcome the presumption of unreasonableness that attaches to all warrantless home entries. An important factor to be considered when determining whether any exigency exists is the gravity of the underlying offense for which the arrest is being made. Moreover, although no exigency is created simply because there is probable cause to believe that a serious crime has been committed, application of the exigent-circumstances exception in the context of a home entry should rarely be sanctioned when there is probable cause to believe that only a minor offense has been committed. Petitioner's warrantless arrest in the privacy of his own bedroom for a non-criminal traffic offense cannot be justified on the basis of the "hot pursuit" doctrine, because there was no immediate or continuous pursuit of the petitioner from the scene of a crime, or on the basis of a threat to public safety, because petitioner had already arrived home and had abandoned his car at the scene of the accident. Nor can the arrest be justified as necessary to preserve evidence of petitioner's blood-alcohol level. Even assuming that the underlying facts would support a finding of this exigent circumstance, given the fact that the State had chosen to classify the first offense for driving while intoxicated as a non-criminal, civil forfeiture offense for which no imprisonment was possible, a warrantless home arrest cannot be upheld simply because evidence of the petitioner's blood-alcohol level might have dissipated while the police obtained a warrant.

C

Vacated and remanded.

Chimel v. California

395 U.S. 752 (1969)

FACTS

Police officers (plaintiffs) arrived at Defendant Chimel's home with a warrant for his arrest for the burglary of a coin shop. Armed with an arrest warrant but not a search warrant, the police were admitted to petitioner's home by his wife, where they awaited petitioner's arrival. When he entered he was served with the warrant. Although he denied the officers' request to "look around," they conducted a search of the entire house "on the basis of the lawful arrest." The officers thoroughly searched the entire three-bedroom house and seized numerous coins and metals. At petitioner's trial on burglary charges, items taken from his home were admitted over objection that they had been unconstitutionally seized. His conviction was affirmed by the California appellate courts, which held, despite their acceptance of petitioner's contention that the arrest warrant was invalid, that since the arresting officers had procured the warrant "in good faith," and since in any event they had had sufficient information to constitute probable cause for the arrest, the arrest was lawful. The courts also held that the search was justified as incident to a valid arrest.

I Is a warrantless search of a person's entire premises justified when it was made incident to the arrest of the person?

R A search incident to arrest but without a warrant may extend only to the person of the arrestee and the area within his immediate control.

A An arresting officer may search the arrestee's person to discover and remove weapons and to seize evidence to prevent its concealment or destruction, and may search the area "within the immediate control" of the person arrested, meaning the area from which he might gain possession of a weapon or destructible evidence. For the routine search of rooms other than that in which an arrest occurs, or for searching desk drawers or other closed or concealed areas in that room itself, absent well-recognized exceptions, a search warrant is required. While the reasonableness of a search incident to arrest depends upon "the facts and circumstances - the total atmosphere of the case," those facts and circumstances must be viewed in the light of established Fourth Amendment principles. Therefore, it is reasonable for an officer to search the person he is arresting to remove weapons the person might use to resist or to escape. It is also reasonable for an officer to search for and seize any evidence on the arrestee's person to prevent its concealment or destruction. Likewise, it is reasonable for the officer to search the area within the immediate control of the arrestee, meaning the area within which the arrestee might reach to grab a weapon or destructible evidence. However, there is no justification for routinely searching incident to an arrest any room, other than that in which the arrest occurs, or for searching closed drawers or concealed areas. Thus, the application of sound Fourth Amendment principles to the facts of this case produces a clear result. The search here went far beyond the petitioner's person and the area from within which he might have obtained either a weapon or something that could have been used as evidence against him. There was no constitutional justification, in the absence of a search warrant, for extending the search beyond that area. The scope of the search was, therefore, "unreasonable" under the Fourth and Fourteenth Amendments, and the petitioner's conviction cannot stand.

C Reversed.

United States v. Robinson

414 U.S. 218 (1973)

FACTS

As a result of a previous check of respondent's operator's permit, and having probable cause to arrest respondent for driving while his license was revoked, a police officer made a full-custody arrest of respondent for such offense. In accordance with prescribed procedures, the officer made a search of respondent's person, in the course of which he found in a coat pocket a cigarette package containing heroin. The heroin was admitted into evidence at the District Court trial and defendant was convicted for its possession and concealment. The Court of Appeals reversed and held that the heroin was the fruit of an legal search.

I

Does any lawful custodial arrest justify a full search of the arrestee's person?

R

Any lawful custodial arrest justifies a full search of the arrestee's person.

A

A search incident to a valid arrest is not limited to a frisk of the suspect's outer clothing and removal any such weapons but may also include other evidence obtained during the search. Moreover, a custodial arrest of a suspect based on probable cause is a reasonable intrusion under the Fourth Amendment and a search incident to the arrest requires no additional justification, such as the probability in a particular arrest situation that weapons or evidence would in fact be found upon the suspect's person; and whether or not there was present one of the reasons supporting the authority for a search of the person incident to a lawful arrest need not be litigated in each case. Lastly, since the custodial arrest here gave rise to the authority to search, it is immaterial that the arresting officer did not fear that the respondent or suspect was armed. The Court of Appeals decided that police may not ordinarily fully search an arrestee, but may conduct a limited search for weapons. In effect, the court decided that the only reason that would support a full search incident to an arrest was the possibility of discovery of evidence or fruits. We disagree. In *Terry* we clearly recognized the difference between a search incident to an arrest and a protective frisk, and held that different rules governing these two types of searches. We hold that when there is a lawful custodial arrest, a full search of the arrestee is not only exception to the warrant requirement of the Fourth Amendment, but is also a reasonable search on to that Amendment. Because the officer in this case made a lawful custodial arrest of the defendant, the search he conducted was permissible.

C

Reversed.

New York v. Belton

453 U.S. 454 (1981)

FACTS

An automobile in which respondent was one of the occupants was stopped by a New York State policeman for traveling at an excessive rate of speed. In the process of discovering that none of the occupants owned the car or was related to the owner, the policeman smelled burnt marihuana and saw on the floor of the car an envelope suspected of containing marihuana. He then directed the occupants to get out of the car and arrested them for unlawful possession of marihuana. After searching each of the occupants, he searched the passenger compartment of the car, found a jacket belonging to respondent, unzipped one of the pockets, and discovered cocaine. Subsequently, respondent was indicted for criminal possession of a controlled substance. After the trial court had denied his motion to suppress the cocaine seized from his jacket pocket, respondent pleaded guilty to a lesser included offense, while preserving his claim that the cocaine had been seized in violation of the Fourth and Fourteenth Amendments. The Appellate Division of the New York Supreme Court upheld the constitutionality of the search and seizure, but the New York Court of Appeals reversed.

I

Does the constitutionality permissible scope of a search incident to an arrest of an occupant of an automobile automatically extend to and include the passenger compartment of that automobile?

R

An officer who makes a lawful custodial arrest of an occupant of an automobile may constitutionally search the passenger compartment of that automobile.

A

The search of respondent's jacket was a search incident to a lawful custodial arrest, and hence did not violate the Fourth and Fourteenth Amendments. The jacket, being located inside the passenger compartment of the car, was "within the arrestee's immediate control" within the meaning of *Chimel v. California*, wherein it was held that a lawful custodial arrest creates a situation justifying the contemporaneous warrantless search of the arrestee and of the immediately surrounding area. Not only may the police search the passenger compartment of the car in such circumstances, they may also examine the contents of any containers found in the passenger compartment. And such a container may be searched whether it is open or closed, since the justification for the search is not that the arrestee has no privacy interest in the container but that the lawful custodial arrest justifies the infringement of any privacy interest the arrestee may have.

C

Judgment reversed.

Whren v. United States

517 U.S. 806 (1996)

FACTS

Plainclothes policemen patrolling a "high drug area" in an unmarked vehicle observed a truck driven by petitioner Brown waiting at a stop sign at an intersection for an unusually long time; the truck then turned suddenly, without signaling, and sped off at an "unreasonable" speed. The officers stopped the vehicle, apparently to warn the driver about traffic violations, and upon approaching the truck observed plastic bags of crack cocaine in petitioner Whren's hands. Petitioners were arrested. Prior to trial on federal drug charges, they moved for suppression of the evidence, arguing that the stop had not been justified by either a reasonable suspicion or probable cause to believe petitioners were engaged in illegal drug-dealing activity, and that the officers' traffic-violation ground for approaching the truck was pretextual. The motion to suppress was denied, petitioners were convicted, and the Court of Appeals affirmed.

I

Can an officer's subjective motives invalidate conduct if it is supported by probable cause?

R

An officer's subjective motives will not invalidate conduct if it is supported by probable cause, even if outside standard police practices and procedures.

A

The temporary detention of a motorist upon probable cause to believe that he has violated the traffic laws does not violate the Fourth Amendment's prohibition against unreasonable seizures, even if a reasonable officer would not have stopped the motorist absent some additional law enforcement objective. Detention of a motorist is reasonable where probable cause exists to believe that a traffic violation has occurred. Petitioners claim that, because the police may be tempted to use commonly occurring traffic violations as means of investigating violations of other laws, the Fourth Amendment test for traffic stops should be whether a reasonable officer would have stopped the car for the purpose of enforcing the traffic violation at issue. However, this Court's cases foreclose the argument that ulterior motives can invalidate police conduct justified on the basis of probable cause. Subjective intentions play no role in ordinary, probable-cause Fourth Amendment analysis. Although framed as an empirical question--whether the officer's conduct deviated materially from standard police practices--petitioners' proposed test is plainly designed to combat the perceived danger of pretextual stops. It is thus inconsistent with this Court's cases, which make clear that the Fourth Amendment's concern with "reasonableness" allows certain actions to be taken in certain circumstances, whatever the subjective intent. Nor can the Fourth Amendment's protections be thought to vary from place to place and from time to time, which would be the consequence of assessing the reasonableness of police conduct in light of local law enforcement practices. Interests inherent in Fourth Amendment inquiries does not support enforcement of minor traffic laws by plainclothes police in unmarked vehicles, since that practice only minimally advances the government's interest in traffic safety while subjecting motorists to inconvenience, confusion, and anxiety. Where probable cause exists, this Court has found it necessary to engage in balancing only in cases involving searches or seizures conducted in a manner unusually harmful to the individual. The making of a traffic stop out-of-uniform does not remotely qualify as such an extreme practice.

C

Affirmed

Chambers v. Maroney

399 U.S. 42 (1970)

FACTS

Petitioner was one of four men arrested after the auto in which they were riding was stopped by police shortly after an armed robbery of a service station. The arrests resulted from information supplied by the service station attendant and bystanders. The car was driven to a police station, where a search disclosed two revolvers, one loaded with dumdum bullets, and cards bearing the name of an attendant at another service station who had been robbed at gunpoint a week earlier. In a warrant-authorized search of petitioner's home the next day police found and seized ammunition, including dumdum bullets similar to those found in one of the guns in the car. At his first trial, which ended in a mistrial, petitioner was represented by a Legal Aid Society attorney. Another Legal Aid Society attorney, who represented him at the second trial, did not confer with petitioner until a few minutes before that trial began. The materials taken from the car and the bullets seized from petitioner's home were introduced in evidence and petitioner was convicted of robbery of both service stations. Petitioner did not take a direct appeal, but sought, unsuccessfully, a writ of habeas corpus in the Pennsylvania courts and in the federal courts, challenging the admissibility of the materials taken from the car and the ammunition seized in his home, and claiming that he was denied the effective assistance of counsel. The Court of Appeals dealt with the claim that the attorney's lack of preparation resulted in the failure to exclude the guns and ammunition by finding harmless error in the admission of the bullets and ruling that the materials seized from the car were admissible in evidence, and concluded that the claim of prejudice from substitution of counsel was without substantial basis.

I

If the police have probable cause justifying an immediate warrantless search of an automobile, can they also conduct a delayed search without a warrant?

R

If the police have probable cause justifying an immediate warrantless search of an automobile, they can also conduct a delayed search without a warrant.

A

The warrantless search of the automobile was valid and the materials seized therefrom were properly introduced in evidence. The search, made at the police station some time after the arrest, cannot be justified as incident to the arrest. Just as there was probable cause to arrest the occupants of the car, there was probable cause to search the car for guns and stolen money. If there is probable cause, an automobile, because of its mobility, may be searched without a warrant in circumstances that would not justify a warrantless search of a house or office. Given probable cause, there is no difference under the Fourth Amendment between (1) seizing and holding a car before presenting the issue of probable cause to a magistrate, and (2) carrying out an immediate warrantless search. The findings of the District Court and the Court of Appeals that, if there was error in admitting in evidence the ammunition seized from petitioner's house, it was harmless error beyond a reasonable doubt, are affirmed on the basis of the Court's review of the record. Based on a careful examination of the state court record, the Court of Appeals' judgment denying a hearing as to the adequacy of representation by counsel, is not disturbed.

C

Affirmed.

California v. Carney

471 U.S. 386 (1985)

FACTS

A Drug Enforcement Administration (DEA) agent, who had information that respondent's (Carney) mobile motor home was being used to exchange marihuana for sex, watched respondent approach a youth who accompanied respondent to the motor home, which was parked in a lot in downtown San Diego. The agent and other agents then kept the vehicle under surveillance, and stopped the youth after he left the vehicle. He told them that he had received marihuana in return for allowing respondent sexual contacts. At the agents' request, the youth returned to the motor home and knocked on the door; respondent stepped out. Without a warrant or consent, one agent then entered the motor home and observed marihuana. A subsequent search of the motor home at the police station revealed additional marihuana, and respondent was charged with possession of marihuana for sale. After his motion to suppress the evidence discovered in the motor home was denied, respondent was convicted in California Superior Court on a plea of *nolo contendere* ("no contest"). The California Court of Appeal affirmed. The California Supreme Court reversed, holding that the search of the motor home was unreasonable and that the motor vehicle exception to the warrant requirement of the Fourth Amendment did not apply, because expectations of privacy in a motor home are more like those in a dwelling than in an automobile.

I

Is a search warrant required by law enforcement when they have probable cause to believe a motor vehicle capable of traveling the public roadways contains evidence of a crime?

R

Without first obtaining a search warrant, any vehicle that is readily mobile and suspect to the pervasive laws regulating motor vehicles may be searched so long as there is probable cause supporting the search.

A

The warrantless search of respondent's motor home did not violate the Fourth Amendment. When a vehicle is being used on the highways or is capable of such use and is found stationary in a place not regularly used for residential purposes, the two justifications for the vehicle exception come into play. First, the vehicle is readily mobile, and, second, there is a reduced expectation of privacy stemming from the pervasive regulation of vehicles capable of traveling on highways. Here, while respondent's vehicle possessed some attributes of a home, it clearly falls within the vehicle exception. To distinguish between respondent's motor home and an ordinary sedan for purposes of the vehicle exception would require that the exception be applied depending on the size of the vehicle and the quality of its appointments. Moreover, to fail to apply the exception to vehicles such as a motor home would ignore the fact that a motor home lends itself easily to use as an instrument of illicit drug traffic or other illegal activity. While ready mobility was perhaps the original justification for the automobile exception, it is not the only one. The reasons for the exception are twofold. Besides the element of mobility, automobiles garner a lesser expectation of privacy than once home or office. This reduced expectation of privacy derives not from the fact that the area to be searched is in plain view, but from the

---

pervasive regulation of vehicles readily capable of traveling on the public highways. The fact that this is a motor "home" is irrelevant given its fulfillment of the requirements of the automobile exception. Our application of the automobile exception had never turn on other uses to which a vehicle might be put. Therefore, we hold that this search was not unreasonable; it was plainly one that the magistrate could authorize if presented with these facts. The DEA agents had fresh, direct, uncontradicted evidence that the respondent was distributing a controlled substance from the vehicle, apart from evidence of other possible offenses. The agents thus had abundant probable cause to enter and search the vehicle for evidence of a crime notwithstanding its possible use as a dwelling place.

C

The judgment of the California Supreme Court is reversed, and the case is remanded for further proceedings not inconsistent with this opinion.

United States v. Chadwick

433 U.S. 1 (1977)

FACTS

When respondents arrived by train in Boston from San Diego, they were arrested at their waiting automobile by federal narcotics agents, who had been alerted that respondents were possible drug traffickers. A double-locked footlocker, which respondents had transported on the train and which the agents had probable cause to believe contained narcotics, had been loaded in the trunk of the automobile. Respondents, together with the automobile and footlocker, which was admittedly under the agents' exclusive control, were then taken to the Federal Building in Boston. An hour and a half after the arrests the agents opened the footlocker without respondents' consent or a search warrant and found large amounts of marihuana in it. Respondents were subsequently indicted for possession of marihuana with intent to distribute it. The District Court granted their pretrial motion to suppress the marihuana obtained from the footlocker, holding that warrantless searches are per se unreasonable under the Fourth Amendment unless they fall within some established exception to the warrant requirement, and that the footlocker search was not justified under either the "automobile exception" or as a search incident to a lawful arrest; the Court of Appeals affirmed.

I Can the warrantless search of another property seized at the time of an arrest be justified as a search incident to that arrest if the search is remote in time or place and no exigency exists?

R The warrantless search of another property seized at the time of an arrest cannot justified as a search incident to that arrest if the search is remote in time or place and no exigency calling for an immediate search exists.

A Respondents were entitled to the protection of the Warrant Clause of the Fourth Amendment, with the evaluation of a neutral magistrate, before their privacy interests in the contents of the footlocker were invaded. A fundamental purpose of the Fourth Amendment is to safeguard individuals from unreasonable government invasions of legitimate privacy interests, and not simply those interests inside the four walls of the home. By placing personal effects inside a double-locked footlocker, respondents manifested an expectation that the contents would remain free from public examination, and no less than one who locks the doors of his home against intruders, one who safeguards his personal possessions in this manner is due the protection of the Fourth Amendment's Warrant Clause; since there was no exigency calling for an immediate search, it was unreasonable for the Government to conduct the search without the safeguards a judicial warrant provides. The footlocker search was not justified under the "automobile exception," since a person's expectations of privacy in personal luggage are substantially greater than in an automobile. In this connection, the footlocker's mobility did not justify dispensing with a search warrant, because once the federal agents had seized the footlocker at the railroad station and safely transferred it to the Federal Building under their exclusive control, there was not the slightest danger that it or its contents could have been removed before a valid search warrant could be obtained. Nor was the footlocker search justified as a search incident to a lawful arrest, where the search was remote in time or place from the arrest and no exigency existed, the search having been conducted more than an hour after the federal agents had gained exclusive control of the footlocker and long after respondents were securely in custody.

C

Affirmed.

California v. Acevedo

500 U.S. 565 (1991)

FACTS

Police observed respondent Acevedo (defendant) leave an apartment, known to contain marijuana, with a brown paper bag the size of marijuana packages they had seen earlier. He placed the bag in his car's trunk, and, as he drove away, they stopped the car, opened the trunk and the bag, and found marijuana. Acevedo's motion to suppress the marijuana was denied, and he pleaded guilty to possession of marijuana for sale. The California Court of Appeals held that the marijuana should have been suppressed. Finding that the officers had probable cause to believe that the bag contained drugs but lacked probable cause to suspect that the car, itself, otherwise contained contraband, the court concluded that the case was controlled by *United States v. Chadwick*, which held that police could seize movable luggage or other closed containers, but could not open them without a warrant, since, *inter alia*, a person has a heightened privacy expectation in such containers.

I

Where police lack probable cause to search the entire automobile, must they obtain a warrant to search a container in an automobile when they have probable cause to search the container?

R

If they have probable cause to search the container, the police may search a closed container in an automobile without a warrant.

A

In *Ross*, we held that a warrantless search of an automobile under *Carroll* could include a search of containers found inside the car. In that case, we upheld the search, reasoning that when probable cause justifies the search of an automobile, it also justifies the search of every part of the automobile and its contents that may conceal the object of the search. In *Chadwick*, the police had probable cause to believe a certain footlocker contained drugs. Officers followed as a footlocker was carried from a train to a waiting car, seized it as soon as it was placed in the car's trunk and then search it. Under the *Chadwick/Sanders* rule, the more likely the police are to find drugs in a container, the less authority they have to search it. This rule is a poor guideline for law-enforcement officers. To end the confusion this rule has bred, we interpret *Carroll* to provide one clear cut rule to govern all automobile searches, and eliminate the warrant requirement for closed containers set forth in *Sanders*. That is, the police may search an automobile and the containers within it where they have probable cause to believe contraband or evidence is contained.

C

Reversed and remanded.

Horton v. California

469 U.S. 128 (1990)

FACTS

A California policeman determined that there was probable cause to search petitioner Horton's home for the proceeds of a robbery and the robbers' weapons. His search warrant affidavit referred to police reports that described both the weapons and the proceeds, but the warrant issued by the Magistrate only authorized a search for the proceeds. Upon executing the warrant, the officer did not find the stolen property but did find the weapons in plain view and seized them. The trial court refused to suppress the seized evidence, and Horton was convicted of armed robbery. The California Court of Appeal affirmed. Since the officer had testified that while he was searching Horton's home for the stolen property he was also interested in finding other evidence connecting Horton to the robbery, the seized evidence was not discovered "inadvertently." However, in rejecting Horton's argument that *Coolidge v. New Hampshire* therefore required suppression of that evidence, the Court of Appeal relied on a State Supreme Court decision holding that Coolidge's discussion of the inadvertence limitation on the "plain-view" doctrine was not binding because it was contained in a four-Justice plurality opinion.

I

Does the Fourth Amendment permit the warrantless seizure of evidence in plain view if the seized evidence was not discovered advertently?

R

The Fourth Amendment permits the warrantless seizure of evidence in plain view if (1) the officer has lawfully arrived at the place from which he views the evidence; (2) if the evidence's incriminating character is immediately apparent; and (3) if he has a lawful right of access to the evidence.

A

The Fourth Amendment does not prohibit the warrantless seizure of evidence in plain view even though the discovery of the evidence was not inadvertent. Although inadvertence is a characteristic of most legitimate plain-view seizures, it is not a necessary condition. Coolidge is a binding precedent. However, the second of the Coolidge plurality's two limitations on the plain-view doctrine - that the discovery of evidence in plain view must be inadvertent - was not essential to the Court's rejection of the State's plain-view argument in that case. Rather, the first limitation that plain view alone is never enough to justify a warrantless seizure adequately supports the Court's holding that gunpowder found in vacuum sweepings from one of the automobiles seized in plain view on the defendant's driveway in the course of his arrest could not be introduced against him because the warrantless seizures violated the Fourth Amendment. In order for a warrantless seizure of an object in plain view to be valid, two conditions must be satisfied in addition to the essential predicate that the officer did not violate the Fourth Amendment in arriving at the place from which the object could be plainly viewed. First, the object's incriminating character must be "immediately apparent." Although the cars in Coolidge were obviously in plain view, their probative value remained uncertain until after their interiors were swept and examined microscopically. Second, the officer must have a lawful right of access to the object itself. Justice Harlan, who concurred in the Coolidge judgment but did not join the plurality's plain-view discussion, may well have rested his vote on the fact that the cars' seizure was accomplished by means of a warrantless trespass on the defendant's property. There are two flaws in the Coolidge plurality's conclusion that the inadvertence requirement was necessary to avoid a violation of the Fourth Amendment's mandate that a valid warrant "particularly describ[e] . . . [the] . . . things to be seized." First, evenhanded law enforcement is best achieved by applying objective standards of conduct, rather than standards that depend upon the officer's subjective state of mind. The fact that an officer is interested in an item and fully expects to find it should not invalidate its seizure if the search is confined in area and duration by a warrant's terms or by a valid exception to the warrant requirement. Second, the suggestion that the inadvertence requirement is necessary to prevent the police from conducting general searches, or from converting specific warrants into general warrants, is not persuasive because that interest is already served by the requirements that an unparticularized warrant not be issued and that a warrantless search be circumscribed by the exigencies which justify its initiation. Here, the search's scope was not enlarged by the warrant's omission of reference to the weapons; indeed, no search for the weapons could have taken place if the named items had been found or surrendered at the outset. The prohibition against general searches and warrants is based on privacy concerns, which are not implicated when an officer with a lawful right of access to an item in plain view seizes it without a warrant.

C

Affirmed.

Arizona v. Hicks

480 U.S. 321 (1987)

FACTS

A bullet fired through the floor of respondent's apartment injured a man on the floor below. Police entered the apartment to search for the shooter, for other victims, and for weapons, and there seized three weapons and discovered a stocking-cap mask. While there, one of the policemen noticed two sets of expensive stereo components and, suspecting that they were stolen, read and recorded their serial numbers - moving some of them, including a turntable, to do so - and phoned in the numbers to headquarters. Upon learning that the turntable had been taken in an armed robbery, he seized it immediately. Respondent was subsequently indicted for the robbery, but the state trial court granted his motion to suppress the evidence that had been seized, and the Arizona Court of Appeals affirmed. Relying upon a statement in *Mincey v. Arizona*, that a warrantless search must be "strictly circumscribed by the exigencies which justify its initiation," the Court of Appeals held that the policeman's obtaining the serial numbers violated the Fourth Amendment because it was unrelated to the shooting, the exigent circumstance that justified the initial entry and search. Both state courts rejected the contention that the policeman's actions were justified under the "plain view" doctrine.

I

Is probable cause required to raise the "plain view doctrine?"

R

The "plain view doctrine" may not be used to circumvent the warrant requirement – that is, it may not be used to justify a warrantless search or seizure of a dwelling.

A

The policeman's actions come within the purview of the Fourth Amendment. The mere recording of the serial numbers did not constitute a "seizure" since it did not meaningfully interfere with respondent's possessory interest in either the numbers or the stereo equipment. However, the moving of the equipment was a "search" separate and apart from the search that was the lawful objective of entering the apartment. The fact that the search uncovered nothing of great personal value to respondent is irrelevant. The "plain view" doctrine does not render the search "reasonable" under the Fourth Amendment. The policeman's action directed to the stereo equipment was not ipso facto unreasonable simply because it was unrelated to the justification for entering the apartment. That lack of relationship always exists when the "plain view" doctrine applies. In saying that a warrantless search must be "strictly circumscribed by the exigencies which justify its initiation," *Mincey* was simply addressing the scope of the primary search itself, and was not overruling the "plain view" doctrine by implication. However, the search was invalid because, as the State concedes, the policeman had only a "reasonable suspicion" - i.e., less than probable cause to believe - that the stereo equipment was stolen. Probable cause is required to invoke the "plain view" doctrine as it applies to seizures. It would be illogical to hold that an object is seizable on lesser grounds, during an unrelated search and seizure, than would have been needed to obtain a warrant for it if it had been known to be on the premises. Probable cause to believe the equipment was stolen was also necessary to support the search here, whether legal authority to move the equipment could be found only as the inevitable concomitant of the authority to seize it, or also as a consequence of some independent power to search objects in plain view. The policeman's action cannot be upheld on the ground that it was not a "full-blown search" but was only a "cursory inspection" that could be justified by reasonable suspicion instead of probable cause. A truly cursory inspection - one that involves merely looking at what is already exposed to view, without disturbing it - is not a "search" for Fourth Amendment purposes, and therefore does not even require reasonable suspicion. This Court is unwilling to create a subcategory of "cursory" searches under the Fourth Amendment.

C

Affirmed.

Schneckloth v. Bustamonte

412 U.S. 218 (1973)

FACTS

While on routine patrol in Sunnyvale, California, at approximately 2:40 in the morning, Police Officer James Rand stopped an automobile when he observed that one headlight and its license plate light were burned out. Six men were in the vehicle. Joe Alcala and Defendant-Respondent Robert Bustamonte were in the front seat with Joe Gonzales, the driver. Three older men were seated in the rear. When, in response to the policeman's question, Gonzales could not produce a driver's license, Officer Rand asked if any of the other five had any evidence of identification. Only Alcala produced a license, and he explained that the car was his brother's. After the six occupants had stepped out of the car at the officer's request and after two additional policemen had arrived, Officer Rand asked Alcala if he could search the car. Alcala replied, "Sure, go ahead." Prior to the search no one was threatened with arrest and, according to Officer Rand's uncontradicted testimony, it "was all very congenial at this time." Gonzales testified that Alcala actually helped in the search of the car, by opening the trunk and glove compartment. Gonzales said the police officer asked Joe Alcala if the trunk opened and Joe said, "Yes." He went to the car and got the keys and opened up the trunk." Wadded up under the left rear seat, the police officers found three checks that had previously been stolen from a car wash. The defendant's motion to suppress the evidence on the grounds that his consent was not voluntary was denied and he was convicted. The conviction was affirmed on appeal. The Federal District Court denied defendant's petition for a writ of habeas corpus, but the Ninth Circuit Court of Appeals set aside the District Court order.

I

In order for a search to be valid, must the State prove that one who consents to a search had knowledge of the right to refuse consent?

R

The State need only prove consent was voluntarily given and not the result of duress or coercion, either express or implied; the consent giver need not know his right to refuse consent, although such knowledge is one factor in determining if the consent was voluntary, for a consent search to be deemed valid.

A

Our decision today is a narrow one. We hold only that when the subject of a search is not in custody and the State attempts to justify a search on the basis of his consent, the Fourth and Fourteenth Amendments require that the State demonstrate that the consent was in fact voluntarily given, and not the result of duress or coercion, express or implied. The question of whether consent to a search was voluntary or was the product of duress or coercion, express or implied, is a question of fact to be determined from the totality of all the circumstances; the knowledge of the right to refuse consent being only one factor to be considered. In making the inquiry, all factors must be taken into account, including subtly coercive police questions, as well as the subjective state of mind of the person who consents. Searches based on coerced consent can thus be set aide. And while the subject's knowledge of a right to refuse is a factor to be taken into account, the prosecution is not required to demonstrate such knowledge as a prerequisite to establishing a voluntary consent. Because the California court followed these principles in affirming the respondent's conviction, and because the

Court of Appeals for the Ninth Circuit in remanding for an evidentiary hearing required more, its judgment must be reversed.

C

Reversed.

United States v. Matlock

415 U.S. 164 (1974)

FACTS

Respondent Matlock was arrested in the front yard of a house in which he lived along with a Mrs. Graff (daughter of the lessees) and others. The arresting officers, who did not ask him which room he occupied or whether he would consent to a search, were then admitted to the house by Mrs. Graff and, with her consent but without a warrant, searched the house, including a bedroom, which Mrs. Graff told them was jointly occupied by respondent and herself, and in a closet of which the officers found and seized money. Respondent was indicted for bank robbery, and moved to suppress the seized money as evidence. The District Court held that where consent by a third person is relied upon as justification for a search, the Government must show, inter alia, not only that it reasonably appeared to the officers that the person had authority to consent, but also that the person had actual authority to permit the search, and that the Government had not satisfactorily proved that Mrs. Graff had such authority. Although Mrs. Graff's statements to the officers that she and respondent occupied the same bedroom were deemed admissible to prove the officers' good-faith belief, they were held to be inadmissible extrajudicial statements to prove the truth of the facts therein averred, and the same was held to be true of statements by both Mrs. Graff and respondent that they were married, which was not the case. The Court of Appeals affirmed.

I

Can a 3rd party give lawful consent to police to search a suspect's dwelling jointly occupied by the 3rd party and the suspect?

R

A 3rd party can give lawful consent to police to search a suspect's dwelling jointly occupied by the 3rd party and the suspect and any evidence discovered in that search may used against the suspect [defendant] in a criminal trial.

A

When the prosecution seeks to justify a warrantless search by proof of voluntary consent it is not limited to proof that consent was given by the defendant, but may show that permission to search was obtained from a third party who possessed common authority over or other sufficient relationship to the premises or effects sought to be inspected. It was error to exclude from evidence at the suppression hearings Mrs. Graff's out-of-court statements respecting the joint occupancy of the bedroom, as well as the evidence that both respondent and Mrs. Graff had represented themselves as husband and wife. There is no automatic rule against receiving hearsay evidence in suppression hearings (where the trial court itself can accord such evidence such weight as it deems desirable), and under the circumstances here, where the District Court was satisfied that Mrs. Graff's out-of-court statements had in fact been made and nothing in the record raised doubts about their truthfulness, there was no apparent reason to exclude the declarations in the course of resolving the issues raised at the suppression hearings. Mrs. Graff's statements were against her penal interest, since extramarital cohabitation is a state crime. Thus they carried their own indicia of reliability and should have been admitted as evidence at the suppression hearings, even if they would not have been admissible at respondent's trial. Although, given the admissibility of the excluded statements, the Government apparently sustained its burden of proof as to Mrs. Graff's authority to consent to the search, the District Court should reconsider the sufficiency of the evidence in light of this Court's opinion.

C

Reversed and remanded.

Illinois v. Rodriguez

497 U.S. 177 (1990)

FACTS

Defendant-Respondent Edward Rodriguez was arrested in his apartment and charged with possession of illegal drugs, which the police had observed in plain view and seized. The officers did not have an arrest or search warrant, but gained entry to the apartment with the assistance of Gail Fischer, who represented that the apartment was "our[s]" and that she had clothes and furniture there, unlocked the door with her key, and gave the officers permission to enter. The trial court granted respondent's motion to suppress the seized evidence, holding that at the time she consented to the entry Fischer did not have common authority because she had moved out of the apartment. The court also rejected the State's contention that, even if Fischer did not have common authority, there was no Fourth Amendment violation if the police reasonably believed at the time of their entry that she possessed the authority to consent. The Appellate Court of Illinois affirmed.

I

Is the Fourth Amendment violated where police make a warrantless consent entry based on a reasonable belief that the person giving consent has the authority to do so?

R

The Fourth Amendment is not violated by a warrantless entry based on consent of a third party is reasonable so long as it was objectively reasonable for law enforcement to believe a third party had authority to give consent.

A

The record demonstrates that the State has not satisfied its burden of proving that Fischer had "joint access or control for most purposes" over respondent's apartment, as is required under *United States v. Matlock*, to establish "common authority." A warrantless entry is valid when based upon the consent of a third party whom the police, at the time of the entry, reasonably believe to possess common authority over the premises, but who in fact does not. Because the Appellate Court's opinion does not contain a "plain statement" that its decision rests on an adequate and independent state ground, it is subject to review by this Court. What respondent is assured by the Fourth Amendment is not that no Government search of his house will occur unless he consents; but that no such search will occur that is "unreasonable." As with the many other factual determinations that must regularly be made by Government agents in the Fourth Amendment context, the "reasonableness" of a police determination of consent to enter must be judged not by whether the police were correct in their assessment, but by the objective standard of whether the facts available at the moment would warrant a person of reasonable caution in the belief that the consenting party had authority over the premises. If not, then warrantless entry without further inquiry is unlawful unless authority actually exists. But if so, the search is valid. Since we find the ruling from below to be in error, we remand for consideration of the reasonableness of the officer's belief in the case.

C

No. The Fourth Amendment is not violated by a warrantless entry based on consent of a third party is reasonable so long as it was objectively reasonable for law enforcement to believe a third party had authority to give consent.

Terry v. Ohio

392 U.S. 1 (1968)

FACTS

A Cleveland detective (McFadden), on a downtown beat which he had been patrolling for many years, observed two strangers (Defendant-Petitioner Terry and another man, Chilton) on a street corner. He saw them proceed alternately back and forth along an identical route, pausing to stare in the same store window, which they did for a total of about 24 times. Each completion of the route was followed by a conference between the two on a corner, at which time they were joined by a third man (Katz) who left swiftly. Suspecting the two men of "casing a job, a stick-up," the officer followed them and saw them rejoin the third man a couple of blocks away in front of a store. The officer approached the three, identified himself as a policeman, and asked their names. The men "mumbled something," whereupon McFadden spun petitioner around, patted down his outside clothing, and found in his overcoat pocket, but was unable to remove, a pistol. The officer ordered the three into the store. He removed petitioner's overcoat, took out a revolver, and ordered the three to face the wall with their hands raised. He patted down the outer clothing of Chilton and Katz and seized a revolver from Chilton's outside overcoat pocket. He did not put his hands under the outer garments of Katz (since he discovered nothing in his pat-down which might have been a weapon), or under petitioner's or Chilton's outer garments until he felt the guns. The three were taken to the police station. Petitioner and Chilton were charged with carrying concealed weapons and Terry moved to suppress the weapon as evidence. The motion was denied. Both the state Appeals Court and the state Supreme Court denied defendant's appeals.

I

May an officer conduct a limited frisk for weapons under circumstances that would lead the officer to reasonably believe that a suspect is armed where probable cause to seize and search is lacking?

R

The officer may conduct a frisk of limited scope when searching for a weapon if he observes conduct that leads him to reasonably believe that a suspect is armed and dangerous.

A

The issue before us is a narrow one; whether it is always unreasonable for a police man to seize a person and make a limited search for weapons, unless there is probable cause for an arrest. Our analysis begins with the understanding that whenever a police officer "accosts" an individual and keeps them from leaving, he has seized that person. Also where there is a patting down of the outer surfaces of a person's clothing, there is a search. Thus, the Fourth Amendment is implicated even when the officer stops short of a full-blown search and or arrest. In the instant case then, it is conceded that Defendant Terry was seized and search by Officer McFadden. However, we must now determine if Officer McFadden's actions were reasonable, both at the onset and whether they were reasonably related in scope to the circumstances that justified the interference in the first instance. The job of a Police officer is a dangerous one. So it follows that there is an essential need for officers to protect themselves and others even in situations where they lack probable cause to arrest. Such a search, however, must be strictly limited by the demands that justify it. Specifically, it must be limited to actions necessary to discover weapons and no further.

Thus if a police officer has reason to believe he's dealing with an armed and dangerous suspect, even without probable cause to arrest, the officer must be free to take the necessary actions to neutralize that danger. Absolute certainty that the person is armed is not required; the test is whether a reasonable prudent person in a similar circumstance and under like conditions would believe that his safety or the safety of others is in danger. In making this determination, the officer may draw upon his experience to formulate specific reasonable inferences based on the facts presented. Thus, we conclude on these facts that the gun seized from the defendant was properly admitted into evidence against him.

C Affirmed.

Dunaway v. New York

442 U.S. 200 (1979)

FACTS

A Rochester, N.Y., police detective questioned a jail inmate, the supposed source of a lead implicating petitioner Dunaway in an attempted robbery and homicide, but learned nothing that supplied "enough information to get a warrant" for petitioner's arrest. Nevertheless, the detective ordered other detectives to "pick up" petitioner and "bring him in." Petitioner was then taken into custody, and although not told that he was under arrest, he would have been physically restrained if he had attempted to leave. He was driven to police headquarters and placed in an interrogation room, where he was questioned by officers after being given the warnings required by *Miranda v. Arizona*. He waived counsel and eventually made statements and drew sketches that incriminated him in the crime. At his state-court trial, his motions to suppress the statements and sketches were denied, and he was convicted. The New York appellate courts affirmed the conviction, but this Court vacated the judgment, and remanded for further consideration in light of the supervening decision in *Brown v. Illinois*, which held that there is no per se rule that Miranda warnings in and of themselves suffice to cure a Fourth Amendment violation involved in obtaining inculpatory statements during custodial interrogation following a formal arrest on less than probable cause, and that in order to use such statements, the prosecution must show not only that the statements meet the Fifth Amendment voluntariness standard, but also that the causal connection between the statements and the illegal arrest is broken sufficiently to purge the primary taint of the illegal arrest in light of the distinct policies and interests of the Fourth Amendment. On remand from the New York Court of Appeals, the trial court granted petitioner's motion to suppress, but the Appellate Division of the New York Supreme Court reversed, holding that although the police lacked probable cause to arrest petitioner, law enforcement officials may detain an individual upon reasonable suspicion for questioning for a reasonable period of time under carefully controlled conditions which are ample to protect the individual's Fifth and Sixth Amendment rights, and that even if petitioner's detention were illegal, the taint of such detention was sufficiently attenuated to allow the admission of his statements and sketches.

I

Can a seizure for the purposes of custodial interrogation be justified by reasonable suspicion?

R

A seizure for the purposes of custodial interrogation cannot justified by reasonable suspicion – the police must have probable cause to believe a crime has been committed.

A

The Rochester police violated the Fourth and Fourteenth Amendments when, without probable cause to arrest, they seized petitioner and transported him to the police station for interrogation. Petitioner was "seized" in the Fourth Amendment sense when he was taken involuntarily to the police station, and the State concedes that the police lacked probable cause to arrest him before his incriminating statement during interrogation. *Terry v. Ohio*, which held that limited "stop and frisk" searches for weapons are so substantially less intrusive than arrests that the general rule requiring probable cause to make Fourth Amendment "seizures" reasonable can be replaced by a test balancing the limited violation of individual privacy against the opposing interests in crime prevention and detection and in the police officer's safety, and the Terry case's progeny, do not support the application of a balancing test so as to hold that "seizures" such as that in this case may be justified by mere "reasonable suspicion." The narrow intrusions in Terry and its progeny were judged by a balancing test rather than the general rule requiring probable cause only because those intrusions fell so far short of the kind of intrusion associated with an arrest. For all but those narrowly defined intrusions, the requisite balancing has been performed in centuries of precedent and is embodied in the principle that seizures are reasonable only if supported by probable cause. The treatment of petitioner, whether or not technically characterized as an arrest, was in important respects indistinguishable from a traditional arrest and must be supported by probable cause. Detention for custodial interrogation - regardless of its label - intrudes so severely on interests protected by the Fourth Amendment as necessarily to trigger the traditional safeguards against illegal arrest. The connection between the unconstitutional police conduct and the incriminating statements and sketches obtained during petitioner's illegal detention was not sufficiently attenuated to permit the use at trial of the statements and sketches. Even though proper Miranda warnings may have been given and petitioner's statements may have been "voluntary" for purposes of the Fifth Amendment, "[t]he exclusionary rule, . . . when utilized to effectuate the Fourth Amendment, serves interests and policies that are distinct from those it serves under the Fifth." *Brown v. Illinois*. While a confession after proper Miranda warnings may be found "voluntary" for Fifth Amendment purposes, this type of "voluntariness" is merely a threshold requirement for Fourth Amendment analysis. Under Fourth Amendment analysis, which focuses on "the causal connection between the illegality and the confession," *Brown v. Illinois*, factors to be considered in determining whether the confession is obtained by exploitation of an illegal arrest include: the temporal proximity of the arrest and the confession, the presence of intervening circumstances, and, particularly, the purpose and flagrancy of the official misconduct. Here, petitioner was admittedly seized without probable cause in the hope that something might turn up, and confessed without any intervening event of significance.

C

Reversed.

United States v. Mendenhall

446 U.S. 544 (1980)

FACTS

Respondent Mendenhall, prior to trial in Federal District Court on a charge of possessing heroin with intent to distribute it, moved to suppress the introduction in evidence of the heroin on the ground that it had been acquired through an unconstitutional search and seizure by Drug Enforcement Administration (DEA) agents. At the hearing on the motion, it was established that when respondent arrived at the Detroit Metropolitan Airport on a flight from Los Angeles, two DEA agents, observing that her conduct appeared to be characteristic of persons unlawfully carrying narcotics, approached her as she was walking through the concourse, identified themselves as federal agents, and asked to see her identification and airline ticket. After respondent produced her driver's license, which was in her name, and her ticket, which was issued in another name, the agents questioned her briefly as to the discrepancy and as to how long she had been in California. After returning the ticket and driver's license to her, one of the agents asked respondent if she would accompany him to the airport DEA office for further questions, and respondent did so. At the office the agent asked respondent if she would allow a search of her person and handbag and told her that she had the right to decline the search if she desired. She responded: "Go ahead," and handed her purse to the agent. A female police officer, who arrived to conduct the search of respondent's person, also asked respondent if she consented to the search, and respondent replied that she did. When the policewoman explained that respondent would have to remove her clothing, respondent stated that she had a plane to catch and was assured that if she was carrying no narcotics there would be no problem. Respondent began to disrobe without further comment and took from her undergarments two packages, one of which appeared to contain heroin, and handed them to the policewoman. Respondent was then arrested for possessing heroin. The District Court denied the motion to suppress, concluding that the agents' conduct in initially approaching the respondent and asking to see her ticket and identification was a permissible investigative stop, based on facts justifying a suspicion of criminal activity, that respondent had accompanied the agents to the DEA office voluntarily, and that respondent voluntarily consented to the search in the DEA office. Respondent was convicted after trial, but the Court of Appeals reversed, finding that respondent had not validly consented to the search.

I

Is the detention of a person for questioning without an arrest an unlawful seizure violative of the Fourth Amendment?

R

A person is seized when a reasonable person would have believed that he or she was not free to leave.

A

The detention of a person for questioning without an arrest is not always an unlawful seizure violative of the Fourth Amendment. Respondent's Fourth Amendment rights were not violated when she went with the agents from the concourse to the DEA office. Whether her consent to accompany the agents was in fact voluntary or was the product of duress or coercion is to be determined by the totality of all the circumstances. Under this test, the evidence - including evidence that respondent was not told that she had to go to the office, but was simply asked if she would accompany the officers, and that there were neither threats nor any show of force - was plainly adequate to support the District Court's finding that respondent voluntarily consented to accompany the officers. The facts that the respondent was 22 years old, had not been graduated from high school, and was a Negro accosted by white officers, while not irrelevant, were not decisive. The evidence also clearly supported the District Court's view that respondent's consent to the search of her person at the DEA office was freely and voluntarily given. She was plainly capable of a knowing consent, and she was twice expressly told by the officers that she was free to withhold consent and only thereafter explicitly consented to the search. The trial court was entitled to view her statement, made when she was told that the search would require the removal of her clothing, that "she had a plane to catch," as simply an expression of concern that the search be conducted quickly, not as indicating resistance to the search. MR. JUSTICE STEWART, joined by MR. JUSTICE REHNQUIST, concluded that no "seizure" of respondent, requiring objective justification, occurred when the agents approached her on the concourse and asked questions of her. A person has been "seized" within the meaning of the Fourth Amendment only if, in view of all of the circumstances surrounding the incident, a reasonable person would have believed that he was not free to leave, and as long as the person to whom questions are put remains free to disregard the questions and walk away, there has been no intrusion upon that person's liberty or privacy as would require some particularized and objective justification. Nothing in the record suggests that respondent had any objective reason to believe that she was not free to end the conversation in the concourse and proceed on her way. MR. JUSTICE POWELL, joined by THE CHIEF JUSTICE and MR. JUSTICE BLACKMUN, concluded that the question whether the DEA agents "seized" respondent within the meaning of the Fourth Amendment should not be reached because neither of the courts below considered the question; and that, assuming that the stop did constitute a seizure, the federal agents, in light of all the circumstances, had reasonable suspicion that respondent was engaging in criminal activity and, therefore, did not violate the Fourth Amendment by stopping her for routine questioning.

C

Reversed and remanded.

Florida v. Bostick

501 U.S. 429 (1991)

FACTS

As part of a drug interdiction effort, Broward County Sheriff's Department officers routinely board buses at scheduled stops and ask passengers for permission to search their luggage. Two officers boarded respondent Bostick's bus and, without articulable suspicion, questioned him and requested his consent to search his luggage for drugs, advising him of his right to refuse. He gave his permission, and the officers, after finding cocaine, arrested Bostick on drug trafficking charges. His motion to suppress the cocaine on the ground that it had been seized in violation of the Fourth Amendment was denied by the trial court. The Florida Court of Appeal affirmed, but certified a question to the State Supreme Court. That court, reasoning that a reasonable passenger would not have felt free to leave the bus to avoid questioning by the police, adopted a per se rule that the sheriff's practice of "working the buses" is unconstitutional.

I Are the actions of the police in randomly searching buses and passengers for evidence of criminal activity considered a seizure violative of the Fourth Amendment?

R The actions of the police in randomly searching buses and passengers for evidence of criminal goings-on are not per se considered a seizure violative of the Fourth Amendment.

A The Florida Supreme Court erred in adopting a per se rule that every encounter on a bus is a seizure. The appropriate test is whether, taking into account all of the circumstances surrounding the encounter, a reasonable passenger would feel free to decline the officers' requests or otherwise terminate the encounter. A consensual encounter does not trigger Fourth Amendment scrutiny. Even when officers have no basis for suspecting a particular individual, they may generally ask the individual questions, *Florida v. Rodriguez*, ask to examine identification, *INS v. Delgdo*, and request consent to search luggage, *Florida v. Royer*, provided they do not convey a message that compliance with their requests is required. Thus, there is no doubt that, if this same encounter had taken place before Bostick boarded the bus or in the bus terminal, it would not be a seizure. That this encounter took place on a bus is but one relevant factor in determining whether or not it was of a coercive nature. The state court erred in focusing on the "free to leave" language of *Michigan v. Chesternut*, rather than on the principle that those words were intended to capture. This inquiry is not an accurate measure of an encounter's coercive effect when a person is seated on a bus about to depart, has no desire to leave, and would not feel free to leave even if there were no police present. The more appropriate inquiry is whether a reasonable passenger would feel free to decline the officers' request or otherwise terminate the encounter. Thus, this case is analytically indistinguishable from *INS v. Delgado*. There, no seizure occurred when INS agents visited factories at random, stationing some agents at exits while others questioned workers, because, even though workers were not free to leave without being questioned, the agents' conduct gave them no reason to believe that they would be detained if they answered truthfully or refused to answer. Such a refusal, alone, does not furnish the minimal level of objective justification needed for detention or seizure. This case is remanded for the Florida courts to evaluate the seizure question under the correct legal standard. The trial court made no express findings of fact, and the State Supreme Court rested its decision on a single fact - that the encounter took place on a bus - rather than on the totality of the circumstances. Rejected, however, is Bostick's argument that he must have been seized because no reasonable person would freely consent to a search of luggage containing drugs, since the "reasonable person" test presumes an innocent person.

C Reversed and remanded.

California v. Hodari D.

499 U.S. 621 (1991)

FACTS

A group of youths, including respondent Hodari D., fled at the approach of an unmarked police car on an Oakland, California, street. Officer Pertoso, who was wearing a jacket with "Police" embossed on its front, left the car to give chase. Pertoso did not follow Hodari directly, but took a circuitous route that brought the two face to face on a parallel street. Hodari, however, was looking behind as he ran and did not turn to see Pertoso until the officer was almost upon him, whereupon Hodari tossed away a small rock. Pertoso tackled him, and the police recovered the rock, which proved to be crack cocaine. In the juvenile proceeding against Hodari, the court denied his motion to suppress the evidence relating to the cocaine. The State Court of Appeal reversed, holding that Hodari had been "seized" when he saw Pertoso running towards him; that this seizure was "unreasonable" under the Fourth Amendment, the State having conceded that Pertoso did not have the "reasonable suspicion" required to justify stopping Hodari; and therefore that the evidence of cocaine had to be suppressed as the fruit of the illegal seizure.

I

Can a seizure occur even when the suspect does not yield when police engage in the show of authority with physical force?

R

An arrest requires either physical force or submission to the officer's "show of authority."

A

The only issue presented here - whether, at the time he dropped the drugs, Hodari had been "seized" within the meaning of the Fourth Amendment - must be answered in the negative. To answer this question, this Court looks to the common law of arrest. To constitute a seizure of the person, just as to constitute an arrest - the quintessential "seizure of the person" under Fourth Amendment jurisprudence - there must be either the application of physical force, however slight, or, where that is absent, submission to an officer's "show of authority" to restrain the subject's liberty. No physical force was applied in this case, since Hodari was untouched by Pertoso before he dropped the drugs. Moreover, assuming that Pertoso's pursuit constituted a "show of authority" enjoining Hodari to halt, Hodari did not comply with that injunction, and therefore was not seized until he was tackled. Thus, the cocaine abandoned while he was running was not the fruit of a seizure, and his motion to exclude evidence of it was properly denied. *United States v. Mendenhall* and its progeny, distinguished.

C

Reversed and remanded.

Alabama v. White

496 U.S. 325 (1990)

FACTS

Police received an anonymous telephone tip that respondent White would be leaving a particular apartment at a particular time in a particular vehicle, that she would be going to a particular motel, and that she would be in possession of cocaine. They immediately proceeded to the apartment building, saw a vehicle matching the caller's description, observed White as she left the building and entered the vehicle, and followed her along the most direct route to the motel, stopping her vehicle just short of the motel. A consensual search of the vehicle revealed marijuana and, after White was arrested, cocaine was found in her purse. The Court of Criminal Appeals of Alabama reversed her conviction on possession charges, holding that the trial court should have suppressed the marijuana and cocaine because the officers did not have the reasonable suspicion necessary under Terry v. Ohio, to justify the investigatory stop of the vehicle.

I

Can an anonymous tip, as corroborated by independent police work, exhibit sufficient indicia of reliability to provide reasonable suspicion to make an investigatory stop?

R

The anonymous tip, as corroborated by independent police work, exhibited sufficient indicia of reliability to provide reasonable suspicion to make the investigatory stop.

A

Under *Adams v. Williams*, an informant's tip may carry sufficient "indicia of reliability" to justify a Terry stop even though it may be insufficient to support an arrest or search warrant. Moreover, *Illinois v. Gates*, adopted a "totality of the circumstances" approach to determining whether an informant's tip establishes probable cause, whereby the informant's veracity, reliability, and basis of knowledge are highly relevant. These factors are also relevant in the reasonable-suspicion context, although allowance must be made in applying them for the lesser showing required to meet that standard. Standing alone, the tip here is completely lacking in the necessary indicia of reliability, since it provides virtually nothing from which one might conclude that the caller is honest or his information reliable and gives no indication of the basis for his predictions regarding White's criminal activities. However, although it is a close question, the totality of the circumstances demonstrates that significant aspects of the informant's story were sufficiently corroborated by the police to furnish reasonable suspicion. Although not every detail mentioned by the tipster was verified - e.g., the name of the woman leaving the apartment building or the precise apartment from which she left - the officers did corroborate that a woman left the building and got into the described vehicle. Given the fact that they proceeded to the building immediately after the call and that White emerged not too long thereafter, it also appears that her departure was within the timeframe predicted by the caller. Moreover, since her 4-mile route was the most direct way to the motel, but nevertheless involved several turns, the caller's prediction of her destination was significantly corroborated even though she was stopped before she reached the motel. Furthermore, the fact that the caller was able to predict her future behavior demonstrates a special familiarity with her affairs.

Alabama v. White

496 U.S. 325 (1990)

Thus, there was reason to believe that the caller was honest and well informed, and to impart some degree of reliability to his allegation that White was engaged in criminal activity.

C Reversed and remanded.

Illinois v. Wardlow

528 U.S. 119 (2000)

FACTS

Respondent Wardlow fled upon seeing a caravan of police vehicles converge on an area of Chicago known for heavy narcotics trafficking. When Officers Nolan and Harvey caught up with him on the street, Nolan stopped him and conducted a protective pat-down search for weapons because in his experience there were usually weapons in the vicinity of narcotics transactions. Discovering a handgun, the officers arrested Wardlow. The Illinois trial court denied his motion to suppress, finding the gun was recovered during a lawful stop and frisk. He was convicted of unlawful use of a weapon by a felon. In reversing, the State Appellate Court found that Nolan did not have reasonable suspicion to make the stop under *Terry* v. *Ohio*. The State Supreme Court affirmed, determining that sudden flight in a high crime area does not create a reasonable suspicion justifying a *Terry* stop because flight may simply be an exercise of the right to "go on one's way," see *Florida* v. *Royer*.

I

Is the act of fleeing from the police in an area known for its high crime a sign of wrongdoing?

R

The act of fleeing from the police in an area known for its high crime is not necessarily a sign of wrongdoing, but is suggestive of such.

A

The officers' actions did not violate the Fourth Amendment. This case, involving a brief encounter between a citizen and a police officer on a public street, is governed by *Terry*, under which an officer who has a reasonable, articulable suspicion that criminal activity is afoot may conduct a brief, investigatory stop. While "reasonable suspicion" is a less demanding standard than probable cause, there must be at least a minimal level of objective justification for the stop. An individual's presence in a "high crime area," standing alone, is not enough to support a reasonable, particularized suspicion of criminal activity, but a location's characteristics are relevant in determining whether the circumstances are sufficiently suspicious to warrant further investigation. In this case, moreover, it was also Wardlow's unprovoked flight that aroused the officers' suspicion. Nervous, evasive behavior is another pertinent factor in determining reasonable suspicion and headlong flight is the consummate act of evasion. In reviewing the propriety of an officer's conduct, courts do not have available empirical studies dealing with inferences from suspicious behavior, and this Court cannot reasonably demand scientific certainty when none exists. Thus, the reasonable suspicion determination must be based on commonsense judgments and inferences about human behavior. Officer Nolan was justified in suspecting that Wardlow was involved in criminal activity, and, therefore, in investigating further. Such a holding is consistent with the decision in *Florida* v. *Royer*, that an individual, when approached, has a right to ignore the police and go about his business. Unprovoked flight is the exact opposite of "going about one's business." While flight is not necessarily indicative of ongoing criminal activity, *Terry* recognized that officers can detain individuals to resolve ambiguities in their conduct and thus accepts the risk that officers may stop innocent people. If they do not learn facts rising to the level of probable cause, an individual must be allowed to go on his way. But in this case the officers found that Wardlow possessed a handgun and arrested him for violating a state law. The propriety of that arrest is not before the Court.

C

Reversed and remanded.

United States v. Place

462 U.S. 696 (1983)

FACTS

When respondent's behavior aroused the suspicion of law enforcement officers as he waited in line at the Miami International Airport to purchase a ticket to New York's La Guardia Airport, the officers approached respondent and requested and received identification. Respondent consented to a search of the two suitcases he had checked, but because his flight was about to depart the officers decided not to search the luggage. The officers then found some discrepancies in the address tags on the luggage and called Drug Enforcement Administration (DEA) authorities in New York to relay this information. Upon respondent's arrival at La Guardia Airport, two DEA agents approached him, said that they believed he might be carrying narcotics, and asked for and received identification. When respondent refused to consent to a search of his luggage, one of the agents told him that they were going to take it to a federal judge to obtain a search warrant. The agents then took the luggage to Kennedy Airport where it was subjected to a "sniff test" by a trained narcotics detection dog which reacted positively to one of the suitcases. At this point, 90 minutes had elapsed since the seizure of the luggage. Thereafter, the agents obtained a search warrant for that suitcase and upon opening it discovered cocaine. Respondent was indicted for possession of cocaine with intent to distribute, and the District Court denied his motion to suppress the contents of the suitcase. He pleaded guilty to the charge and was convicted, but reserved the right to appeal the denial of his motion to suppress. The Court of Appeals reversed, holding that the prolonged seizure of respondent's luggage exceeded the limits of the type of investigative stop permitted by *Terry v. Ohio*, and hence amounted to a seizure without probable cause in violation of the Fourth Amendment.

I

May officers detain a suspect's luggage for the purposes of having a narcotics-sniffing dog sniff the luggage for drugs?

R

Officers may temporary detain a suspect's luggage for the purposes of having a narcotics-sniffing dog sniff the luggage for drugs based on reasonable suspicion that the luggage may contain narcotics.

A

Under the circumstances, the seizure of respondent's luggage violated the Fourth Amendment. Accordingly, the evidence obtained from the subsequent search of the luggage was inadmissible, and respondent's conviction must be reversed. When an officer's observations lead him reasonably to believe that a traveler is carrying luggage that contains narcotics, the principles of Terry and its progeny permit the officer to detain the luggage temporarily to investigate the circumstances that aroused the officer's suspicion, provided that the investigative detention is properly limited in scope. The investigative procedure of subjecting luggage to a "sniff test" by a well-trained narcotics detection dog does not constitute a "search" within the meaning of the Fourth Amendment. When the police seize luggage from the suspect's custody, the limitations applicable to investigative detentions of the person should define the permissible scope of an investigative detention of the luggage on less than probable cause. Under this standard, the police conduct here exceeded the permissible limits of a Terry-type investigative stop. The length of the detention of respondent's luggage alone precludes the conclusion that the seizure was reasonable in the absence of probable cause. This Fourth Amendment violation was exacerbated by the DEA agents' failure to inform respondent accurately of the place to which they were transporting his luggage, of the length of time he might be dispossessed, and of what arrangements would be made for return of the luggage if the investigation dispelled the suspicion.

C

Affirmed.

Michigan v. Long

463 U.S. 1032 (1983)

FACTS

Two police officers, patrolling in a rural area at night, observed a car traveling erratically and at excessive speed. When the car swerved into a ditch, the officers stopped to investigate and were met by respondent, the only occupant of the car, at the rear of the car. Respondent Long, who "appeared to be under the influence of something," did not respond to initial requests to produce his license and registration, and when he began walking toward the open door of the car, apparently to obtain the registration, the officers followed him and saw a hunting knife on the floorboard of the driver's side of the car. The officers then stopped respondent and subjected him to a patdown search, which revealed no weapons. One of the officers shined his flashlight into the car, saw something protruding from under the armrest on the front seat, and upon lifting the armrest saw an open pouch that contained what appeared to be marihuana. Respondent was then arrested for possession of marihuana. A further search of the car's interior revealed no more contraband, but the officers decided to impound the vehicle and more marihuana was found in the trunk. The Michigan state trial court denied respondent's motion to suppress the marihuana taken from both the car's interior and its trunk, and he was convicted of possession of marihuana. The Michigan Court of Appeals affirmed, holding that the search of the passenger compartment was valid as a protective search under *Terry v. Ohio*, and that the search of the trunk was valid as an inventory search under South *Dakota v. Opperman.* However, the Michigan Supreme Court reversed, holding that Terry did not justify the passenger compartment search, and that the marihuana found in the trunk was the "fruit" of the illegal search of the car's interior.

I

Can the police conduct a protective search [for weapons] of the passenger compartment of an automobile?

R

A search of the passenger compartment for weapons is permitted if (1) the police have a reasonable belief (2) based on specific and articulable facts and (3) the rational inferences from those facts indicate that the suspect is dangerous and may gain immediate control of the weapon(s).

A

This Court does not lack jurisdiction to decide the case on the asserted ground that the decision below rests on an adequate and independent state ground. Because of respect for the independence of state courts and the need to avoid rendering advisory opinions, this Court, in determining whether state court references to state law constitute adequate and independent state grounds, will no longer look beyond the opinion under review, or require state courts to reconsider cases to clarify the grounds of their decisions. Accordingly, when a state court decision fairly appears to rest primarily on federal law, or to be interwoven with federal law, and when the adequacy and independence of any possible state law ground is not clear from the face of the opinion, this Court will accept as the most reasonable explanation that the state court decided the case the way it did because it believed that federal law required it to do so. If the state court decision indicates clearly and expressly that it is alternatively based on bona fide separate, adequate, and independent state grounds, this Court will not undertake to review the decision. In this case, apart from two citations to the State

---

Constitution, the court below relied exclusively on its understanding of Terry and other federal cases. Even if it is accepted that the Michigan Constitution has been interpreted to provide independent protection for certain rights also secured under the Fourth Amendment, it fairly appears that the Michigan Supreme Court rested its decision primarily on federal law. The protective search of the passenger compartment of respondent's car was reasonable under the principles articulated in Terry and other decisions of this Court. Although Terry involved the stop and subsequent patdown search for weapons of a person suspected of criminal activity, it did not restrict the preventive search to the person of the detained suspect. Protection of police and others can justify protective searches when police have a reasonable belief that the suspect poses a danger. Roadside encounters between police and suspects are especially hazardous, and danger may arise from the possible presence of weapons in the area surrounding a suspect. Thus, the search of the passenger compartment of an automobile, limited to those areas in which a weapon may be placed or hidden, is permissible if the police officer possesses a reasonable belief based on specific and articulable facts which, taken together with the rational inferences from those facts, reasonably warrant the officer to believe that the suspect is dangerous and the suspect may gain immediate control of weapons. If, while conducting a legitimate Terry search of an automobile's interior, the officer discovers contraband other than weapons, he cannot be required to ignore the contraband, and the Fourth Amendment does not require its suppression in such circumstances. The circumstances of this case justified the officers in their reasonable belief that respondent posed a danger if he were permitted to reenter his vehicle. Nor did they act unreasonably in taking preventive measures to ensure that there were no other weapons within respondent's immediate grasp before permitting him to reenter his automobile. The fact that respondent was under the officers' control during the investigative stop does not render unreasonable their belief that he could injure them. Because the Michigan Supreme Court suppressed the marihuana taken from the trunk as a fruit of what it erroneously held was an illegal search of the car's interior, the case is remanded to enable it to determine whether the trunk search was permissible under *Opperman* or other decisions of this Court.

C Reversed and remanded.

Maryland v. Buie

494 U.S. 325 (1990)

FACTS

Following a Maryland armed robbery by two men, one of whom was wearing a red running suit, police obtained arrest warrants for respondent Buie and his suspected accomplice and executed the warrant for Buie at his house. After Buie was arrested upon emerging from the basement, one of the officers entered the basement "in case there was someone else" there and seized a red running suit lying in plain view. The trial court denied Buie's motion to suppress the running suit, the suit was introduced into evidence, and Buie was convicted of armed robbery and a weapons offense. The intermediate appellate court affirmed the denial of the suppression motion, but the State Court of Appeals reversed, ruling that the running suit was inadmissible because the officer who conducted the "protective sweep" of the basement did not have probable cause to believe that a serious and demonstrable potentiality for danger existed.

I

Can the police conduct a protective sweep of a home without violating the Fourth Amendment?

R

The Fourth Amendment permits a properly limited protective sweep in conjunction <u>with an in-home arrest</u> when the searching officer possesses a reasonable belief based on specific and articulable facts that the area to be swept harbors an individual posing a danger to those on the arrest scene.

A

In holding that, respectively, an on-the-street "frisk" and a roadside search of an automobile's passenger compartment were reasonable despite the absence of a warrant or probable cause, Terry and Long balanced the Fourth Amendment interests of the persons with whom they were dealing against the immediate interests of the police in protecting themselves from the danger posed by hidden weapons. Here, the police had an analogous interest in taking steps to assure themselves that Buie's house was not harboring other persons who were dangerous and who could unexpectedly launch an attack, and the fact that Buie had an expectation of privacy in rooms that were not examined by the police prior to the arrest does not mean that such rooms were immune from entry. No warrant was required, and as an incident to the arrest the officers could, as a precautionary matter and without probable cause or reasonable suspicion, look in closets and other spaces immediately adjoining the place of arrest from which an attack could be launched. Beyond that, however, just as in Terry and Long, there must be [494 U.S. 325, 326] articulable facts which, taken together with the rational inferences from those facts, would warrant a reasonably prudent officer in believing that the area to be swept harbors an individual posing a danger. Such a protective sweep is not a full search of the premises, but may extend only to a cursory inspection of those spaces where a person may be found. The sweep lasts no longer than is necessary to dispel the reasonable suspicion of danger and in any event no longer than it takes to complete the arrest and depart the premises. *Chimel v. California*, which held that in the absence of a search warrant, the justifiable search incident to an in-home arrest could not extend beyond the arrestee's person and the area from within which he might have obtained a weapon, is distinguished. First, *Chimel* was concerned with a full-blown, top-to-bottom search of an entire house for evidence of the crime for which the arrest was made, not the more limited intrusion contemplated by a protective sweep. Second, the justification for the search incident to arrest in *Chimel* was the threat posed by the arrestee, not the safety threat posed by the house, or more properly by unseen third parties in the house. The Court of Appeals applied an unnecessarily strict Fourth Amendment standard in requiring a protective sweep to be justified by probable cause. The case is remanded for application of the proper standard.

C

Vacated and remanded.

Michigan Department of State Police v. Sitz

496 U.S. 444 (1990)

FACTS

Petitioners, the Michigan State Police Department and its director, established a highway sobriety checkpoint program with guidelines governing checkpoint operations, site selection, and publicity. During the only operation to date, 126 vehicles passed through the checkpoint, the average delay per vehicle was 25 seconds, and two drivers were arrested for driving under the influence of alcohol. The day before that operation, respondents, licensed Michigan drivers, filed suit in a county court seeking declaratory and injunctive relief from potential subjection to the checkpoints. After a trial, at which the court heard extensive testimony concerning, among other things, the "effectiveness" of such programs, the court applied the balancing test of *Brown v. Texas* and ruled that the State's program violated the Fourth Amendment. The State Court of Appeals affirmed, agreeing with the lower court's findings that the State has a "grave and legitimate" interest in curbing drunken driving; that sobriety checkpoint programs are generally ineffective and, therefore, do not significantly further that interest; and that, while the checkpoints' objective intrusion on individual liberties is slight, their "subjective intrusion" is substantial.

I

Is the petitioners' highway sobriety checkpoint program consistent with the Fourth Amendment?

R

A Petitioners' highway sobriety checkpoint program is consistent with the Fourth Amendment.

A

United States v. Martinez-Fuerte, which utilized a balancing test in upholding checkpoints for detecting illegal aliens, and *Brown v. Texas*, are the relevant authorities to be used in evaluating the constitutionality of the State's program. *Treasury Employees v. Von Raab* was not designed to repudiate this Court's prior cases dealing with police stops of motorists on public highways and, thus, does not forbid the use of a balancing test here. A Fourth Amendment "seizure" occurs when a vehicle is stopped at a checkpoint. Thus, the question here is whether such seizures are "reasonable." There is no dispute about the magnitude of, and the States' interest in eradicating, the drunken driving problem. The courts below accurately gauged the "objective" intrusion, measured by the seizure's duration and the investigation's intensity, as minimal. However, they misread this Court's cases concerning the degree of "subjective intrusion" and the potential for generating fear and surprise. The "fear and surprise" to be considered are not the natural fear of one who has been drinking over the prospect of being stopped at a checkpoint but, rather, the fear and surprise engendered in law-abiding motorists by the nature of the particular stop, such as one made by a roving patrol operating on a seldom-traveled road. Here, checkpoints are selected pursuant to guidelines, and uniformed officers stop every vehicle. The resulting intrusion is constitutionally indistinguishable from the stops upheld in *Martinez-Fuerte*. The Court of Appeals also erred in finding that the program failed the "effectiveness" part of the Brown test. This balancing factor - which Brown actually describes as "the degree to which the seizure advances the public interest" - was not meant to transfer from politically accountable officials to the courts the choice as to which among reasonable alternative law enforcement techniques should be employed to deal with a serious public danger. Moreover, the court mistakenly relied on *Martinez-Fuerte* and *Delaware v. Prouse* to provide a basis for its "effectiveness" review. Unlike *Delaware v. Prouse,* this case involves neither random stops nor a complete absence of empirical data indicating that the stops would be an effective means of promoting roadway safety. And there is no justification for a different conclusion here than in *Martinez-Fuerte*, where the ratio of illegal aliens detected to vehicles stopped was approximately 0.5 percent, as compared with the approximately 1.6 percent detection ratio in the one checkpoint conducted by Michigan and with the 1 percent ratio demonstrated by other States' experience.

C

Reversed and remanded.

Murray v. United States

487 U.S. 533 (1988)

FACTS

After receiving a robbery report, police stopped the suspected getaway car, which the owner was driving and in which petitioners were passengers. Upon searching the car, the police found a box of rifle shells in the glove compartment and a sawed-off rifle under the front passenger seat and arrested petitioners. Subsequently, petitioners were convicted in an Illinois court of armed robbery at a trial in which the rifle and shells were admitted as evidence. Before trial petitioners had moved to suppress the rifle and shells on Fourth Amendment grounds, but the trial court denied the motion on the ground that petitioners lacked standing to object to the lawfulness of the search of the car because they did not own either the car or the rifle and shells. The Appellate Court affirmed.

I

May Fourth Amendment rights be vicariously asserted by a third person (i.e. a non-owner passenger of a car)?

R

Fourth Amendment rights are personal rights which may not be vicariously asserted, and a person aggrieved by an illegal search and seizure only through the introduction of damaging evidence secured by a search of a third person's premises or property has not had any of his Fourth Amendment rights infringed.

A

"Fourth Amendment rights are personal rights which . . . may not be vicariously asserted," *Alderman v. United States*, and a person aggrieved by an illegal search and seizure only through the introduction of damaging evidence secured by a search of a third person's premises or property has not had any of his Fourth Amendment rights infringed. The rule of standing to raise vicarious Fourth Amendment claims should not be extended by a so-called "target" theory whereby any criminal defendant at whom a search was "directed" would have standing to contest the legality of that search and object to the admission at trial of evidence obtained as a result of the search. In any event, the better analysis of the principle that Fourth Amendment rights are personal rights that may not be asserted vicariously should focus on the extent of a particular defendant's rights under that Amendment, rather than on any theoretically separate but invariably intertwined concept of standing. The phrase "legitimately on premises" coined in *Jones v. United States*, creates "too broad a gauge" for measurement of Fourth Amendment rights. The holding in Jones can best be explained by the fact that Jones had a legitimate expectation of privacy in the premises he was using and therefore could claim the protection of the Fourth Amendment. Petitioners, who asserted neither a property nor a possessory interest in the automobile searched nor an interest in the property seized and who failed to show that they had any legitimate expectation of privacy in the glove compartment or area under the seat of the car in which they were merely passengers, were not entitled to challenge a search of those areas.

C

Affirmed.

Minnesota v. Carter

525 U.S. 83 (1998)

FACTS

A police officer looked in an apartment window through a gap in the closed blind and observed Defendants-Respondents Carter and Johns and the apartment's lessee bagging cocaine. After respondents were arrested, they moved to suppress the cocaine and other evidence obtained from the apartment and their car, arguing that the officer's initial observation was an unreasonable search in violation of the Fourth Amendment. Respondents were convicted and the Minnesota trial court held that since they were not overnight social guests, they were not entitled to Fourth Amendment protection, and that the officer's observation was not a search under the Amendment. The State Court of Appeals held that Carter did not have "standing" to object to the officer's actions because the evidence indicated that he used the apartment for a business purpose, to package drugs, and, separately, affirmed Johns' conviction without addressing the "standing" issue. In reversing, the State Supreme Court held that respondents had "standing" to claim Fourth Amendment protection because they had a legitimate expectation of privacy in the invaded place and that the officer's observation constituted an unreasonable search.

I

Does a casual social guest in another's home have a right to object to an illegal search of that home?

R

A casual social guest in another's home does not have standing to challenge a search of the home as being unreasonable under the Fourth Amendment, without more.

A

We hold that any search that may have occurred did not violate respondents' Fourth Amendment rights. The state courts' analysis of respondents' expectation of privacy under the rubric of "standing" doctrine was expressly rejected in *Rakas v. Illinois*. To claim Fourth Amendment protection, a defendant must demonstrate that he personally has an expectation of privacy in the place searched, and that his expectation is reasonable. The Fourth Amendment protects persons against unreasonable searches of "their persons [and] houses," and thus indicates that it is a personal right that must be invoked by an individual. But the extent to which the Amendment protects people may depend upon where those people are. While an overnight guest may have a legitimate expectation of privacy in someone else's home, one who is merely present with the consent of the householder may not. An expectation of privacy in commercial property is different from, and less than, a similar expectation in a home. Here, the purely commercial nature of the transaction, the relatively short period of time that respondents were on the premises, and the lack of any previous connection between them and the householder all lead to the conclusion that their situation is closer to that of one simply permitted on the premises. Any search which may have occurred did not violate their Fourth Amendment rights. Because respondents had no legitimate expectation of privacy, the Court need not decide whether the officer's observation constituted a "search." No. A casual day guest in another's home does not have standing to challenge a search of the home as being unreasonable under the Fourth Amendment, without more. Reversed and remanded.

Mapp v. Ohio

367 U.S. 643 (1961)

FACTS

On May 23, 1957, three police officers arrived at the Defendant Mapp's residence armed with information that "a person was hiding out in the home was wanted for questioning in connection with a recent bombing, and that there was a large amount of policy paraphernalia being hidden in the home." Miss Mapp and her daughter by a former marriage lived on the top floor of the two-family dwelling. Upon their arrival at that house, the officers knocked on the door and demanded entrance but appellant, after telephoning her attorney, refused to admit them without a search warrant. They advised their headquarters of the situation and undertook a surveillance of the house. The officers again sought entrance some three hours later when four or more additional officers arrived on the scene. When Miss Mapp did not come to the door immediately, at least one of the several doors to the house was forcibly opened and the policemen gained admittance. The officers conducted a widespread search and found obscene materials. No search warrant was ever produced, nor was this failure explained it anyway. Defendant was convicted on the strength of the evidence seized. The Ohio Supreme Court, after acknowledging that no warrant was ever produced, affirmed the conviction.

I

Does the exclusionary rule apply to evidence used in state court proceedings as well?

R

The federal exclusionary rule applies equally to both the state and federal Governments.

A

The federal exclusionary rule requiring evidence gathered in violation of the Fourth Amendment to be excluded from criminal proceedings applies equally to both the state and federal Governments. Prior to *Wolf*, almost two thirds of the States were opposed to the use of the exclusionary rule. Now more than half of the states have wholly or partially adopted or adhered to the *Weeks* rule requiring exclusion of the evidence seized in violation of the Fourth Amendment. Thus, the rationale supporting the failure of the *Wolf* court to extend the exclusionary rule to the states can no longer be deemed controlling. We therefore hold that all evidence obtained by searches and seizures in violation of the Constitution is, by that same authority, inadmissible in state court. Our decision today gives to the individual no more than that which the Constitution guarantees him, to the police officer no less than that to which honest Law enforcement is entitled, and, to the courts, that judicial integrity so necessary in the true administration of justice.

C

Yes. The exclusionary rule applies equally to both the state and federal Governments.

United States v. Leon

468 U.S. 897 (1984)

FACTS

Acting on the basis of information from a confidential informant, officers of the Burbank, California Police Department initiated a drug-trafficking investigation involving surveillance of respondents' activities. Based on an affidavit summarizing the police officers' observations, Officer Rombach prepared an application for a warrant to search three residences and Defendant-Respondent Leon and others' automobiles for an extensive list of items. The application was reviewed by several Deputy District Attorneys, and a facially valid search warrant was issued by a state court judge. Ensuing searches produced large quantities of drugs and other evidence. Respondents were indicted for federal drug offenses, and filed motions to suppress the evidence seized pursuant to the warrant. After an evidentiary hearing, the District Court granted the motions in part, concluding that the affidavit was insufficient to establish probable cause. Although recognizing that Officer Rombach had acted in good faith, the court rejected the Government's suggestion that the Fourth Amendment exclusionary rule should not apply where evidence is seized in reasonable, good faith reliance on a search warrant. The Court of Appeals affirmed, also refusing the Government's invitation to recognize a good faith exception to the rule. The Government's petition for certiorari presented only the question whether a good-faith exception to the exclusionary rule should be recognized.

I

Does the exclusionary rule apply to evidence seized by police who have acted based on a reasonable, good-faith reliance on a facial valid search warrant issued by a neutral and detached magistrate?

R

Where there is a good faith reliance on a facially valid search warrant, evidence obtained pursuant to the warrant is admissible. That is, the exclusionary rule does NOT apply.

A

This case presents the question whether the Fourth Amendment exclusionary rule should be modified so as not to bar the use in the prosecution's case-in-chief of evidence obtained by officers acting in reasonable reliance on a search warrant issued by a detached and neutral magistrate but ultimately found to be unsupported by probable cause. We conclude that it should and, accordingly, reverse the judgment of the Court of Appeals. The Fourth Amendment exclusionary rule should not be applied so as to bar the use in the prosecution's case-in- chief of evidence obtained by officers acting in reasonable reliance on a search warrant issued by a detached and neutral magistrate but ultimately found to be invalid. An examination of the Fourth Amendment's origin and purposes makes clear that the use of fruits of a past unlawful search or seizure works no new Fourth Amendment wrong. The question whether the exclusionary sanction is appropriately imposed in a particular case as a judicially created remedy to safeguard Fourth Amendment rights through its deterrent effect, must be resolved by weighing the costs and benefits of preventing the use in the prosecution's case-in-chief of inherently trustworthy tangible evidence. Indiscriminate application of the exclusionary rule - impeding the criminal justice system's truth-finding function and allowing some guilty defendants to go free – may well generate disrespect

---

for the law and the administration of justice. Application of the exclusionary rule should continue where a Fourth Amendment violation has been substantial and deliberate, but the balancing approach that has evolved in determining whether the rule should be applied in a variety of contexts - including criminal trials - suggests that the rule should be modified to permit the introduction of evidence obtained by officers reasonably relying on a warrant issued by a detached and neutral magistrate. The deference accorded to a magistrate's finding of probable cause for the issuance of a warrant does not preclude inquiry into the knowing or reckless falsity of the affidavit on which that determination was based, and the courts must also insist that the magistrate purport to perform his neutral and detached function and not serve merely as a rubber stamp for the police. Moreover, reviewing courts will not defer to a warrant based on an affidavit that does not provide the magistrate with a substantial basis for determining the existence of probable cause. However the exclusionary rule is designed to deter police misconduct rather than to punish the errors of judges and magistrates. Admitting evidence obtained pursuant to a warrant while at the same time declaring that the warrant was somehow defective will not reduce judicial officers' professional incentives to comply with the Fourth Amendment, encourage them to repeat their mistakes, or lead to the granting of all colorable warrant requests. Even assuming that the exclusionary rule effectively deters some police misconduct and provides incentives for the law enforcement profession as a whole to conduct itself in accord with the Fourth Amendment, it cannot be expected, and should not be applied, to deter objectively reasonable law enforcement activity. In the ordinary case, an officer cannot be expected to question the magistrate's probable-cause determination or his judgment that the form of the warrant is technically sufficient. Once the warrant issues, there is literally nothing more the policeman can do in seeking to comply with the law, and penalizing the officer for the magistrate's error, rather than his own, cannot logically contribute to the deterrence of Fourth Amendment violations. A police officer's reliance on the magistrate's probable-cause determination and on the technical sufficiency of the warrant he issues must be objectively reasonable. Suppression remains an appropriate remedy if the magistrate or judge in issuing a warrant was misled by information in an affidavit that the affiant knew was false or would have known was false except for his reckless disregard of the truth, or if the issuing magistrate wholly abandoned his detached and neutral judicial role. Nor would an officer manifest objective good faith in relying on a warrant based on an affidavit so lacking in indicia of probable cause as to render official belief in its existence entirely unreasonable. Finally, depending on the circumstances of the particular case, a warrant may be so facially deficient - e.g., in failing to particularize the place to be searched or the things to be seized - that the executing officers cannot reasonably presume it to be valid. In view of the modification of the exclusionary rule, the Court of Appeals' judgment cannot stand in this case. Only respondent Leon contended that no reasonably well trained police officer could have believed that there existed probable cause to search his house. However, the record establishes that the police officers' reliance on the state court judge's determination of probable cause was objectively reasonable.

C

No. Where there is a good faith reliance on a facially valid search warrant, evidence obtained pursuant to the warrant is admissible. That is, the exclusionary rule does not apply. Reversed

Siverthorne Lumber Company v. United States

251 U.S. 385 (1919)

FACTS

This is a writ of error brought to reverse a judgment of the District Court fining the Silverthorne Lumber Company $250 for contempt of court and ordering Frederick W. Silverthorne to be imprisoned until he should purge himself of a similar contempt. The contempt in question was a refusal to obey subpoenas and an order of Court to produce books and documents of the company before the grand jury to be used in regard to alleged violation of the statutes of the United States by the said Silverthorne and his father. One ground of the refusal was that the order of the Court infringed the rights of the parties under the Fourth Amendment of the Constitution of the United States.

An indictment upon a single specific charge was brought against Silverthorne and he was arrested at his homes early in the morning of February 25, and was detained in custody a number of hours. While detained, representatives of the Department of Justice and the United States marshal without authority went to the office of their company and made a clean sweep of all the books, papers and documents found there. All the employees were taken or directed to go to the office of the District Attorney of the United States to which also the books, etc., were taken at once. An application was made as soon as might be to the District Court for a return of what thus had been taken unlawfully. Photographs and copies of material papers were made and a new indictment was framed based upon the knowledge thus obtained. The District Court ordered a return of the originals but impounded the photographs and copies. Subpoenas to produce the originals then were served and on the refusal of the plaintiffs in error to produce them the Court made an order that the subpoenas should be complied with, although it had found that all the papers had been seized in violation of the parties' constitutional rights. The refusal to obey this order is the contempt alleged. The Government now, while in form repudiating and condemning the illegal seizure, seeks to maintain its right to avail itself of the knowledge obtained by that means which otherwise it would not have had.

I Can the prosecution avail itself of the information contained in the books, documents and papers obtained in an illegal search and seizure?

R The prosecution may avail itself of the information contained in the books, documents and papers if such evidence was obtained by way of an illegal search and seizure unless an independent source of the information is shown.

A The proposition could not be presented more nakedly. It is that although of course its seizure was an outrage which the Government now regrets, it may study the papers before it returns them, copy them, and then may use the knowledge that it has gained to call upon the owners in a more regular form to produce them; that the protection of the Constitution covers the physical possession but not any advantages that the Government can gain over the object of its pursuit by doing the forbidden act. *Weeks v. United States*, to be sure, had established that laying the papers directly before the grand jury was unwarranted, but it is taken to mean only that two steps are required instead of one. In our opinion such is not the law. It reduces the

Fourth Amendment to a form of words. The essence of a provision forbidding the acquisition of evidence in a certain way is not that evidence so acquired shall not be used before the Court, but that it shall not be used at all. Of course this does not mean that the facts thus obtained become sacred and inaccessible. If knowledge of them is gained from an independent source they may be proved like any others, but the knowledge gained by the Government's own wrong cannot be used by it in the way proposed. But the rights of a corporation against unlawful search and seizure are to be protected even if the same result might have been achieved in a lawful way.

C

Judgment reversed.

Wong Sun v. United States

371 U.S. 471 (1963)

FACTS

In a trial in a Federal District Court without a jury, petitioners Toy and Sun were convicted of fraudulent and knowing transportation and concealment of illegally imported heroin, in violation of 21 U.S.C. 174. Although the Court of Appeals held that the arrests of both petitioners without warrants were illegal, because not based on "probable cause" within the meaning of the Fourth Amendment nor "reasonable grounds" within the meaning of the Narcotics Control Act of 1956, it affirmed their convictions, notwithstanding the admission in evidence over their timely objections of (1) statements made orally by petitioner Toy in his bedroom at the time of his arrest; (2) heroin surrendered to the agents by a third party as a result of those statements; and (3) unsigned statements made by each petitioner several days after his arrest, and after being lawfully arraigned and released on his own recognizance. The Court of Appeals held that these items were not the fruits of the illegal arrests, and, therefore, were properly admitted in evidence.

I

(1) Should statements made by Toy in his bedroom be excluded as "fruits of the poisonous tree?" (2) Does the exclusion of Toy's declaration make the narcotics taken from Yee inadmissible against Toy? (3) Was the unsigned confession of Wong Sun the fruit of an unlawful arrest and therefore inadmissible against Sun at trial? (4) Were the drugs surrendered by Yee admissible against Sun?

R

Evidence that derives so immediately from an unlawful search or seizure is inadmissible as "fruit of the poisonous tree" unless it was obtained from an independent source or so attenuated as to dispel the taint.

A

On the record in this case, there was neither reasonable grounds nor probable cause for Toy's arrest, since the information upon which it was based was too vague and came from too untested a source to accept it as probable cause for the issuance of an arrest warrant; and this defect was not cured by the fact that Toy fled when a supposed customer at his door early in the morning revealed that he was a narcotics agent. On the record in this case, the statements made by Toy in his bedroom at the time of his unlawful arrest were the fruits of the agents' unlawful action, and they should have been excluded from evidence. The narcotics taken from a third party as a result of statements made by Toy at the time of his arrest were likewise fruits of the unlawful arrest, and they should not have been admitted as evidence against Toy. After exclusion of the foregoing items of improperly admitted evidence, the only proofs remaining to sustain Toy's conviction are his and his codefendant's unsigned statements; any admissions of guilt in Toy's statement require corroboration; no reference to Toy in his codefendant's statement constitutes admissible evidence corroborating any admission by Toy; and Toy's conviction must be set aside for lack of competent evidence to support it. In view of the fact that, after his unlawful arrest, petitioner Wong Sun had been lawfully arraigned and released on his own recognizance and had returned voluntarily several days later when he made his unsigned statement, the connection between his unlawful arrest and the making of that statement was so attenuated that the unsigned statement was not the fruit of the unlawful arrest and, therefore, it was properly admitted in evidence. The seizure of the narcotics admitted in evidence invaded no right of privacy of person or premises which would entitle Wong Sun to object to its use at his trial. Any references to Wong Sun in his codefendant's statement were incompetent to corroborate Wong Sun's admissions, and Wong Sun is entitled to a new trial, because it is not clear from the record whether or not the trial court relied upon his codefendant's statement as a source of corroboration of Wong Sun's confession.

C

Reversed and remanded.

Murray v. United States

487 U.S. 533 (1988)

FACTS

While watching petitioner Murray and others suspected of illegal drug activities, federal agents observed both petitioners driving vehicles into, and later out of, a warehouse, and, upon petitioners' exit, saw that the warehouse contained a tractor-trailer rig bearing a long container. Petitioners later turned over their vehicles to other drivers, who were in turn followed and ultimately arrested, and the vehicles were lawfully seized and found to contain marijuana. After receiving this information, several agents forced their way into the warehouse and observed in plain view numerous burlap-wrapped bales. The agents left without disturbing the bales and did not return until they had obtained a warrant to search the warehouse. In applying for the warrant, they did not mention the prior entry or include any recitations of their observations made during that entry. Upon issuance of the warrant, they reentered the warehouse and seized 270 bales of marijuana and other evidence of crime. The District Court denied petitioners' pretrial motion to suppress the evidence, rejecting their arguments that the warrant was invalid because the agents did not inform the Magistrate about their prior warrantless entry, and that the warrant was tainted by that entry. Petitioners were subsequently convicted of conspiracy to possess and distribute illegal drugs. The Court of Appeals affirmed, assuming for purposes of its decision on the suppression question that the first entry into the warehouse was unlawful.

I

Does the Fourth Amendment require the suppression of evidence initially discovered during police officers' illegal entry of private premises, if that evidence is also discovered during a later search pursuant to a valid warrant that is wholly independent of the initial illegal entry?

R

The Fourth Amendment does not require the suppression of evidence initially discovered during police officers' illegal entry of private premises, if that evidence is also discovered during a later search pursuant to a valid warrant that is wholly independent of the initial illegal entry.

A

The "independent source" doctrine permits the introduction of evidence initially discovered during, or as a consequence of, an unlawful search, but later obtained independently from lawful activities untainted by the initial illegality. There is no merit to petitioners' contention that allowing the doctrine to apply to evidence initially discovered during an illegal search, rather than limiting it to evidence first obtained during a later lawful search, will encourage police routinely to enter premises without a warrant. Although the federal agents' knowledge that marijuana was in the warehouse was assuredly acquired at the time of the unlawful entry, it was also acquired at the time of entry pursuant to the warrant, and if that later acquisition was not the result of the earlier entry, the independent source doctrine allows the admission of testimony as to that knowledge. This same analysis applies to the tangible evidence, the bales of marijuana. *United States v. Silvestri* is unpersuasive insofar as it distinguishes between tainted intangible and tangible evidence. The ultimate question is whether the search pursuant to warrant was in fact a genuinely independent source of the information and tangible evidence at issue. This would not have been the case if the agents' decision to seek the warrant was prompted by what they had seen during the initial entry or if information obtained during that entry was presented to the Magistrate and affected his decision to issue the warrant. Because the District Court did not explicitly find that the agents would have sought a warrant if they had not earlier entered the warehouse, the cases are remanded for a determination whether the warrant-authorized search of the warehouse was an independent source in the sense herein described.

C Vacated and remanded.

Brown v. Mississippi

297 U.S. 278 (1936)

FACTS

Petitioners were indicted for the murder of one Raymond Stewart, whose death occurred on March 30, 1934. They were indicted on April 4, 1934, and were then arraigned and pleaded not guilty. Counsel were appointed by the court to defend them. Trial was begun the next morning and was concluded on the following day, when they were found guilty and sentenced to death. Aside from the confessions, there was no evidence sufficient to warrant the submission of the case to the jury. After a preliminary inquiry, testimony as to the confessions was received over the objection of defendants' counsel. Defendants then testified that the confessions were false and had been procured by physical torture. The case went to the jury with instructions, upon the request of defendants' counsel, that if the jury had reasonable doubt as to the confessions having resulted from coercion, and that they were not they were not to be considered as evidence. On their appeal to the Supreme Court of the State, defendants assigned as error the inadmissibility of the confessions. The judgment was affirmed.

I

Are convictions, which rest solely upon confessions shown to have been extorted by officers of the state by brutality and violence, consistent with the due process of law required by the Fourteenth Amendment of the Constitution of the United States?

R

Convictions, which rest solely upon confessions shown to have been extorted by officers of the state by brutality and violence, are inconsistent with the due process of law required by the Fourteenth Amendment of the Constitution of the United States.

A

In the instant case, the trial court was fully advised by the undisputed evidence of the way in which the confessions had been procured. The trial court knew that there was no other evidence upon which conviction and sentence could be based. Yet it proceeded to permit conviction and to pronounce sentence. The conviction and sentence were void for want of the essential elements of due process, and the proceeding thus vitiated could be challenged in any appropriate manner. It was challenged before the Supreme Court of the State by the express invocation of the Fourteenth Amendment. That court entertained the challenge, considered the federal question thus presented, but declined to enforce petitioners' constitutional right. The court thus denied a federal right fully established and specially set up and claimed, and the judgment must be reversed.

C

Judgment reversed.

Lisenba v. California

314 U.S. 219 (1941)

FACTS

James employed Mary E. Busch as a manicurist in his barber shop in March, 1935, and, about a month later, went through a marriage ceremony with her, which was not legal as he then had a living wife. While they were affianced, insurance was negotiated on her life, with James as beneficiary. Upon the annulment of the earlier marriage a lawful ceremony was performed. The petitioner made sure that the policies were not annulled by the fact that when they were issued Mary had not been his lawful wife. The allegation is that James enlisted one Hope in a conspiracy to do away with Mary and collect and divide the insurance on her life. Hope testified that, at James' instigation, he procured rattlesnakes which were to bite and kill Mary; that they appeared not to be sufficiently venomous for the purpose but he ultimately purchased others and delivered them to James; that James, on August 4, 1935, blindfolded his wife's eyes, tied her to a table, had Hope bring one of the snakes into the room and caused the reptile to bite her foot; that, during the night James told Hope the bite did not have the desired effect and, in the early morning of August 5, he told Hope that he was going to drown his wife; that later he said to Hope, 'That is that', and still later, at his request, Hope aided him in carrying the body to the yard, and James placed the body face down at the edge of a fish pond with the head and shoulders in the water. James was at his barber shop on August 5. On that evening he took two friends home for dinner. When they arrived the house was dark and empty, and, upon a search of the grounds, his wife's body was found in the position indicated. An autopsy showed the lungs were almost filled with water. The left great toe showed a puncture and the left leg was greatly swollen and almost black. Nothing came of the investigation of the death. James attempted to collect double indemnity; the insurers refused to pay; suits were instituted and one of them settled. As a result of this activity, a fresh investigation of Mary James' death was instituted. On April 19, 1936, officers arrested James for the crime of incest. He was booked on this charge on the morning of April 21, was given a hearing and remanded to jail. On May 2 and 3 he made statements respecting his wife's death to the prosecuting officials. At the trial, in addition to that of Hope, testimony was adduced as to the finding and condition of the body, other [314 U.S. 219, 225] evidence to connect James with the death, and expert testimony that the condition of the left leg could be attributed to rattlesnake bites. The purchase of snakes by Hope was proved by him and several other witnesses one of whom said he sold the two snakes to Hope, one of which Hope claimed had bitten Mary James. Two snakes were brought into court which the witness identified as those sold to Hope and by Hope resold to the witness. James' statements were offered in evidence. Objection was made that they were not voluntary. Before they were admitted the trial judge heard testimony offered by the State and the defendant on that issue. He ruled that the confessions were admissible, and they were received in evidence.

The petitioner was convicted of murder and sentenced to death in the Superior Court of California for Los Angeles County. The Supreme Court of California affirmed the judgment March 21, 1939, two judges dissenting. A rehearing was granted, the case was reargued and, October 5, 1939, the decision was reaffirmed and the former opinion adopted and amplified, two justices dissenting. No question arising under the Constitution of the United States had been raised or decided. In a second petition for rehearing the petitioner, for the first time, asserted that his conviction violated the

Lisenba v. California

314 U.S. 219 (1941)

Fourteenth Amendment. On November 3, 1939, the Court ruled that the petition for a rehearing herein was denied.

I Does the use of a voluntary confession to convict a defendant of a capital crime violate due process?

R The use of a voluntary confession to convict a defendant of a capital crime does not violate due process.

A Like the Supreme Court of California, we disapprove the violations of law involved in the treatment of the petitioner, and we think it right to add that where a prisoner held incommunicado is subjected to questioning by officers for long periods, and deprived of the advice of counsel, we shall scrutinize the record with care to determine whether, by the use of his confession, he is deprived of liberty or life through tyrannical or oppressive means. Officers of the law must realize that if they indulge in such practices they may, in the end, defeat rather than further the ends of justice. Their lawless practices here took them close to the line. But on the facts as we have endeavored fairly to set them forth, and in the light of the findings in the State courts, we cannot hold that the illegal conduct in which the law enforcement officers of California indulged by the prolonged questioning of the prisoner before arraignment, and in the absence of counsel, or their questioning on May 2, coerced the confessions, the introduction of which is the infringement of due process of which the petitioner complains. The petitioner has said that the interrogation would never have drawn an admission from him had his confederate not made a statement; he admits that no threats, promises, or acts of physical violence were offered him during this questioning or for eleven days preceding it. Counsel had been afforded full opportunity to see him and had advised him. He exhibited a self-possession, a coolness, and an acumen throughout his questioning, and at his trial, which negatives the view that he had so lost his freedom of action that the statements made were not his but were the result of the deprivation of his free choice to admit, to deny, or to refuse to answer.

C The Judgments are affirmed.

Spano v. New York

360 U.S. 315 (1959)

FACTS

After petitioner, a foreign-born young man of 25 with a junior-high-school education and no previous criminal record, had been indicted for first-degree murder, he retained counsel and surrendered to police at 7:10 p. m. He was then subjected to persistent and continuous questioning by an assistant prosecutor and numerous police officers for virtually eight hours until he confessed, after he had repeatedly requested, and had been denied, an opportunity to consult his counsel. At his trial in a state court, his confession was admitted in evidence over his objection, and he was convicted and sentenced to death. Held: On the record in this case, petitioner's will was overborne by official pressure, fatigue and sympathy falsely aroused; his confession was not voluntary; and its admission in evidence violated the Due Process Clause of the Fourteenth Amendment.

I

When a confession is obtained through relentless questioning and based on emotional distress, does it comply with due process?

R

A confession obtained through relentless questioning and based on emotional distress does not comply with due process because it is not considered voluntary.

A

Petitioner was a foreign-born young man of 25 with no past history of law violation or of subjection to official interrogation, at least insofar as the record shows. He had progressed only one-half year into high school and the record indicates that he had a history of emotional instability. He did not make a narrative statement, but was subject to the leading questions of a skillful prosecutor in a question and answer confession. He was subjected to questioning not by a few men, but by many. They included Assistant District Attorney Goldsmith, one Hyland of the District Attorney's Office, Deputy Inspector Halks, Lieutenant Gannon, Detective Ciccone, Detective Motta, Detective Lehrer, Detective Marshal, Detective Farrell, Detective Leira, Detective Murphy, Detective Murtha, Sergeant Clarke, Patrolman Bruno and Stenographer Baldwin. All played some part, and the effect of such massive official interrogation must have been felt. Petitioner was questioned for virtually eight straight hours before he confessed, with his only respite being a transfer to an arena presumably considered more appropriate by the police for the task at hand. Nor was the questioning conducted during normal business hours, but began in early evening, continued into the night, and did not bear fruition until the not-too-early morning. The drama was not played out, with the final admissions obtained, until almost sunrise. In such circumstances slowly mounting fatigue does, and is calculated to, play its part. The questioners persisted in the face of his repeated refusals to answer on the advice of his attorney, and they ignored his reasonable requests to contact the local attorney whom he had already retained and who had personally delivered him into the custody of these officers in obedience to the bench warrant.

We conclude that petitioner's will was overborne by official pressure, fatigue and sympathy falsely aroused, after considering all the facts in their post-indictment setting.

Spano v. New York

360 U.S. 315 (1959)

Here a grand jury had already found sufficient cause to require petitioner to face trial on a charge of first-degree murder, and the police had an eyewitness to the shooting. The police were not therefore merely trying to solve a crime, or even to absolve a suspect. They were rather concerned primarily with securing a statement from defendant on which they could convict him. The undeviating intent of the officers to extract a confession from petitioner is therefore patent. When such an intent is shown, this Court has held that the confession obtained must be examined with the most careful scrutiny, and has reversed a conviction on facts less compelling than these. Accordingly, we hold that petitioner's conviction cannot stand under the Fourteenth Amendment.

C

Reversed.

Colorado v. Connelly

479 U.S. 157 (1986)

FACTS

Respondent approached a Denver police officer and stated that he had murdered someone and wanted to talk about it. The officer advised respondent of his Miranda rights, and respondent said that he understood those rights but still wanted to talk about the murder. Shortly thereafter, a detective arrived and again advised respondent of his rights. After respondent answered that he had come all the way from Boston to confess to the murder, he was taken to police headquarters. He then openly detailed his story to the police and subsequently pointed out the exact location of the murder. He was held overnight, and the next day he became visibly disoriented during an interview with the public defender's office and was sent to a state hospital for evaluation. Interviews with a psychiatrist revealed that respondent was following the "voice of God" in confessing to the murder. On the basis of the psychiatrist's testimony that respondent suffered from a psychosis that interfered with his ability to make free and rational choices and, although not preventing him from understanding his rights, motivated his confession, the trial court suppressed respondent's initial statements and custodial confession because they were "involuntary," notwithstanding the fact that the police had done nothing wrong or coercive in securing the confession. The court also found that respondent's mental state vitiated his attempted waiver of the right to counsel and the privilege against self-incrimination. The Colorado Supreme Court affirmed, holding that the Federal Constitution requires a court to suppress a confession when the defendant's mental state, at the time he confessed, interfered with his "rational intellect" and his "free will," the very admission of the evidence in a court of law being sufficient state action to implicate the Due Process Clause of the Fourteenth Amendment. The court further held that respondent's mental condition precluded his ability to make a valid waiver of his Miranda rights and that the State had not met its burden of proving a waiver by "clear and convincing evidence."

I

Is a confession consider voluntary if it obtained by an individual diagnosed as a paranoid schizophrenic and given in response to "command hallucinations?"

R

A confession obtained from a individual suffering from an undetected mental condition is not a deprivation of due process in the absence of police misconduct.

A

Coercive police activity is a necessary predicate to finding that a confession is not "voluntary" within the meaning of the Due Process Clause. Here, the taking of respondent's statements and their admission into evidence constituted no violation of that Clause. While a defendant's mental condition may be a "significant" factor in the "voluntariness" calculus, this does not justify a conclusion that his mental condition, by itself and apart from its relation to official coercion, should ever dispose of the inquiry into constitutional "voluntariness." Whenever the State bears the burden of proof in a motion to suppress a statement allegedly obtained in violation of the Miranda doctrine, the State need prove waiver only by a preponderance of the evidence. Thus, the Colorado Supreme Court erred in applying a "clear and convincing evidence" standard. That court also erred in its analysis of the question whether respondent had waived his Miranda rights. Notions of "free will" have no place in this area of constitutional law. Respondent's perception of coercion flowing from the "voice of God" is a matter to which the Federal Constitution does not speak.

C

Reversed and remanded.

Bram v. United States

168 U.S. 532 (1897)

FACTS

This writ of error is prosecuted to a verdict and sentence thereon, by which the plaintiff was found guilty of murder, and condemned to suffer death. The homicide was committed on board the American ship *Herbert Fuller* while on the high seas, bound from Boston to a port in South America. The accused was the first officer of the ship, and the deceased, of whose murder he was convicted, was the master of the vessel. The bill of exceptions, after stating the sailing of the vessel from Boston on July 2, 1896, with a cargo of lumber, gives a general summary of the facts leading up to and surrounding the homicide, as follows: The captain of the ship was Charles I. Nash and one Bram, the defendant; was the first officer. Shortly before 2:00 a.m., the captain was found dead in his room. A few days later, one Brown was suspected of the murder and seized on board the ship. Thereafter Brown informed his shipmates that he saw Bram commit the murder from a window into the captain's cabin. The bill of exceptions further states that, when the ship arrived at Halifax, Bram and Brown were held in custody by the chief of police at that place, and that, while in such custody, the accused was taken from prison to the office of a detective, and there questioned, under circumstances to be hereafter stated. Subsequently to this occurrence at Halifax, all the officers, the crew, and the passenger were examined before the American consul, and gave their statements, which were reduced to writing and sworn to. They were thereafter, at the request of the American consul, sent to Boston, where the accused was indicted for the murder of Nash, the captain, of Mrs. Nash, and the second mate, Blomberg. The trial and the conviction now under review related to the first of these charges.

I

Can an involuntary confession be used as evidence against the accused in a criminal trial?

R

The Fifth Amendment privilege against self-incrimination bars an involuntary confession from being admitted as evidence against the accused.

A

The fact, then, is that the language of the accused, which was offered in evidence as a confession, was made use of by him as a reply to the statement of the detective that Bram's co-suspect had charged him with the crime; and, although the answer was in the form of a denial, it was doubtless offered as a confession. But the situation of the accused, and the nature of the communication made to him by the detective, necessarily place in doubt any possible implication that his reply to the detective could have been the result of a purely voluntary mental action; that is to say, when all the surrounding circumstances are considered in their true relations, not only is the claim that the statement was voluntary placed in doubt, but the impression is irresistibly produced that it must necessarily have been the result of either hope or fear, or both, operating on the mind. It cannot be doubted that, placed in the position in which the accused was when the statement was made to him that the other suspected person had charged him with crime, the result was to produce upon his mind the fear that, if he remained silent, it would be considered an admission of guilt, and therefore render certain his being committed for trial as the guilty person; and it cannot be conceived that the converse impression would not also have naturally arisen that, by denying, there was hope of removing the suspicion from himself. If this must have been the state of mind of one situated as was the prisoner when the confession was made, how, in reason, can it be said that the answer which he gave, and which was required by the situation, was wholly voluntary? It was not.

It cannot be doubted that, placed in the position in which the accused was when the statement was made to him that the other suspected person had charged him with crime, the result was to produce upon his mind the fear that, if he remained silent, it would be considered an admission of guilt, and therefore render certain his being committed for trial as the guilty person; and it cannot be conceived that the converse impression would not also have naturally arisen that, by denying, there was hope of removing the suspicion from himself. If this must have been the state of mind of one situated as was the prisoner when the confession was made, how, in reason, can it be said that the answer which he gave, and which was required by the situation, was wholly voluntary..

C

The judgment is reversed, and the cause remanded, with directions to set aside the verdict and to order a new trial.

Miranda v. Arizona

384 U.S. 436 (1966)

FACTS

On March 13, 1963, Defendant-Petitioner, Ernesto Miranda, an indigent, semi-educated, and possibly schizophrenic Mexican was arrested at his home and taken in custody to a Phoenix police station on suspicion of kidnapping and rape. He was there identified by the complaining witness. The police then took him to "Interrogation Room No. 2" of the detective bureau. There he was questioned by two police officers. The officers admitted at trial that Miranda was not advised that he had a right to have an attorney present. Two hours later, the officers emerged from the interrogation room with a written confession signed by Miranda. At the top of the statement was a typed paragraph stating that the confession was made voluntarily, without threats or promises of immunity and "with full knowledge of my legal rights, understanding any statement I make may be used against me." At trial, the state prosecution introduced the confession, and the defendant was convicted of kidnapping and rape. Defendant appealed. The Appellate Court affirmed, finding that defendant never specifically requested counsel. Miranda appealed.

I

Is a confession produced after custodial interrogation in which the suspect was not informed of his privilege against self-incrimination and right to counsel, admissible?

R

Confessions produced by way of custodial interrogation are admissible if the suspect was informed (1) of his right to silence, (2) of the consequences of waiving that right, (3) of his right to retain or appoint counsel, and (4) if he waived those rights knowingly and intelligently.

A

The Fifth Amendment provides "no person shall be compelled to any criminal case to be a witness against himself" and "the accused shall have the assistance of counsel." From the testimony of the officers and by the admission of respondent, it is clear that Ernesto Miranda was not in any way apprised of his right to consult with an attorney and to have one present during the interrogation, nor was his right not to be compelled to incriminate himself effectively protected in any other manner. Without these warnings the statements were inadmissible. The mere fact that he signed a statement which contained a typed-in clause stating that he had "full knowledge" of his "legal rights" does not approach the knowing and intelligent waiver required to relinquish constitutional rights. Thus, confessions produced by custodial interrogation are inadmissible unless the suspect was informed of (1) his right to silence, (2) the consequences of waving his right, (3) his right to retain or appoint counsel, and (4) if he waived those rights knowingly and intelligently.

C

Reversed.

Oregon v. Mathiason

429 U.S. 492 (1977)

FACTS

Respondent Carl Mathiason was convicted of first-degree burglary after a bench trial in which his confession was critical to the State's case. At trial he moved to suppress the confession as the fruit of questioning by the police not preceded by the warnings required in *Miranda v. Arizona*. The trial court refused to exclude the confession because it found that Mathiason was not in custody at the time of the confession. The Oregon Court of Appeals affirmed respondent's conviction, but on his petition for review in the Supreme Court of Oregon that court by a divided vote reversed the conviction. It found that although Mathiason had not been arrested or otherwise formally detained, "the interrogation took place in a `coercive environment'" of the sort to which Miranda was intended to apply. The court conceded that its holding was contrary to decisions in other jurisdictions, and referred in particular to *People v. Yukl*. The State of Oregon has petitioned for certiorari to review the judgment of the Supreme Court of Oregon.

I

Where a respondent voluntarily came to a police station for questioning about a burglary and was immediately informed that he was not under arrest, and at the close of a half-hour interview left the station without hindrance, should his confession to a burglary obtained during such interview be suppressed at his state criminal trial because he was not given Miranda warnings prior to being questioned?

R

An individual who appears voluntarily at a police officer's request to be questioned, and who is not placed under arrest, is not in a custodial setting such that Miranda warnings must be given.

A

We think that the court has read Miranda too broadly, and we therefore reverse its judgment. In the present case, however, there is no indication that the questioning took place in a context where respondent's freedom to depart was restricted in any way. He came voluntarily to the police station, where he was immediately informed that he was not under arrest. At the close of a 1/2-hour interview respondent did in fact leave the police station without hindrance. It is clear from these facts that Mathiason was not in custody "or otherwise deprived of his freedom of action in any significant way." Such a non-custodial situation is not converted to one in which Miranda applies simply because a reviewing court concludes that, even in the absence of any formal arrest or restraint on freedom of movement, the questioning took place in a "coercive environment." Any interview of one suspected of a crime by a police officer will have coercive aspects to it, simply by virtue of the fact that the police officer is part of a law enforcement system which may ultimately cause the suspect to be charged with a crime. But police officers are not required to administer Miranda warnings to everyone whom they question. Nor is the requirement of warnings to be imposed simply because the questioning takes place in the station house, or because the questioned person is one whom the police suspect. Miranda warnings are required only where there has been such a restriction on a person's freedom as to render him "in custody." It was that sort of coercive environment to which Miranda by its terms was made applicable, and to which it is limited. The officer's false statement about having discovered Mathiason's fingerprints at the scene was found by the Supreme Court of Oregon to be another circumstance contributing to the coercive environment which makes the Miranda rationale applicable. Whatever relevance this fact may have to other issues in the case, it has nothing to do with whether respondent was in custody for purposes of the Miranda rule. The petition for certiorari is granted, the judgment of the Oregon Supreme Court is reversed, and the case is remanded for proceedings not inconsistent with this opinion.

C

Reversed and remanded.

Berkemer v. McCarty

468 U.S. 420 (1984)

FACTS

After observing respondent's car weaving in and out of a highway lane, an officer of the Ohio State Highway Patrol forced respondent to stop and asked him to get out of the car. Upon noticing that respondent was having difficulty standing, the officer concluded that respondent would be charged with a traffic offense and would not be allowed to leave the scene, but respondent was not told that he would be taken into custody. When respondent could not perform a field sobriety test without falling, the officer asked him if he had been using intoxicants, and he replied that he had consumed two beers and had smoked marihuana a short time before. The officer then formally arrested respondent and drove him to a county jail, where a blood test failed to detect any alcohol in respondent's blood. Questioning was then resumed, and respondent again made incriminating statements, including an admission that he was "barely" under the influence of alcohol. At no point during this sequence was respondent given the warnings prescribed by *Miranda v. Arizona*. Respondent was charged with the misdemeanor under Ohio law of operating a motor vehicle while under the influence of alcohol and/or drugs, and when the state court denied his motion to exclude the various incriminating statements on the asserted ground that their admission into evidence would violate the Fifth Amendment because respondent had not been informed of his constitutional rights prior to his interrogation, he pleaded "no contest" and was convicted. After the conviction was affirmed on appeal by the Franklin County Court of Appeals and the Ohio Supreme Court denied review, respondent filed an action in Federal District Court for habeas corpus relief. The District Court dismissed the petition, but the Court of Appeals reversed, holding that Miranda warnings must be given to all individuals prior to custodial interrogation, whether the offense investigated is a felony or a misdemeanor traffic offense, and that respondent's post-arrest statements, at least, were inadmissible.

I

Is a motorist who is detained for questioning pursuant to a traffic stop considered "in custody" for *Miranda* purposes?

R

A detainee, in an ordinary traffic stop is not considered "in custody" for *Miranda* purposes.

A

A person subjected to custodial interrogation is entitled to the benefit of the procedural safeguards enunciated in Miranda, regardless of the nature or severity of the offense of which he is suspected or for which he was arrested. Thus, respondent's statements made at the station house were inadmissible since he was "in custody" at least as of the moment he was formally arrested and instructed to get into the police car, and since he was not informed of his constitutional rights at that time. To create an exception to the Miranda rule when the police arrest a person for allegedly committing a misdemeanor traffic offense and then question him without informing him of his constitutional rights would substantially undermine the rule's simplicity and clarity and would introduce doctrinal complexities, particularly with respect to situations where the police, in conducting custodial interrogations, do not know whether the person has committed a misdemeanor or a felony. The purposes of the Miranda safeguards as to ensuring that the police do not coerce or trick captive suspects into confessing, relieving the inherently compelling pressures generated by the custodial setting itself, and freeing courts from the task of scrutinizing individual cases to determine, after the fact, whether particular confessions were voluntary, are implicated as much by in-custody questioning of persons suspected of misdemeanors as they are by questioning of persons suspected of felonies. The roadside questioning of a motorist detained pursuant to a routine traffic stop does not constitute "custodial interrogation" for the purposes of the Miranda rule. Although an ordinary traffic stop curtails the "freedom of action" of the detained motorist and imposes some pressures on the detainee to answer questions, such pressures do not sufficiently impair the detainee's exercise of his privilege against self-incrimination to require that he be warned of his constitutional rights. A traffic stop is usually brief, and the motorist expects that, while he may be given a citation, in the end he most likely will be allowed to continue on his way. Moreover, the typical traffic stop is conducted in public, and the atmosphere surrounding it is substantially less "police dominated" than that surrounding the kinds of interrogation at issue in Miranda and subsequent cases in which Miranda has been applied. However, if a motorist who has been detained pursuant to a traffic stop thereafter is subjected to treatment that renders him "in custody" for practical purposes, he is entitled to the full panoply of protections prescribed by Miranda. In this case, the initial stop of respondent's car, by itself, did not render him "in custody," and respondent has failed to demonstrate that, at any time between the stop and the arrest, he was subjected to restraints comparable to those associated with a formal arrest. Although the arresting officer apparently decided as soon as respondent stepped out of his car that he would be taken into custody and charged with a traffic offense, the officer never communicated his intention to respondent. A policeman's unarticulated plan has no bearing on the question whether a suspect was "in custody" at a particular time; the only relevant inquiry is how a reasonable man in the suspect's position would have understood his situation. Since respondent was not taken into custody for the purposes of Miranda until he was formally arrested, his statements made prior to that point were admissible against him. A determination of whether the improper admission of respondent's post-arrest statements constituted "harmless error" will not be made by this Court for the cumulative reasons that (i) the issue was not presented to the Ohio courts or to the federal courts below, (ii) respondent's admissions made at the scene of the traffic stop and the statements he made at the police station were not identical, and (iii) the procedural posture of the case makes the use of harmless-error analysis especially difficult because respondent, while preserving his objection to the denial of his pretrial motion to exclude the evidence, elected not to contest the prosecution's case against him and thus has not yet had an opportunity to try to impeach the State's evidence or to present evidence of his own.

C Affirmed.

Rhode Island v. Innis

446 U.S. 291 (1980)

FACTS

Shortly after a taxicab driver, who had been robbed by a man wielding a sawed-off shotgun, identified a picture of Defendant-Respondent Innis as that of his assailant, Providence, R. I., patrolman spotted respondent, who was unarmed, on the street, arrested him, and advised him of his rights under *Miranda v. Arizona*. When other police officers arrived at the arrest scene, respondent was twice again advised of his Miranda rights, and he stated that he understood his rights and wanted to speak with a lawyer. Innis was then placed in a police car to be driven to the central station in the company of three officers, who were instructed not to question respondent or intimidate him in any way. While en route to the station, two of the officers engaged in a conversation between themselves concerning the missing shotgun. One of the officers stated that there were "a lot of handicapped children running around in this area" because a school for such children was located nearby, and "God forbid one of them might find a weapon with shells and they might hurt themselves." Respondent interrupted the conversation, stating that the officers should turn the car around so he could show them where the gun was located. Upon returning to the scene of the arrest where a search for the shotgun was in progress, respondent was again advised of his *Miranda* rights, replied that he understood those rights but that he "wanted to get the gun out of the way because of the kids in the area in the school," and then led the police to the shotgun. Before trial on charges of kidnapping, robbery, and murder of another taxi-cab driver, the trial court denied respondent's motion to suppress the shotgun and the statements he had made to the police regarding its discovery, ruling that respondent had waived his *Miranda* rights, and respondent was subsequently convicted. The Rhode Island Supreme Court set aside the conviction and held that respondent was entitled to a new trial, concluding that respondent had invoked his Miranda right to counsel and that, contrary to *Miranda's* mandate that, in the absence of counsel, all custodial interrogation then cease, the police officers in the vehicle had "interrogated" respondent without a valid waiver of his right to counsel. The prosecution appealed.

I Is a police officer's statement which elicits an incriminating response from the suspect an "interrogation" which requires *Miranda* safeguards if the suspect is in police custody?

R Police officers' statements are not deemed "interrogation" unless they are either express questions or equivalent statements which are reasonably likely to elicit an incriminating response and in fact elicit such a response when a suspect is in police custody.

A The respondent was not "interrogated" in violation of his right under *Miranda* to remain silent until he had consulted with a lawyer. The *Miranda* safeguards come into play whenever a person in custody is subjected to either express questioning or its functional equivalent. That is, the term "interrogation" under *Miranda* refers not only to express questioning, but also to any words or actions on the part of the police (other than those normally attendant to arrest and custody) that the police should know are reasonably likely to elicit an incriminating response from the suspect. The latter portion of this definition focuses primarily upon the perceptions of the suspect, rather than the intent of the police. Here, there was no express questioning of respondent; the conversation between the two officers was, at least in form, nothing more than a dialogue between them to which no response from respondent was invited. Moreover, respondent was not subjected to the "functional equivalent" of questioning, since it cannot be said that the officers should have known that their conversation was reasonably likely to elicit an incriminating response from respondent. There is nothing in the record to suggest that the officers were aware that respondent was peculiarly susceptible to an appeal to his conscience concerning the safety of handicapped children, or that the police knew that respondent was unusually disoriented or upset at the time of his arrest. Nor does the record indicate that, in the context of a brief conversation, the officers should have known that respondent would suddenly be moved to make a self-incriminating response. While it may be said that respondent was subjected to "subtle compulsion," it must also be established that a suspect's incriminating response was the product of words or actions on the part of the police that they should have known were reasonably likely to elicit an incriminating response, which was not established here. There is no evidence on record suggesting the officer's remarks were designed to elicit a response from the defendant and the defendant's incriminating statement was not caused by the police's words.

C

Reversed.

North Carolina v. Butler

441 U.S. 369 (1979)

FACTS

Respondent, while under arrest for certain crimes and after being advised of his rights under *Miranda v. Arizona*, made incriminating statements to the arresting officers. His motion to suppress evidence of these statements on the ground that he had not waived his right to assistance of counsel at the time the statements were made was denied by a North Carolina trial court, and he was subsequently convicted. The North Carolina Supreme Court reversed, holding that Miranda requires that no statement of a person under custodial interrogation may be admitted in evidence against him unless, at the time the statement was made, he explicitly waived the right to the presence of a lawyer.

I Does *Miranda* require that no statement of a person under custodial interrogation may be admitted in evidence against him unless, at the time the statement was made, he explicitly waived the right to the presence of a lawyer?

R An explicit statement of waiver is not invariably necessary to support a finding that the defendant waived the right to counsel guaranteed by the *Miranda* case.

A An explicit statement of waiver is not invariably necessary to support a finding that the defendant waived the right to counsel guaranteed by the *Miranda* case. The question of waiver must be determined on the particular facts and circumstances surrounding the case, and there is no reason in a case such as this for a per se rule, such as that of the North Carolina Supreme Court. By creating an inflexible rule that no implicit waiver can ever suffice, that court has gone beyond the requirements of federal organic law, and thus its judgment cannot stand, since a state court can neither add to nor subtract from the mandates of the United States Constitution.

C Vacated and remanded.

Edwards v. Arizona

451 U.S. 477 (1981)

FACTS

After being arrested on a state criminal charge, and after being informed of his rights as required by *Miranda v. Arizona*, petitioner Edwards was questioned by the police on January 19, 1976, until he said that he wanted an attorney. Questioning then ceased, but on January 20 police officers came to the jail and, after stating that they wanted to talk to him and again informing petitioner of his Miranda rights, obtained his confession when he said that he was willing to talk. The trial court ultimately denied petitioner's motion to suppress his confession, finding the statement to be voluntary, and he was thereafter convicted. The Arizona Supreme Court held that during the January 20 meeting he waived his right to remain silent and his right to counsel when he voluntarily gave his statement after again being informed of his rights.

I

When the accused invokes his right to counsel during a custodial interrogation, does his response to further police-initiated interrogation, after being re-advised of his rights, constitute a valid waiver?

R

An accused, having expressed his desire to deal with the police only through counsel, is not subject to further interrogation until counsel has been made available to him, unless the accused has himself initiated further communication, exchanges, or conversations with the police.

A

The use of petitioner's confession against him at his trial violated his right under the Fifth and Fourteenth Amendments to have counsel present during custodial interrogation, as declared in Miranda, supra. Having exercised his right on January 19 to have counsel present during interrogation, petitioner did not validly waive that right on the 20th. A waiver of the right to counsel, once invoked, not only must be voluntary, but also must constitute a knowing and intelligent relinquishment of a known right or privilege. Here, however, the state courts applied an erroneous standard for determining waiver by focusing on the voluntariness of petitioner's confession rather than on whether he understood his right to counsel and intelligently and knowingly relinquished it. When an accused has invoked his right to have counsel present during custodial interrogation, a valid waiver of that right cannot be established by showing only that he responded to police-initiated interrogation after being again advised of his rights. An accused, such as petitioner, having expressed his desire to deal with the police only through counsel, is not subject to further interrogation until counsel has been made available to him, unless the accused has himself initiated further communication, exchanges, or conversations with the police. Here, the interrogation of petitioner on January 20 was at the instance of the authorities, and his confession, made without having had access to counsel, did not amount to a valid waiver and hence was inadmissible.

C

Reversed.

New York v. Quarles
467 U.S. 649 (1984)

FACTS

Defendant-Respondent Quarles was charged in a New York state court with criminal possession of a weapon. The record showed that a woman approached two police officers who were on road patrol, told them that she had just been raped, described her assailant, and told them that the man had just entered a nearby supermarket and was carrying a gun. While one of the officers radioed for assistance, the other (Officer Kraft) entered the store and spotted respondent, who matched the description given by the woman. Respondent ran toward the rear of the store, and Officer Kraft pursued him with a drawn gun but lost sight of him for several seconds. Upon regaining sight of respondent, Officer Kraft ordered him to stop and put his hands over his head; frisked him and discovered that he was wearing an empty shoulder holster; and, after handcuffing him, asked him where the gun was. Respondent nodded toward some empty cartons and responded that "the gun is over there." Officer Kraft then retrieved the gun from one of the cartons, formally arrested respondent, and read him his rights under *Miranda v. Arizona*. Respondent indicated that he would answer questions without an attorney being present and admitted that he owned the gun and had purchased it in Florida. The trial court excluded respondent's initial statement and the gun because the respondent had not yet been given the Miranda warnings, and also excluded respondent's other statements as evidence tainted by the Miranda violation. Both the Appellate Division of the New York Supreme Court and the New York Court of Appeals affirmed. The prosecution appealed.

I

If a police officer asks an arrestee where his gun is hidden, when in police custody, is the arrestee's answer and any evidence (the gun) admissible?

R

Police may ask questions reasonably necessary to ensure public safety without reciting *Miranda* warnings and suspects' replies are admissible, when the suspect is in police custody.

A

The Court of Appeals erred in affirming the exclusion of respondent's initial statement and the gun because of Officer Kraft's failure to read respondent his *Miranda* rights before attempting to locate the weapon. Accordingly, it also erred in affirming the exclusion of respondent's subsequent statements as illegal fruits of the *Miranda* violation. This case presents a situation where concern for public safety must be paramount to adherence to the literal language of the prophylactic rules enunciated in *Miranda*. Although respondent was in police custody when he made his statements and the facts come within the ambit of *Miranda*, nevertheless on these facts there is a "public safety" exception to the requirement that Miranda warnings be given before a suspect's answers may be admitted into evidence, and the availability of that exception does not depend upon the motivation of the individual officers involved. The doctrinal underpinnings of *Miranda* do not require that it be applied in full force to a situation in which police officers ask questions reasonably prompted by a concern for the public safety. In this case, as long as the gun was concealed somewhere in the supermarket, it posed more than one danger to the public safety: an accomplice might make use of it, or a customer or employee might later come upon it. Procedural safeguards that deter a suspect from responding, and increase the possibility of fewer convictions, were deemed acceptable in *Miranda* in order to protect the Fifth Amendment privilege against compulsory self-incrimination. However, if *Miranda* warnings had deterred responses to Officer Kraft's question about the whereabouts of the gun, the cost would have been something more than merely the failure to obtain evidence useful in convicting respondent. An answer was needed to insure that future danger to the public did not result from the concealment of the gun in a public area. The narrow exception to the Miranda rule recognized here will to some degree lessen the desirable clarity of that rule. However, the exception will not be difficult for police officers to apply because in each case it will be circumscribed by the exigency which justifies it. Police officers can and will distinguish almost instinctively between questions necessary to secure their own safety or the safety of the public and questions designed solely to elicit testimonial evidence from a suspect. We thus conclude that the need to ask questions necessary to protect public safety outweighs the need to uphold the Fifth Amendment privilege against self-incrimination.

C Yes. Police may ask questions reasonably necessary to ensure public safety without reciting *Miranda* warnings and suspects' replies are admissible, when the suspect is in police custody.

Dickerson v. United States

530 U.S. 428 (2000)

FACTS

In the wake of *Miranda* v. *Arizona*, in which the Court held that certain warnings must be given before a suspect's statement made during custodial interrogation could be admitted in evidence, Congress enacted 18 U. S. C. §3501, which in essence makes the admissibility of such statements turn solely on whether they were made voluntarily. Defendant-Petitioner Dickerson, under indictment for bank robbery and related federal crimes, moved to suppress a statement he had made to the Federal Bureau of Investigation (FBI), on the ground he had not received "*Miranda* warnings" before being interrogated. The District Court granted his motion, and the Government took an interlocutory appeal. In reversing, the Court of Appeals for the Fourth Circuit acknowledged that petitioner had not received *Miranda* warnings, but held that §3501 (Crime Control Act of 1968, which limits *Miranda* and the *McNabb-Mallory* rule in federal prosecutions by giving judges the option of admitting confessions obtained without informing the suspect of his right to silence and/or counsel, if they are deemed involuntary) was satisfied. It also concluded that *Miranda* was not a constitutional holding, and that, therefore, Congress could by statute have the final say on the admissibility question. Dickerson sought review by the United States Supreme Court.

I May Congress legislatively supersede the decision in *Miranda v. Arizona*?

R Congress MAY NOT legislatively supersede *Miranda v. Arizona* as it announced a constitutional rule.

A *Miranda* and its progeny in this Court govern the admissibility of statements made during custodial interrogation in both state and federal courts. *Miranda*, being a constitutional decision of this Court, may not be in effect overruled by an Act of Congress. Given §3501's express designation of voluntariness as the touchstone of admissibility, its omission of any warning requirement, and its instruction for trial courts to consider the totality of the circumstances surrounding the giving of the confession, this Court agrees with the Fourth Circuit that Congress intended §3501 to overrule *Miranda.* The law is clear as to whether Congress has constitutional authority to do so. This Court has supervisory authority over the federal courts to prescribe binding rules of evidence and procedure. *Carlisle v. United States.* While Congress has ultimate authority to modify or set aside any such rules that are not constitutionally required, *e.g., Palermo v. United States,* it may not supersede this Court's decisions interpreting and applying the Constitution, see, *e.g., City of Boerne v. Flores.* The conclusion that *Miranda* is constitutionally based is also supported by the fact that that case is replete with statements indicating that the majority thought it was announcing a Constitutional rule. Although *Miranda* invited legislative action to protect the constitutional right against coerced self-incrimination, it stated that any legislative alternative must be 'at least as effective in appraising accused persons of their right of silence and in assuring a continuous opportunity to exercise it.'

This Court declines to overrule *Miranda.* Whether or not this Court would agree with *Miranda*'s reasoning and its rule in the first instance, *stare decisis* weighs heavily against overruling it now. Even in Constitutional cases, *stare decisis* carries such persuasive force that the Court has always required a departure from precedent to be supported by some special justification. There is no such justification here. *Miranda* has become embedded in routine police practice to the point where the warnings have become part of our national culture. While the Court has overruled precedents when subsequent cases have undermined their doctrinal underpinnings, this has not happened to *Miranda.* If anything, subsequent cases have reduced *Miranda*'s impact on legitimate law enforcement while reaffirming the decision's core ruling. But experience suggests that §3501's totality-of-the-circumstances test is more difficult than *Miranda* for officers to conform to, and for courts to apply consistently. The requirement that *Miranda* warnings be given does not dispense with the voluntariness inquiry, but cases in which a defendant can make a colorable argument that a self-incriminating statement was compelled despite officers' adherence to *Miranda* are rare.

Finally, although the Court agrees with the court-appointed *amicus curiae* that there are more remedies available for abusive police conduct than there were when *Miranda* was decided (*e.g.*, a suit under *Bivens v. Six Unknown Named Agents*) it does not agree that such additional measures supplement §3501's protections sufficiently to create an adequate substitute for the *Miranda* warnings. *Miranda* requires procedures that will warn a suspect in custody of his right to remain silent and assure him that the exercise of that right will be honored, see, *e.g.*, while §3501 explicitly eschews a requirement of pre-interrogation warnings in favor of an approach that looks to the administration of such warnings as only one factor in determining the voluntariness of a suspect's confession. Section 3501, therefore, cannot be sustained if *Miranda* is to remain the law

C

No. Congress may not legislatively supersede *Miranda v. Arizona* as it announced a constitutional rule.

Massiah v. United States

377 U.S. 201 (1964)

FACTS

The petitioner was indicted for violating the federal narcotics laws. He retained a lawyer, pleaded not guilty, and was released on bail. While he was free on bail a federal agent succeeded by surreptitious means in listening to incriminating statements made by him. Evidence of these statements was introduced against the petitioner at his trial over his objection. He was convicted, and the Court of Appeals affirmed. The U.S. Supreme Court granted certiorari to consider whether, under the circumstances here presented, the prosecution's use at the trial of evidence of the petitioner's own incriminating statements deprived him of any right secured to him under the Federal Constitution.

I Do incriminating statements, deliberately elicited by federal agents from the petitioner, in the absence of his attorney, deprive a defendant of his right to counsel under the Sixth Amendment?

R Incriminating statements thus deliberately elicited by federal agents from the petitioner, in the absence of his attorney, deprived the petitioner of his right to counsel under the Sixth Amendment; therefore such statements could not constitutionally be used as evidence against him in his trial.

A In *Spano v. New York*, we reversed a state criminal conviction because a confession had been wrongly admitted into evidence against the defendant at his trial. In that case the defendant had already been indicted for first-degree murder at the time he confessed. The Court held that the defendant's conviction could not stand under the Fourteenth Amendment. While the Court's opinion relied upon the totality of the circumstances under which the confession had been obtained, four concurring Justices pointed out that the Constitution required reversal of the conviction upon the sole and specific ground that the confession had been deliberately elicited by the police after the defendant had been indicted, and therefore at a time when he was clearly entitled to a lawyer's help. Ever since this Court's decision in the *Spano* case, the New York courts have unequivocally followed this constitutional rule. "Any secret interrogation of the defendant, from and after the finding of the indictment, without the protection afforded by the presence of counsel, contravenes the basic dictates of fairness in the conduct of criminal causes and the fundamental rights of persons charged with crime." Here we deal not with a state court conviction, but with a federal case, where the specific guarantee of the Sixth Amendment directly applies. We hold that the petitioner was denied the basic protections of that guarantee when there was used against him at his trial evidence of his own incriminating words, which federal agents had deliberately elicited from him after he had been indicted and in the absence of his counsel. It is true that in the *Spano* case the defendant was interrogated in a police station, while here the damaging testimony was elicited from the defendant without his knowledge while he was free on bail. But, as Judge Hays pointed out in his dissent in the Court of Appeals, "if such a rule is to have any efficacy it must apply to indirect and surreptitious interrogations as well as those conducted in the jailhouse. In this case, Massiah was more seriously imposed upon because he did not even know that he was under interrogation by a government agent. We do not question that in this case, as in many cases, it was entirely proper to continue an investigation of the suspected criminal activities of the defendant and his alleged confederates, even though the defendant had already been indicted. All that we hold is that the defendant's own incriminating statements, obtained by federal agents under the circumstances here disclosed, could not constitutionally be used by the prosecution as evidence against him at his trial. Reversed.

C Reversed

Brewer v. Williams

430 U.S. 387 (1977)

FACTS

Defendant-Respondent Williams, an escaped mental patient, was arrested, arraigned, and committed to jail in Davenport, Iowa, for abducting a 10-year-old girl in Des Moines, Iowa. Both his Des Moines lawyer and his lawyer at the Davenport arraignment advised respondent not to make any statements until after consulting with the Des Moines lawyer upon being returned to Des Moines, and the police officers who were to accompany respondent on the automobile drive back to Des Moines agreed not to question him during the trip. During the trip respondent expressed no willingness to be interrogated in the absence of an attorney but instead stated several times that he would tell the whole story after seeing his Des Moines lawyer. However, one of the police officers, who knew that respondent was a former mental patient and was deeply religious, sought to obtain incriminating remarks from respondent by stating to him during the drive that he felt they should stop and locate the girl's body because her parents were entitled to a Christian burial for the girl, who was taken away from them on Christmas Eve. Respondent eventually made several incriminating statements in the course of the trip and finally directed the police to the girl's body. Respondent was tried and convicted of murder, over his objections to the admission of evidence relating to or resulting from any statements he made during the automobile ride and the Iowa Supreme Court affirmed, holding, as did the trial court, that respondent had waived his constitutional right to the assistance of counsel. Respondent then petitioned for habeas corpus in Federal District Court, which held that the evidence in question had been wrongly admitted at respondent's trial on the ground, *inter alia*, that he had been denied his constitutional right to the assistance of counsel, and further ruled that he had not waived that right. The Court of Appeals affirmed. Petitioner Williams claims that the District Court in making its findings of fact disregarded 28 U.S.C. §2254(d), which provides that, subject to certain exceptions, federal habeas corpus courts shall accept as correct the factual determinations made by state courts.

I

When incriminating statements are obtained from the accused after judicial proceedings have been initiated and counsel retained, is the accused's right to counsel violated?

R

When incriminating statements are obtained from the accused after judicial proceedings have been initiated and counsel retained, the accused's right to counsel is violated.

A

The District Court correctly applied 28 U.S.C. §2254 (d) in its resolution of the disputed evidentiary facts, where it appears that it made no findings of fact in conflict with those of the Iowa courts, and that its additional findings of fact based upon its examination of the state-court record were conscientiously and carefully explained and were approved by the Court of Appeals as being supported by the record. Respondent was deprived of his constitutional right to assistance of counsel. The right to counsel granted by the Sixth and Fourteenth Amendments means at least that a person is entitled to a lawyer's help at or after the time that judicial proceedings have been initiated against him, and here there is no doubt that judicial proceedings had been initiated against respondent before the automobile trip started, since a warrant had been issued for his arrest, he had been arraigned, and had been committed to jail. An individual against whom adversary proceedings have commenced has a right to legal representation when the Government interrogates him, *Massiah v. United States*, and since here the police officer's "Christian burial speech" was tantamount to interrogation, respondent was entitled to the assistance of counsel at the time he made the incriminating statements. The Detective, by drawing upon defendant's religious background, set out to elicit information from him, which was probably more effective than a formal interrogation. The Detective knew that defendant was represented by counsel into cities. The circumstances of record provide, when viewed in light of respondent's assertions of his right to counsel, no reasonable basis for finding that respondent waived his right to the assistance of counsel, the record falling far short of sustaining the State's burden to prove "an intentional relinquishment or abandonment of a known right or privilege," *Johnson v. Zerbst.*

C

Yes. When incriminating statements are obtained from the accused after judicial proceedings have been initiated and counsel retained, the accused's right to counsel is violated.

Michigan v. Jackson

475 U.S. 625 (1986)

FACTS

Respondents, at separate arraignments in a Michigan trial court on unrelated murder charges, each requested appointment of counsel. But before respondents had an opportunity to consult with counsel, police officers, after advising respondents of their Miranda rights, questioned them and obtained confessions. Both respondents were convicted over objections to the admission of the confessions in evidence. The Michigan Court of Appeals reversed and remanded in one case, but affirmed in the other. The Michigan Supreme Court considered both cases together, and held that the confessions were improperly obtained in violation of the Sixth Amendment.

I

Must the police refrain from the interrogation of the defendant until his counsel is appointed where the defendant has been formally charged and requests counsel at his arraignment?

R

The Sixth Amendment permits an accused who requests a lawyer to have one present during any custodial interrogation by the police absent a waiver by the accused.

A

The confessions should have been suppressed. Although the rule of *Edwards v. Arizona*, that once a suspect has invoked his right to counsel, police may not initiate interrogation until counsel has been made available to the suspect, rested on the Fifth Amendment and concerned a request for counsel made during custodial interrogation, the reasoning of that case applies with even greater force to these cases. The assertion of the right to counsel is no less significant, and the need for additional safeguards no less clear, when that assertion is made at an arraignment and when the basis for it is the Sixth Amendment. If police initiate an interrogation after a defendant's assertion of his right to counsel at an arraignment or similar proceeding, as in these cases, any waiver of that right for that police-initiated interrogation is invalid.

C

Affirmed.

McNeil v. Wisconsin

501 U.S. 171 (1991)

FACTS

Charged with an armed robbery in West Allis, Wisconsin, petitioner McNeil was represented by a public defender at a bail hearing. While in jail on that charge, he was questioned by police about a murder and related crimes in Caledonia, Wisconsin. He was advised of his Miranda rights, signed forms waiving them, and made statements incriminating himself in the Caledonia offenses. He was then formally charged with the latter crimes, his pretrial motion to suppress his statements was denied, and he was convicted. His conviction was affirmed on appeal, the State Supreme Court holding that an accused's request for counsel at an initial appearance on a charged offense does not constitute an invocation of his Fifth Amendment right to counsel that precludes police interrogation on unrelated, uncharged offenses.

I

When an accused invokes his Sixth Amendment right to counsel during a judicial proceeding, does it also constitute an invocation of his Miranda right to counsel?

R

An accused's invocation of his Sixth Amendment right to counsel during a judicial proceeding does not constitute an invocation of the right to counsel derived by *Miranda* because the Sixth Amendment right does not attach until the initiation of adversary judicial proceedings and is offense-specific.

A

An accused's invocation of his Sixth Amendment right to counsel during a judicial proceeding does not constitute an invocation of the right to counsel derived by *Miranda v. Arizona* from the Fifth Amendment's guarantee against compelled self-incrimination. The identity between the two rights that McNeil asserts is false as a matter of fact. The Sixth Amendment right does not attach until the initiation of adversary judicial proceedings and is offense-specific. Thus, McNeil's invocation of that right with respect to the West Allis robbery poses no bar to the admission of his statements regarding the Caledonia crimes, with which he had not been charged at the time he made the statements. Moreover, although the Miranda right to counsel is non-offense-specific, *Arizona v. Roberson*, and, once asserted, prevents any further police-initiated interrogation outside the presence of counsel, *Edwards v. Arizona*, its assertion cannot be inferred from the invocation of the Sixth Amendment right in light of the differing purposes and effects of the two rights. The Sixth Amendment right is intended to protect the unaided layman at critical confrontations with the government after the initiation of the adversary process with respect to a particular crime, *United States v. Gouveia*. The *Miranda-Edwards* guarantee is intended to protect the suspect's "desire to deal with the police only through counsel." Requesting the assistance of an attorney at a bail hearing does not satisfy the minimum requirement of some statement that can reasonably be construed as an expression of a desire for counsel in dealing with custodial interrogation by the police. Nor will this Court declare as a matter of sound policy (assuming the existence of such expansive power) that assertion of the Sixth Amendment right implies invocation of the Miranda right. McNeil's proposed rule offers only insignificant advantages, and would seriously impede effective law enforcement by precluding uncounseled but uncoerced admissions of guilt pursuant to valid Miranda waivers.

McNeil v. Wisconsin

501 U.S. 171 (1991)

C Affirmed.

Sherman v. United States

356 U.S. 369 (1958)

FACTS

At petitioner's trial in a Federal District Court for selling narcotics in violation of 21 U.S.C. 174, he relied on the defense of entrapment. From the undisputed testimony of the Government's witnesses, it appeared that a government informer had met petitioner at a doctor's office where both were being treated to cure narcotics addiction, the informer asked petitioner to help him to obtain narcotics for his own use, petitioner seemed reluctant to do so, the informer persisted, and finally petitioner made several small purchases of narcotics and let the informer have half of each amount purchased at cost plus expenses. By prearrangement, other government agents then obtained evidence of three similar sales to the informer, for which petitioner was indicted. Except for a record of two convictions nine and five years previously, there was no evidence that petitioner himself was in the trade or that he showed a "ready complaisance" to the informer's request. The factual issue whether the informer had persuaded the otherwise unwilling petitioner to make the sale or whether petitioner was already predisposed to do so and exhibited only the natural hesitancy of one acquainted with the narcotics trade was submitted to the jury, which found petitioner guilty.

I

When a government informant persuades a reluctant recovering drug addict to obtain drugs, must the conviction be set aside on entrapment grounds?

R

Entrapment occurs only when the criminal conduct was "the product of the creative activity" of law-enforcement officials.

A

On the record in this case, entrapment was established as a matter of law, and petitioner's conviction is reversed. Entrapment occurs only when the criminal conduct was "the product of the creative activity" of law-enforcement officials. The undisputed testimony of the Government's witnesses established entrapment as a matter of law. Although the informer was not being paid, the Government cannot disown him or disclaim responsibility for his actions, since he was an active government informer who was himself awaiting trial on narcotics charges, for which he was later given a suspended sentence. It makes no difference that the sales for which petitioner was convicted occurred after a series of sales, since they were not independent acts subsequent to the inducement but were part of a course of conduct which was the product of the inducement. The Government cannot make such use of an informer and then claim disassociation through ignorance of the way in which he operated. The evidence was insufficient to overcome the defense of entrapment by showing that petitioner evinced a "ready complaisance" to accede to the informer's request. We adhere to the doctrine of the Court's opinion in *Sorrells v. United States* and decline to reassess the doctrine of entrapment.

C

Reversed and remanded.

Jacobson v. United States

503 U.S. 540 (1992)

FACTS

At a time when federal law permitted such conduct, Defendant-Petitioner Jacobson ordered and received from a bookstore two Bare Boys magazines containing photographs of nude preteen and teenage boys. Subsequently, the Child Protection Act of 1984 made illegal the receipt through the mails of sexually explicit depictions of children. After finding Jacobson's name on the bookstore mailing list, two Government agencies sent mail to him through five fictitious organizations and a bogus pen pal, to explore his willingness to break the law. Many of those organizations represented that they were founded to protect and promote sexual freedom and freedom of choice, and that they promoted lobbying efforts through catalog sales. Some mailings raised the specter of censorship. Jacobson responded to some of the correspondence. After 2 ½ years on the Government mailing list, Jacobson was solicited to order child pornography. He answered a letter that described concern about child pornography as hysterical nonsense and decried international censorship, and then received a catalog and ordered a magazine depicting young boys engaged in sexual activities. He was arrested after a controlled delivery of a photocopy of the magazine, but a search of his house revealed no materials other than those sent by the Government and the Bare Boys magazines. At his jury trial, he pleaded entrapment and testified that he had been curious to know the type of sexual actions to which the last letter referred, and that he had been shocked by the Bare Boys magazines, because he had not expected to receive photographs of minors. He was convicted, and the Court of Appeals affirmed.

I

Must the Government prove that the defendant's predisposition to commit the crime was not the result of the Government's efforts when entrapment is in issue?

R

The defendant's predisposition must be independent and not the product of the conduct of the Government under a claim of entrapment.

A

The prosecution failed, as a matter of law, to adduce evidence to support the jury verdict that Jacobson was predisposed, independent of the Government's acts and beyond a reasonable doubt, to violate the law by receiving child pornography through the mail. Government agents may not originate a criminal design, implant in an innocent person's mind the disposition to commit a criminal act, and then induce commission of the crime so that the Government may prosecute. Jacobson was not simply offered the opportunity to order pornography, after which he promptly availed himself of that opportunity. He was the target of 26 months of repeated Government mailings and communications and the Government has failed to carry its burden of proving predisposition independent of its attention. The pre-investigation evidence - the Bare Boys magazines - merely indicates a generic inclination to act within a broad range, not all of which is criminal. Furthermore, Jacobson was acting within the law when he received the magazines, as the magazines were lawfully obtained. He also testified that he did not know that they would depict minors. As for the evidence gathered during the investigation, Jacobson's responses to the many communications prior to the criminal act were, at most, indicative of certain personal inclinations, and would not support the inference that Jacobson was predisposed to violate the Child Protection Act. On the other hand, the strong arguable inference is that, by waving the banner of individual rights and disparaging the legitimacy and constitutionality of efforts to restrict the availability of sexually explicit materials, the Government not only excited Jacobson's interest in material banned by law but also exerted substantial pressure on him to obtain and read such material as part of the fight against censorship and the infringement of individual rights. Thus, rational jurors could not find beyond a reasonable doubt that Jacobson possessed the requisite predisposition before the Government's investigation, and that it existed independent of the Government's many and varied approaches to him.

C Yes. The defendant's predisposition must be independent and not the product of the conduct of the Government under a claim of entrapment.

United States v. Wade

388 U.S. 218 (1967)

FACTS

Several weeks after respondent's indictment for robbery of a federally insured bank and for conspiracy, Defendant-Respondent Wade, without notice to his appointed counsel, was placed in a lineup in which each person wore strips of tape on his face, as the robber allegedly had done, and on direction repeated words like those the robber allegedly had used. Two bank employees identified respondent as the robber. At the trial when asked if the robber was in the courtroom, they identified respondent. The prior lineup identifications were elicited on cross-examination. Urging that the conduct of the lineup violated his Fifth Amendment privilege against self-incrimination and his Sixth Amendment right to counsel, respondent filed a motion for judgment of acquittal or, alternatively, to strike the courtroom identifications. The trial court denied the motions and respondent was convicted. The Court of Appeals reversed, holding that though there was no Fifth Amendment deprivation the absence of counsel at the lineup denied respondent his right to counsel under the Sixth Amendment and required the grant of a new trial at which the in-court identifications of those who had made lineup identifications would be excluded.

I If the Government conducted a pretrial lineup without the defendant's counsel present, is an in court identification of an accused at trial admissible?

R Without defendant's counsel present, conducting a lineup violates the defendant's right to counsel, unless the defendant knowingly waives this right.

A Neither the lineup itself nor anything required therein violated respondent's Fifth Amendment privilege against self-incrimination since merely exhibiting his person for observation by witnesses and using his voice as an identifying physical characteristic involved no compulsion of the accused to give evidence of a testimonial nature against himself which is prohibited by that Amendment. The Sixth Amendment guarantees an accused the right to counsel not only at his trial but at any critical confrontation by the prosecution at pretrial proceedings where the results might well determine his fate and where the absence of counsel might derogate from his right to a fair trial. The post-indictment lineup (unlike such preparatory steps as analyzing fingerprints and blood samples) was a critical stage at which respondent was entitled to the aid of counsel. There is a great possibility of unfairness to the accused at that point, (1) because of the manner in which confrontations for identification are frequently conducted, (2) because of dangers inherent in eyewitness identification and suggestibility inherent in the context of the confrontations, and (3) because of the likelihood that the accused will often be precluded from reconstructing what occurred and thereby obtaining a full hearing on the identification issue at trial. This case illustrates the potential for improper influence on witnesses through the lineup procedure, since the bank employees were allowed to see respondent in the custody of FBI agents before the lineup began. The presence of counsel at the lineup will significantly promote fairness at the confrontation and a full hearing at trial on the issue of identification. In-court identification by a witness to whom the accused was exhibited before trial in the absence of counsel must be excluded unless it can be established that such evidence had an independent origin or that error in its admission was harmless. Since it is not clear that the Court of Appeals applied the prescribed rule of exclusion, and since the nature of the in-court identifications here was not an issue in the trial and cannot be determined on the record, the case must be remanded to the District Court for resolution of these issues.

C No. Without defendant's counsel present, conducting a lineup violates the defendant's right to counsel unless the defendant knowingly waives this right.

Stovall v. Denno

388 U.S 293 (1967)

FACTS

Petitioner was convicted and sentenced to death for murdering one Dr. Behrendt. He had been arrested the day after the murder and without being afforded time to retain counsel was taken by police officers, to one of whom he was handcuffed, to be viewed at the hospital by Mrs. Behrendt, who had been seriously wounded by her husband's assailant. After observing him and hearing him speak as directed by an officer, Mrs. Behrendt identified petitioner as the murderer. Mrs. Behrendt and the officers testified at petitioner's trial as to the hospital identification and she also made an in-court identification of the petitioner. Following affirmance of his conviction by the highest state court, petitioner sought habeas corpus in the District Court claiming that Mrs. Behrendt's identification testimony violated his Fifth, Sixth, and Fourteenth Amendment rights. The District Court after hearing argument on an unrelated claim dismissed the petition. The Court of Appeals, en banc, vacated a panel decision reversing the dismissal of the petition on constitutional grounds, and affirmed the District Court.

I

Does a one-on-one showup, as opposed to a lineup, violate the defendant's due process rights?

R

A showup, rather than a lineup, violates the defendant's due process rights if it is unusually suggestive when viewed in light of the totality of the circumstances.

A

The constitutional rule established in today's decisions in *United States v. Wade* and *Gilbert v. California* has application only to cases involving confrontations for identification purposes conducted in the absence of counsel after this date. Though the practice of showing suspects singly for purposes of identification has been widely condemned, a violation of due process of law in the conduct of a confrontation depends on the totality of the surrounding circumstances. There was no due process denial in the confrontation here since Mrs. Behrendt was the only person who could exonerate the suspect; she could not go to the police station for the usual lineup; and there was no way of knowing how long she would live.

C

Affirmed.

Mason v. Brathwaite

432 U.S. 98 (1977)

FACTS

Glover, a trained black undercover state police officer, purchased heroin from a seller through the open doorway of an apartment while standing for two or three minutes within two feet of the seller in a hallway illuminated by natural light. A few minutes later Glover described the seller to another police officer as being "a colored man, approximately five feet eleven inches tall, dark complexion, black hair, short Afro style, and having high cheekbones, and of heavy build." The other police officer, suspecting from the description that respondent might be the seller, left a police photograph of respondent at the office of Glover, who viewed it two days later and identified it as the picture of the seller. In a Connecticut court, respondent was charged with, and convicted of, possession and sale of heroin, and at his trial, held some eight months after the crime, the photograph was received in evidence without objection and Glover testified that there was no doubt that the person shown in the photograph was respondent and also made a positive in-court identification without objection. After the Connecticut Supreme Court affirmed the conviction, respondent filed a petition for habeas corpus in Federal District Court, alleging that the admission of the identification testimony at his state trial deprived him of due process of law in violation of the Fourteenth Amendment. The District Court dismissed the petition, but the Court of Appeals reversed, holding that evidence as to the photograph should have been excluded, regardless of reliability, because the examination of the single photograph was unnecessary and suggestive, and that the identification was unreliable in any event.

I Are a defendant's due process rights violated by a witness identification that might be based on suggestion and that is unnecessary?

R A defendant's due process rights are not violated by a witness's identification which is based on suggestion and is unnecessary, if it is reliable based on the totality of the circumstances.

A The Due Process Clause of the Fourteenth Amendment does not compel the exclusion of the identification evidence. Reliability is the key to determine the admissibility of identification testimony for confrontations that occur prior to and after *Stovall v. Denno*, wherein it was held that the determination depends on the "totality of the circumstances." The factors to be weighed against the corrupting effect of the suggestive procedure in assessing reliability are set out in *Neil v. Biggers*, and include the witness's (1) opportunity to view the criminal at the time of the crime. Here are Glover stood only its couple of feet from the respondent in good light and look directly at him; (2) the witness' degree of attention. Glover was in on duty police officer and was trained to pay scrupulous attention to detail; (3) the accuracy of his prior description of the criminal. No claim has been raised that the respondent does not have the physical characteristics Glover described; (4) the level of certainty demonstrated at the confrontation. Glover stated that he was positive that the photograph was about the suspect from home. He brought the drugs; and (5) the time between the crime and the confrontation. Glover described the suspect to deed within minutes of the crime and identified the photograph only two days later. Finally, there was little pressure on Glover to acquiesce in the suggestive procedure.

C

No. A defendant's due process rights are not violated by a witness's identification which is based on suggestion and is unnecessary, if it is reliable based on the totality of the circumstances. Reversed.

Stack v. Boyle

342 U.S. 1 (1951)

FACTS

The twelve petitioners were arrested on charges of conspiring to violate the Smith Act, 18 U.S.C. (Supp. IV) 371, 2385, and their bail was fixed initially in amounts varying from $2,500 to $100,000. Subsequently, the District Court fixed bail pending trial in the uniform amount of $50,000 for each of them. They moved to reduce bail, claiming that it was "excessive" under the Eighth Amendment, and filed supporting statements of fact which were not controverted. The only evidence offered by the Government was a certified record showing that four other persons previously convicted under the Smith Act in another district had forfeited bail; and there was no evidence relating them to petitioners. The motion to reduce bail was denied.

I

Is bail fixed at $500,000 excessive in light of the crime charged and when compared to other similar crimes?

R

Under the Eighth Amendment, bail must be reasonably fixed to insure that the defendant will appear at trial an must be based upon standards relevant to the purpose of assuring the presence of that defendant - Rule 46 (c) of the Federal Rules of Criminal Procedure.

A

Bail has not been fixed by proper methods in this case. Bail set before trial at a figure higher than an amount reasonably calculated to fulfill the purpose of assuring the presence of the defendant is "excessive" under the Eighth Amendment. The fixing of bail before trial for any individual defendant must be based upon standards relevant to the purpose of assuring the presence of that defendant - Rule 46 (c) of the Federal Rules of Criminal Procedure. If bail in an amount greater than that usually fixed for serious charges of crimes is required in the case of any of the petitioners, that is a matter to which evidence should be directed in a hearing, so that the constitutional rights of each petitioner may be preserved. After their motion to reduce bail was denied, petitioners did not appeal, but applied to the same District Court for habeas corpus. This was denied and the Court of Appeals affirmed.

C

Judgment vacated and case remanded.

United States v. Salerno

481 U.S. 739 (1987)

FACTS

The Bail Reform Act of 1984 (Act) requires courts to detain prior to trial arrestees charged with certain serious felonies if the Government demonstrates by clear and convincing evidence after an adversary hearing that no release conditions "will reasonably assure . . . the safety of any other person and the community." The Act provides arrestees with a number of procedural rights at the detention hearing, including the right to request counsel, to testify, to present witnesses, to proffer evidence, and to cross-examine other witnesses. The Act also specifies the factors to be considered in making the detention decision, including the nature and seriousness of the charges, the substantiality of the Government's evidence, the arrestee's background and characteristics, and the nature and seriousness of the danger posed by his release. Under the Act, a decision to detain must be supported by written findings of fact and a statement of reasons, and is immediately reviewable. After a hearing under the Act, the District Court ordered the detention of Defendants-Respondents Salerno and Cafaro, who had been charged with 35 counts of violating the Racketeer Influenced and Corrupt Organizations Act (RICO), and also mail and wire fraud, extortion, and some gambling violations. Pursuant to the Act, the Government moved for pretrial detention without bail. At the hearing, evidence and testimony was proffered to show that defendant was the boss of the Genovese crime family. The Court of Appeals reversed, holding that the Act's authorization of pretrial detention on the ground of future dangerousness is facially unconstitutional as it violates the Fifth Amendment's substantive due process guarantee.

I May a defendant in a criminal prosecution be detained without bail without violating his constitutional rights?

R A criminal defendant who is a danger to individuals or the community may be detained prior to trial without bail if the Government has shown by clear and convincing evidence that a sufficiently compelling reason exists for doing so.

A We hold that given the Act's legitimate and compelling regulatory purpose and the procedural protections it offers, §3142(e) is not facially invalid under the Due Process Clause. The argument that the Act violates substantive due process because the detention it authorizes constitutes impermissible punishment before trial is unpersuasive. The Act's legislative history clearly indicates that Congress formulated the detention provisions not as punishment for dangerous individuals, but as a potential solution to the pressing societal problem of crimes committed by persons on release. Preventing danger to the community is a legitimate regulatory goal. Moreover, the incidents of detention under the Act are not excessive in relation to that goal, since the Act carefully limits the circumstances under which detention may be sought to the most serious of crimes, the arrestee is entitled to a prompt hearing, the maximum length of detention is limited by the Speedy Trial Act, and detainees must be housed apart from convicts. Thus, the Act constitutes permissible regulation rather than impermissible punishment. The Court of Appeals erred in ruling that the Due Process Clause categorically prohibits pretrial detention that is imposed as a regulatory measure on the ground of community danger. The Government's regulatory interest in community safety can, in appropriate circumstances, outweigh an individual's liberty interest. Such circumstances exist here. The Act narrowly focuses on a particularly acute problem - crime by arrestees - in which the Government's interests are overwhelming. Moreover, the Act operates only on individuals who have been arrested for particular extremely serious offenses, and carefully delineates the circumstances under which detention will be permitted. The Act's extensive procedural safeguards are specifically designed to further the accuracy of the likelihood-of-future-dangerousness determination, and are sufficient to withstand respondents' facial challenge, since they are more than "adequate to authorize the pretrial detention of at least some [persons] charged with crimes." *Schall v. Martin.* Section 3142(e) is not facially unconstitutional as violative of the Excessive Bail Clause of the Eighth Amendment. The contention that the Act violates the Clause because it allows courts essentially to set bail at an infinite amount for reasons not related to the risk of flight is not persuasive. Nothing in the Clause's text limits the Government's interest in the setting of bail solely to the prevention of flight. Where Congress has mandated detention on the basis of some other compelling interest - here, the public safety - the Eighth Amendment does not require release on bail.

C

Yes. A criminal defendant who is a danger to individuals or the community may be detained prior to trial without bail if the Government has shown by clear and convincing evidence that a sufficiently compelling reason exists for doing so. Reversed.

United States v. Armstrong

517 U.S. 456 (1996)

FACTS

In response to their indictment on "crack" cocaine and other federal charges, Defendant-Respondent Armstrong and others filed a motion for discovery or for dismissal, alleging that they were selected for prosecution because they are black. The District Court granted the motion over the Government's argument, among others, that there was no evidence or allegation that it had failed to prosecute non black defendants. When the Government indicated it would not comply with the discovery order, the court dismissed the case. The *en banc* ("by the full court") Ninth Circuit affirmed, holding that the proof requirements for a selective-prosecution claim do not compel a defendant to demonstrate that the Government has failed to prosecute others who are similarly situated. This appeal followed.

I

Must the defendant demonstrate that the Government failed to prosecute others who are similarly situated, in order to obtain discovery in support of a claim of selective prosecution?

R

The defendant must make a credible showing of different treatment of similarly situated persons, in order to obtain discovery in support of a claim of selective prosecution.

A

We hold that for a defendant to be entitled to discovery on a claim that he was singled out for prosecution on the basis of his race, he must make a threshold showing that the Government declined to prosecute similarly situated suspects of other races. Contrary to respondents' contention, Federal Rule of Criminal Procedure 16, which governs discovery in criminal cases, does not support the result reached by the Ninth Circuit in this case. Rule 16(a)(1)(C) - which, *inter alia*, requires the Government to permit discovery of documents that are "material to the preparation of the . . . defense" or "intended for use by the Government as evidence in chief" - applies only to the preparation of the "defense" against the Government's case in chief, not to the preparation of selective-prosecution claims. This reading creates a perceptible symmetry between the types of documents referred to in the Rule. Moreover, its correctness is established beyond peradventure by Rule 16(a)(2), which, as relevant here, exempts from discovery the work product of Government attorneys and agents made in connection with the case's investigation. Respondents' construction of "defense" as including selective-prosecution claims is implausible: It creates the anomaly of a defendant's being able to Page II examine all Government work product under Rule 16(a)(1)(C), except that which is most pertinent, the work product in connection with his own case, under Rule 16(a)(2). Under the equal protection component of the Fifth Amendment's Due Process Clause, the decision whether to prosecute may not be based on an arbitrary classification such as race or religion. In order to prove a selective-prosecution claim, the claimant must demonstrate that the prosecutorial policy had a discriminatory effect and was motivated by a discriminatory purpose. To establish a discriminatory effect in a race case, the claimant must show that similarly situated individuals of a different race were not prosecuted. Although Ah Sin involved federal review of a state conviction, a similar rule applies where the power of a federal court is

---

invoked to challenge an exercise of one of the core powers of the Executive Branch of the Federal Government, the power to prosecute. Discovery imposes many of the costs present when the Government must respond to a prima facie case of selective prosecution. Assuming that discovery is available on an appropriate showing in aid of a selective-prosecution claim, see *Wade v. United States*, the justifications for a rigorous standard of proof for the elements of such a case thus require a correspondingly rigorous standard for discovery in aid of it. Thus, in order to establish entitlement to such discovery, a defendant must produce credible evidence that similarly situated defendants of other races could have been prosecuted, but were not. In this case, respondents have not met this required threshold. The affidavit and accompanying list failed to identify individuals who were not black and could have been prosecuted for the same offenses but were not. Moreover, much of the information provided was either irrelevant or based on hearsay.

C

Yes. The defendant must make a credible showing of different treatment of similarly situated persons, in order to obtain discovery in support of a claim of selective prosecution. Reversed and remanded

Blackledge v. Perry

417 U.S. 21 (1974)

FACTS

Respondent, a North Carolina prison inmate, had an altercation with another prisoner, and was charged with the misdemeanor of assault with a deadly weapon, of which he was convicted in the State District Court. While respondent's subsequent appeal was pending in the Superior Court, where he had the right to a trial de novo, the prosecutor obtained an indictment covering the same conduct for the felony offense of assault with a deadly weapon with intent to kill and inflict serious bodily injury, to which respondent pleaded guilty. Thereafter, respondent applied for a writ of habeas corpus in Federal District Court, claiming, inter alia, that the felony indictment deprived him of due process. The District Court granted the writ, and the Court of Appeals affirmed.

I

Does the indictment on a felony charge violate a defendant's due process rights when the state brings the charge against the defendant after the defendant exercises a statutory right to challenge a misdemeanor conviction arising from the same period?

R

The indictment on the felony charge contravened the Due Process Clause of the Fourteenth Amendment, since a person convicted of a misdemeanor in North Carolina is entitled to pursue his right under state law to a trial de novo without apprehension that the State will retaliate by substituting a more serious charge for the original one and thus subject him to a significantly increased potential period of incarceration..

A

The indictment on the felony charge contravened the Due Process Clause of the Fourteenth Amendment, since a person convicted of a misdemeanor in North Carolina is entitled to pursue his right under state law to a trial de novo without apprehension that the State will retaliate by substituting a more serious charge for the original one and thus subject him to a significantly increased potential period of incarceration. Since North Carolina, having chosen originally to proceed against respondent on the misdemeanor charge in the State District Court, was precluded by the Due Process Clause from even prosecuting respondent for the more serious charge in the Superior Court, respondent's guilty plea to the felony charge did not bar him from raising his constitutional claim in the federal habeas corpus proceeding.

C

Affirmed.

Coleman v. Alabama

399 U.S. 1 (1970)

FACTS

Petitioners were convicted in an Alabama Circuit Court of assault with intent to murder in the shooting of one Reynolds after he and his wife parked their car on an Alabama highway to change a flat tire. The Alabama Court of Appeals affirmed. They argue that (1) the in-court identifications that were made of them were fatally tainted by a prejudicial station-house lineup (which occurred prior to United *States v. Wade* and *Gilbert v. California*, requiring the exclusion of such tainted in-court identification evidence), and (2) that Alabama's failure to provide them with appointed counsel at the preliminary hearing, a "critical stage" of the prosecution, unconstitutionally denied them the assistance of counsel. The victim testified that, "in the car lights" while "looking straight at him," he saw the petitioner who shot him and saw the other petitioner "face to face." He also stated that he identified the gunman at the station house before the formal lineup began, and identified the other before he spoke the words used by the assailants. The sole purposes of a preliminary hearing under Alabama law are to determine whether there is sufficient evidence to warrant presenting the case to a grand jury, and to fix bail for bailable offenses. The trial court scrupulously followed *Pointer v. Texas*, which prohibits the use of testimony given at a pretrial proceeding where the accused did not have the benefit of cross-examination by and through counsel. Held: The convictions are vacated and the case is remanded to determine whether the denial of counsel at the preliminary hearing was harmless error.

I

Is a criminal defendant entitled to counsel at a preliminary hearing?

R

A criminal defendant entitled to counsel at a preliminary hearing because preliminary hearings are a critical stage of the prosecution.

A

MR. JUSTICE BRENNAN, joined by MR. JUSTICE DOUGLAS, MR. JUSTICE WHITE, and MR. JUSTICE MARSHALL, for the three points enumerated directly below, and by MR. JUSTICE BLACK, for the third point, concluded that: On this record the trial court did not err in finding that the victim's in-court identifications did not stem from a lineup procedure "so impermissibly suggestive as to give rise to a very substantial likelihood of irreparable misidentification." The preliminary hearing is a "critical stage" of Alabama's criminal process at which the indigent accused is "as much entitled to such aid [of counsel] . . . as at the trial itself." Although nothing that occurred at the preliminary hearing was used at the trial, the record does not reveal whether petitioners were otherwise prejudiced by absence of counsel at the hearing, and the question whether the denial of counsel was harmless error should be answered in the first instance by the Alabama courts. MR. JUSTICE BLACK concluded that: Petitioners had a right to the assistance of counsel at the preliminary hearing not because it is deemed part of a "fair trial" by judges but because the Sixth Amendment establishes a right to counsel "[i]n all criminal prosecutions" and in Alabama the preliminary hearing is a definite part or stage of a criminal prosecution. The trial court did not err in permitting courtroom identification of petitioners by the victim who had previously identified them at the lineup, as the requirements of the Fifth and Sixth Amendments were satisfied when the prosecution declined at trial to introduce the lineup identifications into evidence. MR. JUSTICE HARLAN concurs in the conclusion that petitioners' constitutional rights were violated when they were refused counsel at the preliminary hearing.

C

Vacated and remanded.

United States v. Williams

504 U.S. 36 (1992)

FACTS

Respondent Williams was indicted by a federal grand jury for alleged violations of 18 U.S.C. 1014. On his motion, the District Court ordered the indictment dismissed without prejudice because the Government had failed to fulfill its obligation under Circuit precedent to present "substantial exculpatory evidence" to the grand jury. Following that precedent, the Court of Appeals affirmed.

I

In a criminal case, does a prosecutor have a duty to present exculpatory evidence to the grand jury?

R

A prosecutor does not have a duty to present exculpatory evidence to the grand jury.

A

The argument that the petition should be dismissed as improvidently granted because the question presented was not raised below was considered and rejected when this Court granted certiorari, and is rejected again here. The Court will not review a question that was neither pressed nor passed on below, but there is no doubt that the Court of Appeals passed on the crucial issue of the prosecutor's duty to present exculpatory evidence to the grand jury. It is appropriate to review an important issue expressly decided by a federal court where, as here, although the petitioner did not contest the issue in the case immediately at hand, it did so as a party to the recent proceeding upon which the lower courts relied for their resolution of the issue, and did not concede in the current case the correctness of that precedent. A district court may not dismiss an otherwise valid indictment because the Government failed to disclose to the grand jury "substantial exculpatory evidence" in its possession. Imposition of the Court of Appeals' disclosure rule is not supported by the courts' inherent "supervisory power" to formulate procedural rules not specifically required by the Constitution or the Congress. This Court's cases relying upon that power deal strictly with the courts' control over their own procedures, whereas the grand jury is an institution separate from the courts, over whose functioning the courts do not preside. Any power federal courts may have to fashion, on their own initiative, rules of grand jury procedure is very limited, and certainly would not permit the reshaping of the grand jury institution that would be the consequence of the proposed rule here. The Court of Appeals' rule would neither preserve nor enhance the traditional functioning of the grand jury that the "common law" of the Fifth Amendment demands. To the contrary, requiring the prosecutor to present exculpatory, as well as inculpatory, evidence would alter the grand jury's historical role, transforming it from an accusatory body that sits to assess whether there is adequate basis for bringing a criminal charge into an adjudicatory body that sits to determine guilt or innocence. Because it has always been thought sufficient for the grand jury to hear only the prosecutor's side, and, consequently that the suspect has no right to present, and the grand jury no obligation to consider, exculpatory evidence, it would be incompatible with the traditional system to impose upon the prosecutor a legal obligation to present such evidence. Moreover, motions to quash indictments based upon the sufficiency of the evidence relied upon by the grand jury have never been allowed, and it would make little sense to abstain from reviewing the evidentiary support for the grand jury's judgment while scrutinizing the sufficiency of the prosecutor's presentation. This Court need not pursue respondent's argument that the Court of Appeals' rule would save valuable judicial time. If there is any advantage to the proposal, Congress is free to prescribe it.

C

Reversed and remanded.

Ohio v. Reiner

532 U.S. 17 (2001)

FACTS

Respondent was charged with involuntary manslaughter in connection with the death of his 2-month-old son Alex. The coroner testified at trial that Alex died from "shaken baby syndrome," the result of child abuse. He estimated that Alex's injury most likely occurred minutes before the child stopped breathing. Alex died two days later when he was removed from life support. Evidence produced at trial revealed that Alex had a broken rib and a broken leg at the time of his death. His twin brother Derek, who was also examined, had several broken ribs. Respondent had been alone with Alex for half an hour immediately before Alex stopped breathing. Respondent's experts testified that Alex could have been injured several hours before his respiratory arrest. Alex was in the care of the family's babysitter, Susan Batt, at that time. Batt had cared for the children during the day for about two weeks prior to Alex's death. The defense theory was that Batt, not respondent, was the culpable party. Batt informed the court in advance of testifying that she intended to assert her Fifth Amendment privilege. At the State's request, the trial court granted her transactional immunity from prosecution pursuant to Ohio Rev. Code Ann. §2945.44 (1999). She then testified to the jury that she had refused to testify without a grant of immunity on the advice of counsel, although she had done nothing wrong. Batt denied any involvement in Alex's death. She testified that she had never shaken Alex or his brother at any time, specifically on the day Alex suffered respiratory arrest. She said she was unaware of and had nothing to do with the other injuries to both children. The jury found respondent guilty of involuntary manslaughter, and he appealed. The Court of Appeals of Ohio, Sixth District, reversed respondent's conviction on grounds not relevant to our decision here. The Supreme Court of Ohio affirmed the reversal, on the alternative ground that Batt had no valid Fifth Amendment privilege and that the trial court's grant of immunity under §2945.44 was therefore unlawful. The court found that the wrongful grant of immunity prejudiced respondent, because it effectively told the jury that Batt did not cause Alex's injuries.

I

Is the Fifth Amendment privilege against self incrimination available to those who claim innocence?

R

The Fifth Amendment privilege against self incrimination is available to all those who have "reasonable cause" to apprehend danger from a direct answer, even those who claim innocence.

A

The Fifth Amendment provides that "[n]o person ... shall be compelled in any criminal case to be a witness against himself." U. S. Const., Amendment 5. As the Supreme Court of Ohio acknowledged, this privilege extends not only "to answers that would in themselves support a conviction ... but likewise embraces those which would furnish a link in the chain of evidence needed to prosecute the claimant" and. "it need only be evident from the implications of the question, in the setting in which it is asked, that a responsive answer to the question or an explanation of why it cannot be answered might be dangerous because injurious disclosure could result." We have held that the privilege's protection extends only to witnesses who have "reasonable cause to apprehend danger from a direct answer." That inquiry is for the court; the witness' assertion does not by itself establish the risk of incrimination. A danger of "imaginary and unsubstantial character" will not suffice. But we have never held, as the Supreme Court of Ohio did, that the privilege is unavailable to those who claim innocence. To the contrary, we have emphasized that one of the Fifth Amendment's "basic functions ... is to protect *innocent* men ... 'who otherwise might be ensnared by ambiguous circumstances.' " The Supreme Court of Ohio's determination that Batt did not have a valid Fifth Amendment privilege because she denied any involvement in the abuse of the children clearly conflicts with *Hoffman* and *Grunewald.* Batt had "reasonable cause" to apprehend danger from her answers if questioned at respondent's trial. Batt spent extended periods of time alone with Alex and his brother in the weeks immediately preceding discovery of their injuries. She was with Alex within the potential timeframe of the fatal trauma. The defense's theory of the case was that Batt, not respondent, was responsible for Alex's death and his brother's uncharged injuries. In this setting, it was reasonable for Batt to fear that answers to possible questions might tend to incriminate her. Batt therefore had a valid Fifth Amendment privilege against self-incrimination. We do not, of course, address the question whether immunity from suit under §2945.44 was appropriate. Because the Supreme Court of Ohio mistakenly held that the witness' assertion of innocence deprived her of her Fifth Amendment privilege against self-incrimination, the petition for a writ of certiorari is granted, the court's judgment is reversed, and this case is remanded for further proceedings not inconsistent with this opinion.

C

Reversed and remanded.

United States v. Bagley

473 U.S. 667 (1985)

FACTS

Defendant-Respondent Bagley was indicted on charges of violating federal narcotics and firearms statutes. Before trial, he filed a discovery motion requesting, *inter alia*, "any deals, promises or inducements made to [Government] witnesses in exchange for their testimony." The Government's response did not disclose that any "deals, promises or inducements" had been made to its two principal witnesses, who had assisted the Bureau of Alcohol, Tobacco and Firearms (ATF) in conducting an undercover investigation of respondent. But the Government did produce signed affidavits by these witnesses recounting their undercover dealing with respondent and concluding with the statement that the affidavits were made without any threats or rewards or promises of reward. Respondent waived his right to a jury trial and was tried before the District Court. The two principal Government witnesses testified about both the firearms and narcotics charges, and the court found respondent guilty on the narcotics charges but not guilty on the firearms charges. Subsequently, respondent received copies of ATF contracts signed by the principal Government witnesses during the undercover investigation and stating that the Government would pay money to the witnesses commensurate with the information furnished. Respondent then moved to vacate his sentence, alleging that the Government's failure in response to the discovery motion to disclose these contracts, which he could have used to impeach the witnesses, violated his right to due process under *Brady v. Maryland*, which held that the prosecution's suppression of evidence favorable to an accused upon request violates due process where the evidence is material either to guilt or punishment. The District Court denied the motion, finding beyond a reasonable doubt that had the existence of the ATF contracts been disclosed to it during trial, the disclosure would not have affected the outcome, because the principal Government witnesses' testimony was primarily devoted to the firearms charges on which respondent was acquitted, and was exculpatory on the narcotics charges. The Court of Appeals reversed, holding that the Government's failure to disclose the requested impeachment evidence that respondent could have used to conduct an effective cross-examination of the Government's principal witnesses required automatic reversal. The Government petitioned the Supreme Court for review.

I What is the standard of materiality to be applied in determining whether a conviction should be reversed because the prosecutor failed to disclose requested evidence that could have been used to impeach Government witnesses?

R Under *Brady v. Maryland*, the standard of materiality applied to impeachment evidence is whether it is reasonably probable that the requested, yet undisclosed evidence, would have affected the outcome of the proceedings.

A We hold that the Court of Appeals erred in holding that the prosecutor's failure to disclose evidence that could have been used effectively to impeach important Government witnesses requires automatic reversal. Such nondisclosure constitutes constitutional error and requires reversal of the conviction only if the evidence is material in the sense that its suppression might have affected the outcome of the trial. We also hold that the non-disclosed evidence at issue is material only if there is a reasonable probability that, had the evidence been disclosed to the defense, the result of the proceeding would have been different. A "reasonable probability" is a probability sufficient to undermine confidence in the outcome. This standard of materiality is sufficiently flexible to cover cases of prosecutorial failure to disclose evidence favorable to the defense regardless of whether the defense makes no request, a general request, or a specific request. Although the prosecutor's failure to respond fully to a specific request may impair the adversary process by having the effect of representing to the defense that certain evidence does not exist, this possibility of impairment does not necessitate a different standard of materiality. That is, there is the likelihood that the prosecutor's response to defendant's discovery motion misleadingly induced defense council to believe that O'Connor and Mitchell could not be impeached on the basis of bias or interest arising from inducements offered by the Government. The possibility of a reward, however, gave O'Connor and Mitchell a direct, personal stake in defendant's conviction. Under the standard stated above, the reviewing court may consider directly any adverse effect that the prosecutor's failure to respond might have had on the preparation or presentation of the defendant's case. We adopt the view that there is no reason to elaborate on the relevance of the specificity of the defense's request for disclosure, either generally or with respect to this case, concluded that reversal was mandated simply because the Court of Appeals failed to apply the "reasonable probability" standard of materiality to the non-disclosed evidence in question. Accordingly, we reverse the judgment of the Court of Appeals and remand the case to that court for a determination whether there is a reasonable probability that had the inducement offered by the Government to O'Connor and Mitchell been disclosed to the defense, the result of the trial would have been different.

C

Yes. Under *Brady v. Maryland*, the standard of materiality applied to impeachment evidence is whether it is reasonably probable that the requested, yet undisclosed evidence, would have affected the outcome of the proceedings.

Arizona v. Youngblood

488 U.S. 51 (1988)

FACTS

The victim, a 10-year-old boy, was molested and sodomized by a middle-aged man for 1 1/2 hours. After the assault, the boy was taken to a hospital where a physician used a swab from a "sexual assault kit" to collect semen samples from the boy's rectum. The police also collected the boy's clothing, which they failed to refrigerate. A police criminologist later performed some tests on the rectal swab and the boy's clothing, but he was unable to obtain information about the identity of the boy's assailant. At trial, expert witnesses testified that respondent might have been completely exonerated by timely performance of tests on properly preserved semen samples. Respondent was convicted of child molestation, sexual assault, and kidnapping in an Arizona state court. The Arizona Court of Appeals reversed the conviction on the ground that the State had breached a constitutional duty to preserve the semen samples from the victim's body and clothing.

I

Does the failure of the police to use potentially useful evidence constitute a denial of due process?

R

The failure of the police to use potentially useful evidence does not constitute a denial of due process unless the defendant can show bad faith on the part of the state.

A

The Due Process Clause of the Fourteenth Amendment did not require the State to preserve the semen samples even though the samples might have been useful to respondent. Unless a criminal defendant can show bad faith on the part of the police, failure to preserve potentially useful evidence does not constitute a denial of due process of law. Here, the police's failure to refrigerate the victim's clothing and to perform tests on the semen samples can at worst be described as negligent. None of this information was concealed from respondent at trial, and the evidence - such as it was - was made available to respondent's expert, who declined to perform any tests on the samples. The Arizona Court of Appeals noted in its opinion - and this Court agrees - that there was no suggestion of bad faith on the part of the police. Moreover, the Due Process Clause was not violated because the State failed to perform a newer test on the semen samples. The police do not have a constitutional duty to perform any particular tests.

C

Reversed.

Williams v. Florida

399 U.S. 78 (1970)

FACTS

Florida has a rule of criminal procedure requiring a defendant who intends to rely on an alibi to disclose to the prosecution the names of his alibi witnesses; the prosecution must in turn disclose to the defense the names of witnesses to rebut the alibi. Failure to comply can result in exclusion of alibi evidence at trial (except for the defendant's own testimony) or, in the case of the State, exclusion of the rebuttal evidence. Petitioner Williams, who was charged with robbery, complied with the rule after failing to be relieved of its requirements. His pretrial motion to impanel a 12-man jury, instead of the six-man jury Florida law provides for non-capital cases, was denied. At trial the State used a deposition of petitioner's alibi witness to impeach the witness. Petitioner was convicted and the appellate court affirmed. Petitioner claims that his Fifth Amendment rights were violated, on the ground that the notice-of-alibi rule required him to furnish the State with information useful in convicting him, and that his Sixth Amendment right was violated on the ground that the six-man jury deprived him of the right to "trial by jury" under the Sixth Amendment.

I

Is a criminal defendant compelled to bear witness against himself when he is required to notify the prosecution of a plan to advance an alibi, along with details supporting such a defense?

R

Compelling pretrial notice of a defendant's plans to present an alibi defense along with a list of alibi witnesses DOES NOT constitute compelled self incrimination under the Fifth and 14th Amendments.

A

We conclude that Florida's notice-of-alibi rule does not violate the Fifth Amendment (right against self-incrimination) as made applicable to the States by the 14th Amendment. This discovery rule is designed to enhance the search for truth in criminal trials by giving both the accused and the State opportunity to investigate certain facts crucial to the issue of guilt or innocence and comports with requirements for due process and a fair trial. The rule at most accelerated the timing of petitioner's disclosure of an alibi defense and thus did not violate the privilege against compelled self-incrimination. The constitutional guarantee of a trial by jury does not require that jury membership be fixed at 12, a historically accidental figure. Although accepted at common law, the Framers did not explicitly intend to forever codify as a constitutional requirement a feature not essential to the Sixth Amendment's purpose of interposing between the defendant and the prosecution the commonsense judgment of his peers.

C

No. Compelling pretrial notice of a defendant's plans to present an alibi defense along with a list of alibi witnesses does not constitute compelled self incrimination under the Fifth and 14th Amendments. Affirmed.

State v. Reldan

401 A.2d 563 (1979)

FACTS

This matter comes before the court on a motion, pursuant to R. 3:15-2(b), to order separate trials of counts 1 and 2 of indictment S-63-77. That indictment charges defendant in count 1 with the first degree murder of Susan Heynes and in count 2 with the first degree murder of Susan Reeves. Susan Reeves was reported missing from her home in Demarest, New Jersey, on October 14, 1975, and her nude body was subsequently found in Tallman State Park, Bear Mountain, in Rockland County, New York, on October 28, 1975. The Medical Examiner of Rockland County examined the two bodies and found that the cause of death in both cases was strangulation due to a ligature of pantyhose found around the necks of the victims. Defendant was charged with both murders in separate counts of a single indictment on January 20, 1977. The State maintains that the joinder of the two murders was proper under R. 3:7-6 which permits the specification of two or more offenses in the same indictment if the offenses charged are of the same or similar character. The defendant contends that the joinder is prejudicial and seeks separate trials on each count under R. 3:15-2(b).

I

Is joinder of multiple but related criminal offenses in a single indictment proper?

R

Joinder of multiple but related criminal offenses in a single indictment is proper unless the defendant makes a convincing showing that he has (1) important testimony to give concerning one count and (2) a strong need to refrain from testifying on the other.

A

Evidence of other crimes is admissible to prove a relevant fact in issue such as motive, intent, common plan or scheme, absence of mistake or identity. In this case, the facts of the murders demonstrate sufficient similarity to permit the evidence of one murder to be introduced into evidence with regard to the other. Admission of the evidence was not so prejudicial as to outweigh its probative value. It was therefore unnecessary to sever on a theory that the jury would be improperly hearing evidence of the other crimes in a single trial.

C

Motion denied.

Barker v. Wingo

407 U.S. 514 (1972)

FACTS

Defendant-Petitioner Barker and his accomplice, Silas Manning, were indicted by the Commonwealth of Kentucky on September 15, 1958 for murdering an elderly couple early that same year. Petitioner was not brought to trial for murder until more than five years after he had been arrested, during which time the prosecution obtained numerous continuances, initially for the purpose of first trying petitioner's alleged accomplice so that his testimony, if conviction resulted, would be available at petitioner's trial. Before the accomplice was finally convicted, he was tried six times. Petitioner made no objection to the continuances until three and one-half years after he was arrested. After the accomplice was finally convicted, petitioner, after further delays because of a key prosecution witness' illness, was tried and convicted. In this habeas corpus proceeding the Court of Appeals, concluding that petitioner had waived his right to a speedy trial for the period prior to his demand for trial, and in any event had not been prejudiced by the delay, affirmed the District Court's judgment against petitioner.

I

Does a defendant waive his right to a speedy if he fails to assert it?

R

Courts must perform a balancing test that weighs the conduct of the defendant and that of the prosecution in assessing whether a defendant had been deprived of his right to a speedy trial.

A

A defendant's constitutional right to a speedy trial cannot be established by any inflexible rule but can be determined only on an ad hoc balancing basis, in which the conduct of the prosecution and that of the defendant are weighed. Specifically, the factors which should be assessed in this balancing test are: (1) the length of the delay, (2) the reason for the delay, (3) the defendant's assertion of his right, and (4) prejudice to the defendant. None of these for factors taken alone necessitates a finding of a deprivation of the right to a speedy trial. Rather, they are related factors and must be considered together with other circumstances which may be relevant. Thus, in any case, the defendant's assertion of or failure to assert his right to a speedy trial is only one factor to be considered in an inquiry into the deprivation of that right. The right to a speedy trial is different from any of the rights afforded to those accused of crimes. The right benefits both the individual and society. When the right protects individuals from lengthy incarceration and undue anxiety and concern, it also assures society that those who are guilty will not be released on bond for an extended period, and that the accused will not be tempted to flee the jurisdiction. In this case, the lack of any serious prejudice to petitioner and the fact, as disclosed by the record, that he did not want a speedy trial (this fact is supported by his failure to object to the Commonwealth's first 11 motions for continuances) outweigh opposing considerations and compel the conclusion that petitioner was not deprived of his due process right to a speedy trial. However, we do not rule that they may never be a situation in which an indictment may be dismissed on speedy trial grounds where the defendant has failed to raise the issue. In those cases, extraordinary circumstances may necessitate a dismissal.

C

No. Courts must perform a balancing test that weighs the conduct of the defendant and that of the prosecution in assessing whether a defendant had been deprived of his right to a speedy trial. Affirmed.

Nix v. Whiteside

475 U.S. 157 (1986)

FACTS

In preparing for his Iowa state-court trial on a murder charge, respondent consistently told his attorney (Robinson) that although he had not actually seen a gun in the victim's hand when he stabbed the victim, he was convinced that the victim had a gun. Defendant-Respondent Whiteside's companions, who were present during the stabbing, told counsel that they had not seen a gun and no gun was found. Counsel advised respondent that the existence of a gun was not necessary to establish a claim of self-defense, and that only a reasonable belief that the victim had a gun nearby was necessary even though no gun was actually present. However, during preparation for direct examination shortly before trial, respondent for the first time told counsel that he had seen "something metallic" in the victim's hand. When asked about this, respondent said: "If I don't say I saw a gun, I'm dead." On respondent's insisting that he would testify that he saw "something metallic," counsel told him that if he testified falsely, it would be counsel's duty to advise the court that he felt respondent was committing perjury, and that counsel probably would be allowed to impeach that testimony and would seek to withdraw from representation if respondent insisted on committing perjury. Respondent ultimately testified as originally contemplated, admitting on cross-examination that he had not actually seen a gun in the victim's hand. After the jury found respondent guilty, respondent moved for a new trial, claiming that he had been deprived of a fair trial by counsel's admonitions not to state that he saw a gun or "something metallic." The court denied the motion after a hearing, and the Iowa Supreme Court affirmed the conviction, holding that counsel's actions were not only permissible, but were required under Iowa law. Respondent then sought federal habeas corpus relief, alleging that he had been denied effective assistance of counsel by his attorney's refusal to allow him to testify as he proposed. The District Court denied relief, but the Court of Appeals reversed, concluding that an intent to commit perjury, communicated to counsel, does not alter a defendant's right to effective assistance of counsel, and that counsel's threatened violation of his client's confidences violated the "effective representation" standards set forth in *Strickland v. Washington.* The Government (plaintiff) petitioned the Supreme Court of the United States for review.

I

When the attorney refuses to cooperate with the defendant in presenting perjured testimony at his trial, is the defendant's Sixth Amendment right to assistance of counsel violated?

R

The defendant's attorney does not violate the defendant's Sixth Amendment right to assistance of counsel when he refuses to cooperate in the defendant's presentation of perjured testimony.

A

The Sixth Amendment right of a criminal defendant to assistance of counsel is not violated when an attorney refuses to cooperate with the defendant in presenting perjured testimony at his trial. *Strickland v. Washington* held that to obtain relief by way of federal habeas corpus on a claim of a deprivation of effective assistance of counsel under the Sixth Amendment, the movant must establish both serious attorney error and prejudice. The Sixth Amendment inquiry is into whether the attorney's conduct was "reasonably effective." A court must be careful not to narrow the wide range of attorney conduct acceptable under the Sixth Amendment so restrictively as to constitutionalize particular standards of professional conduct and thereby intrude into a state's proper authority to define and apply the standards of professional conduct applicable to those it admits to practice in its courts. Counsel's conduct here fell within the wide range of professional responses to threatened client perjury acceptable under the Sixth Amendment. Counsel's duty of loyalty to, and advocacy of, the defendant's cause is limited to legitimate, lawful conduct compatible with the very nature of a trial as a search for truth. Although counsel must take all reasonable lawful means to attain his client's objectives, counsel is precluded from taking steps or in any way assisting the client in presenting false evidence or otherwise violating the law. Moreover, accepted norms require that a lawyer disclose his client's perjury and frauds upon the court. The Model Rules of Professional Conduct similarly require attorneys to obey all laws in the course of representing a client and Rule 1.2 provides that a "lawyer shall not counsel a client to engage or assist a client in conduct of the lawyer knows is criminal or fraudulent." Iowa's Code also expressly permits withdrawal from representation as an appropriate response of an attorney when the client threatens to commit perjury. The Court of Appeals' holding is not supported by the record since counsel's action, at most, deprived respondent of his contemplated perjury. Whatever the scope of a constitutional right to testify, it is elementary that such a right does not extend to testifying falsely, and the right to counsel includes no right to have a lawyer who will cooperate with planned perjury. There was no breach of professional duty in counsel's admonition to respondent that he would disclose respondent's perjury to the court. As a matter of law, counsel's conduct here cannot establish the prejudice required for relief under the *Strickland* inquiry. The "conflict of interest" involved was one imposed on the attorney by the client's proposal to commit the crime of fabricating testimony. This is not the kind of conflict of interest that would render the representation constitutionally infirm.

C

No. The defendant's attorney does not violate the defendant's Sixth Amendment right to assistance of counsel when he refuses to cooperate in the defendant's presentation of perjured testimony.

Gideon v. Wainwright

372 U.S. 335 (1963)

FACTS

Defendant Gideon was charged with breaking and entering with the intent to commit a misdemeanor therein. This was a felony in Florida. Gideon could not afford a lawyer, so he asked for one appointed for him by the court. The court denied his request, so the defendant represented himself at trial. Gideon was eventually convicted and sentenced.

I Must the states appoint counsel to indigents in felony cases under the Sixth Amendment's right to counsel?

R The Sixth Amendment's right to counsel requires the states to appoint counsel to indigents in felony cases.

A The Sixth Amendment's right to counsel is a fundamental right. Without it, any person who is too poor to hire a lawyer and made to appear in court cannot be assured a fair trial. In criminal cases, lawyers are essential requirements, not mere luxuries. Thus, we overrule *Betts v. Brady* (the right to counsel based on a case-by-case basis).

C Yes. The Sixth Amendment's right to counsel, through the Fourteenth Amendment, requires states to appoint counsel to indigents in felony cases. Judgment reversed and remanded.

Scott v. Illinois

440 U.S. 367 (1979)

FACTS

Petitioner, an indigent, was convicted of shoplifting and was fined $50 after a bench trial in an Illinois state court. The applicable Illinois statute set the maximum penalty for such an offense at a $500 fine, one year in jail, or both. Petitioner's conviction was ultimately affirmed by the Illinois Supreme Court, over the petitioner's contention that a line of cases culminating in *Argersinger v. Hamlin* requires state provision of counsel whenever imprisonment is an authorized penalty.

I

Does the Sixth Amendment require a state to appoint counsel for an indigent defendant accused of a crime for which imprisonment is merely authorized but not imposed?

R

The Sixth and Fourteenth Amendments require that no indigent criminal defendant be sentenced to a term of imprisonment unless the State has afforded him the right to assistance of appointed counsel in his defense, but do not require a state trial court to appoint counsel for a criminal defendant, such as petitioner, who is charged with a statutory offense for which imprisonment upon conviction is authorized but not imposed.

A

The Sixth and Fourteenth Amendments require that no indigent criminal defendant be sentenced to a term of imprisonment unless the State has afforded him the right to assistance of appointed counsel in his defense, but do not require a state trial court to appoint counsel for a criminal defendant, such as petitioner, who is charged with a statutory offense for which imprisonment upon conviction is authorized but not imposed. *Argersinger v. Hamlin* limits the constitutional right to appointed counsel in state criminal proceedings to a case that actually leads to imprisonment. Even were the matter *res nova, Argersinger's* central premise - that actual imprisonment is a penalty different in kind from fines or the mere threat of imprisonment - is eminently sound and warrants adoption of actual imprisonment as the line defining the constitutional right to appointment of counsel.

C

Affirmed.

Douglas v. California

372 U.S. 353 (1963)

FACTS

Petitioners, Bennie Will Meyes and William Douglas, were jointly tried and convicted in a California court on an information charging them with 13 felonies. A single public defender was appointed to represent them. At the commencement of the trial, the defender moved for a continuance; stating that the case was very complicated, that he was not as prepared as he felt he should be because he was handling a different defense every day, and that there was a conflict of interest between the petitioners requiring the appointment of separate counsel for each of them. This motion was denied. Thereafter, petitioners dismissed the defender, claiming he was unprepared, and again renewed motions for separate counsel and for a continuance. These motions also were denied, and petitioners were ultimately convicted by a jury of all 13 felonies, which included robbery, assault with a deadly weapon, and assault with intent to commit murder. Both were given prison terms. Both appealed as of right to the California District Court of Appeal. That court affirmed their convictions. Both Meyes and Douglas then petitioned for further discretionary review in the California Supreme Court, but their petitions were denied without a hearing. The U.S. Supreme Court granted certiorari.

I Does an indigent defendant have a constitutional right to counsel to pursue a first appeal as of right?

R Where the merits of the one and only appeal an indigent has as of right are decided without benefit of counsel in a state criminal case, there has been a discrimination between the rich and the poor which violates the Fourteenth Amendment.

A Where the merits of the one and only appeal an indigent has as of right are decided without benefit of counsel in a state criminal case, there has been a discrimination between the rich and the poor which violates the Fourteenth Amendment. We are not here concerned with problems that might arise from the denial of counsel for the preparation of a petition for discretionary or mandatory review beyond the stage in the appellate process at which the claims have once been presented by a lawyer and passed upon by an appellate court. We are dealing only with the first appeal, granted as a matter of right to rich and poor alike from a criminal conviction. We need not now decide whether California would have to provide counsel for an indigent seeking a discretionary hearing from the California Supreme Court after the District Court of Appeal had sustained his conviction or whether counsel must be appointed for an indigent seeking review of an appellate affirmance of his conviction in this Court by appeal as of right or by petition for a writ of certiorari which lies within the Court's discretion. When an indigent is forced to run this gantlet of a preliminary showing of merit, the right to appeal does not comport with fair procedure. In the federal courts, on the other hand, an indigent must be afforded counsel on appeal whenever he challenges a certification that the appeal is not taken in good faith. The federal courts must honor his request for counsel regardless of what they think the merits of the case may be; and "representation in the role of an advocate is required," *Ellis v. United States*. In California, however, once the court has "gone through" the record and denied counsel, the indigent has no recourse but to prosecute his appeal on his own, as best he can, no matter how meritorious his case may turn out to be. The present case, where counsel was denied petitioners on appeal, shows that the discrimination is not between "possibly good and obviously bad cases," but between cases where the rich man can require the court to listen to argument of counsel before deciding on the merits, but a poor man cannot. There is lacking that equality demanded by the Fourteenth Amendment where the rich man, who appeals as of right, enjoys the benefit of counsel's examination into the record, research of the law, and marshalling of arguments on his behalf, while the indigent, already burdened by a preliminary determination that his case is without merit, is forced to shift for himself. The indigent, where the record is unclear or the errors are hidden, has only the right to a meaningless ritual, while the rich man has a meaningful appeal. We vacate the judgment of the District Court of Appeal and remand the case to that court for further proceedings not inconsistent with this opinion.

C

Vacated and remanded.

Ross v. Moffitt

417 U.S. 600 (1974)

FACTS

Plaintiff Ross and two others were convicted of forgery in North Carolina (defendant). They wished to make discretionary appeals to either the federal Supreme Court (on writ or certiorari) or North Carolina Supreme Court (on discretionary review). Under North Carolina law, attorneys are appointed only for appeals as a matter of right to the state intermediate Court of Appeals, but not for discretionary appeals to the federal or state Supreme Courts. Plaintiff Ross appealed on a federal writ of habeas corpus, contending that the denial of counsel violated his constitutional due process and equal protection rights. On appeal, the Fourth Circuit held both discretionary state court review and federal Supreme Court certiorari required appointment of counsel, citing *Douglas*. The State appealed.

I

When an indigent convict wishes to make a discretionary appeal to the state Supreme Court or petition the federal Supreme Court for certiorari, must the states appoint him counsel?

R

When an indigent convict makes a discretionary appeal, the states need not appoint counsel for him.

A

When an indigent convict makes a discretionary appeal, the states need not appoint counsel for him. *Griffin* held that states cannot arbitrarily foreclose the appeal rights of indigent persons while leaving open the opportunity of appeal for the wealthy. Following *Griffin*, the court in *Douglas* held that the states must wave both transcript and appeals fees for indigents and provide them counsel on their first appeal as a matter of right. The rational for these cases was never explicitly stated, but can be seen as deriving partly from the 14th Amendment Equal Protection Clause and partly from the Due Process Clause. "Due process" is the administration of justice according to established rules and principles; based on the principle that a person cannot be deprived of life or liberty or property without appropriate legal procedures. "Equal protection" is the constitutional requirement that guarantees that similarly situated persons receive the same rights and are treated the same. In the instant case, we hold that the Due Process Clause does not require North Carolina to provide counsel for discretionary appeals to the State Supreme Court. Unlike a criminal prosecution, the criminal appeal is initiated by the defendant and the Constitution does not require the states to even permit an appeal. The fact that a State allows an appeal does not obligate it to provide counsel to indigents at every stage of the process. Due process violations occur only when indigents are singled out by the State and denied appeals because of their poverty.

C

No. When an indigent convict makes a discretionary appeal, the states need not appoint counsel for him. Reversed.

Faretta v. California

422 U.S. 806 (1975)

FACTS

Anthony Faretta was charged with grand theft in the Superior Court of Los Angeles County, California. At the arraignment, the Superior Court Judge appointed the public defender to represent Faretta. Well before the date of trial, Faretta requested that he be permitted to represent himself. Faretta had once represented himself in a criminal prosecution, he had a high school education, and he did not want to be represented by the public defender because he believed that that office was "very loaded down with . . . a heavy case load." The judge responded that he believed Faretta was "making a mistake." Nevertheless, the judge, in a "preliminary ruling," accepted Faretta's waiver of the assistance of counsel. The judge indicated, however, that he might reverse this ruling if it later appeared that Faretta was unable adequately to represent himself. Several weeks thereafter, but still prior to trial, the judge *sua sponte* held a hearing to inquire into Faretta's ability to conduct his own defense. After consideration of Faretta's answers, and observation of his demeanor, the judge ruled that Faretta had not made an intelligent and knowing waiver of his right to the assistance of counsel and also ruled that Faretta had no constitutional right to conduct his own defense. The judge, accordingly, reversed his earlier ruling and again appointed the public defender to represent Faretta. Faretta's subsequent request for leave to act as co-counsel was rejected, as were his efforts to make certain motions on his own behalf. Throughout the subsequent trial, the judge required that Faretta's defense be conducted only through the appointed lawyer from the public defender's office. At the conclusion of the trial, the jury found Faretta guilty as charged, and the judge sentenced him to prison. The California Court of Appeal, relying upon a then recent California Supreme Court decision that had expressly decided the issue, affirmed the trial judge's ruling that Faretta had no federal or state constitutional right to represent himself. Accordingly, the Appellate Court affirmed the conviction. A petition for rehearing was denied without opinion, and the California Supreme Court denied review. The U.S. Supreme Court granted certiorari.

I

Does a criminal defendant have a constitutional right to proceed in a state criminal trial without counsel when he voluntarily and intelligently elects to do so?

R

A defendant in a state criminal trial has a Sixth Amendment constitutional right to self representation and he may proceed to defend himself without counsel when he voluntarily and intelligently elects to do so.

A

The Sixth Amendment as made applicable to the States by the Fourteenth guarantees that a defendant in a state criminal trial has an independent constitutional right of self-representation and that he may proceed to defend himself without counsel when he voluntarily and intelligently elects to do so. In this case, the state courts erred in forcing petitioner against his will to accept a state-appointed public defender and in denying his request to conduct his own defense. The defendant was literate, competent, possessed understanding and voluntarily exercised his free will. Moreover, the judge warned the defendant of the mistake he was making. But

Faretta v. California

422 U.S. 806 (1975)

his lack of legal knowledge was not relevant to an assessment of his knowing exercise of the right to defend himself. In forcing Faretta to accept a state appointed public defender, the California courts deprived him of his constitutional right to represent himself.

C Yes. A defendant in a state criminal trial has a Sixth Amendment constitutional right to self representation and he may proceed to defend himself without counsel when he voluntarily and intelligently elects to do so. Vacated and remanded.

Godinez v. Moran

509 U.S. 389 (1993)

FACTS

After respondent Moran pleaded not guilty to three counts of first-degree murder and two psychiatrists concluded that he was competent to stand trial, he informed the Nevada trial court that he wished to discharge his attorneys and change his pleas to guilty. The court found that Moran understood "the nature of the criminal charges against him" and was "able to assist in his defense"; that he was "knowingly and intelligently" waiving his right to the assistance of counsel; and that his guilty pleas were "freely and voluntarily" given. He was ultimately sentenced to death. When Moran subsequently sought state post-conviction relief, the trial court held an evidentiary hearing before rejecting his claim that he was mentally incompetent to represent himself, and the State Supreme Court dismissed his appeal. A Federal District Court denied his petition for a writ of habeas corpus, but the Court of Appeals reversed. It concluded that due process required the trial court to hold a hearing to evaluate and determine Moran's competency before it accepted his decisions to waive counsel and plead guilty. It also found that the post-conviction hearing did not cure the error, holding that the trial court's ruling was premised on the wrong legal standard because competency to waive constitutional rights requires a higher level of mental functioning than that required to stand trial. The court reasoned that, while a defendant is competent to stand trial if he has a rational and factual understanding of the proceedings and is capable of assisting his counsel, he is competent to waive counsel or plead guilty only if he has the capacity for reasoned choice among the available alternatives.

I Is the competency standard for pleading guilty or waiving the right to counsel is the same as the competency standard for standing trial?

R The competency standard for pleading guilty or waiving the right to counsel is the same as the competency standard for standing trial: whether the defendant has "sufficient present ability to consult with his lawyer with a reasonable degree of rational understanding" and a "rational as well as factual understanding of the proceedings against him."

A The competency standard for pleading guilty or waiving the right to counsel is the same as the competency standard for standing trial: whether the defendant has "sufficient present ability to consult with his lawyer with a reasonable degree of rational understanding" and a "rational as well as factual understanding of the proceedings against him," *Dusky v. United States*. There is no reason for the competency standard for either of those decisions to be higher than that for standing trial. The decision to plead guilty, though profound, is no more complicated than the sum total of decisions that a defendant may have to make during the course of a trial, such as whether to testify, whether to waive a jury trial, and whether to cross-examine witnesses for the prosecution. Nor does the decision to waive counsel require an appreciably higher level of mental functioning than the decision to waive other constitutional rights. A higher standard is not necessary in order to ensure that a defendant is competent to represent himself, because the ability to do so has no bearing upon his competence to choose self-representation, *Faretta v. California*. When, in

Westbrook v. Arizona, this Court vacated a lower court ruling because there had been no "hearing or inquiry into the issue of [the petitioner's] competence to waive his constitutional right to the assistance of counsel," it did not mean to suggest that the Dusky formulation is not a high enough standard in cases in which the defendant seeks to waive counsel. Rather, the "competence to waive" language was simply a shorthand for the "intelligent and competent waiver" requirement of *Johnson v. Zerbst*. Thus, Westbrook stands only for the unremarkable proposition that, when a defendant seeks to waive his right to counsel, a determination that he is competent to stand trial is not enough; the waiver must also be intelligent and voluntary before it can be accepted. While States are free to adopt competency standards that are more elaborate than the Dusky formulation, the Due Process Clause does not impose them.

C

Reversed and remanded.

Strickland v. Washington

466 U.S. 668 (1984)

FACTS

Respondent Washington pleaded guilty in a Florida trial court to an indictment that included three capital murder charges. In the plea colloquy, respondent told the trial judge that, although he had committed a string of burglaries, he had no significant prior criminal record and that at the time of his criminal spree he was under extreme stress caused by his inability to support his family. The trial judge told respondent that he had "a great deal of respect for people who are willing to step forward and admit their responsibility." In preparing for the sentencing hearing, defense counsel spoke with respondent about his background, but did not seek out character witnesses or request a psychiatric examination. Counsel's decision not to present evidence concerning respondent's character and emotional state reflected his judgment that it was advisable to rely on the plea colloquy for evidence as to such matters, thus preventing the State from cross-examining respondent and from presenting psychiatric evidence of its own. Counsel did not request a pre-sentence report because it would have included respondent's criminal history and thereby would have undermined the claim of no significant prior criminal record. Finding numerous aggravating circumstances and no mitigating circumstance, the trial judge sentenced respondent to death on each of the murder counts. The Florida Supreme Court affirmed, and respondent then sought collateral relief in state court on the ground, *inter alia*, that counsel had rendered ineffective assistance at the sentencing proceeding in several respects, including his failure to request a psychiatric report, to investigate and present character witnesses, and to seek a pre-sentence report. The trial court denied relief, and the Florida Supreme Court affirmed. Respondent then filed a habeas corpus petition in Federal District Court advancing numerous grounds for relief, including the claim of ineffective assistance of counsel. After an evidentiary hearing, the District Court denied relief, concluding that although counsel made errors in judgment in failing to investigate mitigating evidence further than he did, no prejudice to respondent's sentence resulted from any such error in judgment. The Court of Appeals ultimately reversed, stating that the Sixth Amendment accorded criminal defendants a right to counsel rendering "reasonably effective assistance given the totality of the circumstances." After outlining standards for judging whether a defense counsel fulfilled the duty to investigate non-statutory mitigating circumstances and whether counsel's errors were sufficiently prejudicial to justify reversal, the Court of Appeals remanded the case for application of the standards. The U.S. Supreme Court took the matter up on review.

I

Where his counsel fails to render adequate legal assistance, can a defendant be deprived of the right to effective counsel?

R

A conviction based upon ineffectiveness of counsel can be reversed upon a showing by the defendant that (1) counsel's performance was deficient requiring a showing that counsel made errors so serious that counsel was not functioning as counsel guaranteed by the Sixth Amendment; and (2) the deficient performance prejudiced the defense by showing that counsel's errors were so serious as to deprive defendant of a fair trial, a trial whose result is reliable.

Strickland v. Washington

466 U.S. 668 (1984)

A The Sixth Amendment right to counsel is the right to the effective assistance of counsel, and the benchmark for judging any claim of ineffectiveness must be whether counsel's conduct so undermined the proper functioning of the adversarial process that the trial cannot be relied on as having produced a just result. The same principle applies to a capital sentencing proceeding - such as the one provided by Florida law. A convicted defendant's claim that counsel's assistance was so defective as to require reversal of a conviction or setting aside of a death sentence requires that the defendant show (1) that counsel's performance was deficient and, (2) that the deficient performance prejudiced the defense so as to deprive the defendant of a fair trial. The proper standard for judging attorney performance is that of reasonably effective assistance, considering all the circumstances. When a convicted defendant complains of the ineffectiveness of counsel's assistance, the defendant must show that counsel's representation fell below an objective standard of reasonableness. Judicial scrutiny of counsel's performance must be highly deferential, and a fair assessment of attorney performance requires that every effort be made to eliminate the distorting effects of hindsight, to reconstruct the circumstances of counsel's challenged conduct, and to evaluate the conduct from counsel's perspective at the time. A court must indulge a strong presumption that counsel's conduct falls within the wide range of reasonable professional assistance. These standards require no special amplification in order to define counsel's duty to investigate, the duty at issue in this case. With regard to the required showing of prejudice, the proper standard requires the defendant to show that there is a reasonable probability that, but for counsel's unprofessional errors, the result of the proceeding would have been different. A reasonable probability is a probability sufficient to undermine confidence in the outcome. A court hearing an ineffectiveness claim must consider the totality of the evidence before the judge or jury. The principles governing ineffectiveness claims apply in federal collateral proceedings as they do on direct appeal or in motions for a new trial. And in a federal habeas challenge to a state criminal judgment, a state court conclusion that counsel rendered effective assistance is not a finding of fact binding on the federal court to the extent stated by 28 U.S.C. §2254(d), but is a mixed question of law and fact. Applying these standards to the facts of the case, it is clear that the conduct of Washington's counsel was reasonable. Even if we assumed his conduct was unreasonable, defendant suffered insufficient prejudice to warrant the setting aside of his death sentence. Counsel made tactical choices to argue for the mitigation of circumstances with regard to extreme emotional distress, to fully rely on defendant's acceptance of responsibility for his crimes and not to seek more character or psychological evidence. Counsel's strategy was well within the range of those professionally reasonable judgments allowed. With respect to prejudice, the evidence that defendant contends his counsel should have offered at the sentencing hearing would barely have altered the sentencing profile. There is no reasonable probability that the omitted evidence would have changed the end result thus altering the sentence imposed. Thus, we conclude that the District Court properly declined to issue a writ of habeas corpus.

C Yes. A defendant can be deprived of the right to effective counsel where his counsel fails to render adequate legal assistance.

Brady v. United States

397 U.S. 742 (1970)

FACTS

In 1959, petitioner was charged with kidnapping in violation of 18 U.S. C. 1201(a). Since the indictment charged that the victim of the kidnapping was not liberated unharmed, petitioner faced a maximum penalty of death if the verdict of the jury should so recommend. Petitioner, represented by competent counsel throughout, first elected to plead not guilty. Apparently because the trial judge was unwilling to try the case without a jury, petitioner made no serious attempt to reduce the possibility of a death penalty by waiving a jury trial. Upon learning that his codefendant, who had confessed to the authorities, would plead guilty and be available to testify against him, petitioner changed his plea to guilty. His plea was accepted after the trial judge twice questioned him as to the voluntariness of his plea. Petitioner was sentenced to 50 years' imprisonment, later reduced to 30. In 1967, petitioner sought relief under 28 U.S.C. 2255, claiming that his plea of guilty was not voluntarily given because 1201(a) operated to coerce his plea, because his counsel exerted impermissible pressure upon him, and because his plea was induced by representations with respect to reduction of sentence and clemency. It was also alleged that the trial judge had not fully complied with Rule 11 of the Federal Rules of Criminal Procedure. After a hearing, the District Court for the District of New Mexico denied relief. The court held that 1201(a) was constitutional and found that petitioner decided to plead guilty when he learned that his codefendant was going to plead guilty: petitioner pleaded guilty 'by reason of other matters and not by reason of the statute' or because of any acts of the trial judge. The court concluded that 'the plea was voluntarily and knowingly made.' The Court of Appeals for the Tenth Circuit affirmed, determining that the District Court's findings were supported by substantial evidence and specifically approving the finding that petitioner's plea of guilty was voluntary. The U.S. Supreme Court granted certiorari.

I

Must a guilty plea be nullified [a/k/a considered involuntary] simply because it was entered into to avoid the death penalty?

R

A plea of guilty will not be considered involuntary simply because it was entered into to avoid the death penalty.

A

The voluntariness of Brady's plea can be determined only by considering all of the relevant circumstances surrounding it. One of these circumstances was the possibility of a heavier sentence following a guilty verdict after a trial. It may be that Brady, faced with a strong case against him and recognizing that his chances for acquittal were slight, preferred to plead guilty and thus limit the penalty to life imprisonment rather than to elect a jury trial which could result in a death penalty. But even if we assume that Brady would not have pleaded guilty except for the death penalty provision of 1201(a), this assumption merely identifies the penalty provision as a 'but for' cause of his plea. That the statute caused the plea in this sense does not necessarily prove that the plea was coerced and invalid as an involuntary act. The record before us also supports the conclusion that Brady's plea was intelligently made. He was advised by competent counsel, he was made aware of the nature of the charge against him, and there was nothing to indicate that he was incompetent or otherwise not in control of his mental faculties; once his confederate had pleaded guilty and became available to testify, he chose to plead guilty, perhaps to ensure that he would face no more than life imprisonment or a term of years. Brady was aware of precisely what he was doing when he admitted that he had kidnapped the victim and had not released her unharmed. Although Brady's plea of guilty may well have been motivated in part by a desire to avoid a possible death penalty, we are convinced that his plea was voluntarily and intelligently made and we have no reason to doubt that his solemn admission of guilt was truthful.

C

Affirmed.

Henderson v. Morgan

426 U.S. 637 (1976)

FACTS

Respondent Morgan was indicted for first-degree murder, but by agreement with the prosecution and on counsel's advice respondent pleaded guilty to second-degree murder and was sentenced. Subsequently, after exhausting his state remedies in an unsuccessful attempt to have his conviction vacated on the ground that his guilty plea was involuntary, respondent filed a habeas corpus petition in Federal District Court, alleging that his guilty plea was involuntary because, inter alia, he was not aware that intent to cause death was an element of second-degree murder. The District Court ultimately heard the testimony of several witnesses, including respondent and his defense counsel in the original prosecution; and the transcript of the relevant state-court proceedings and certain psychological evaluations of respondent, who was substantially below average intelligence, were made part of the record. On the basis of the evidence thus developed the District Court found that respondent had not been advised by counsel or the state court that an intent to cause death was an essential element of second-degree murder, and, based on this finding, held that the guilty plea was involuntary and had to be set aside. The Court of Appeals affirmed.

I

May a defendant enter a voluntary plea of guilty to a charge of second-degree murder without being informed that intent to cause the death of his victim was an element of the offense?

R

If the defendant did not receive adequate notice of the offense to which he pleaded guilty, then the guilty plea was not made knowingly and intelligently, and, therefore, not voluntarily made.

A

Since respondent did not receive adequate notice of the offense to which he pleaded guilty, his plea was involuntary and the judgment of conviction was entered without due process of law. The plea could not be voluntary in the sense that it constituted an intelligent admission that he committed the offense unless respondent received "real notice of the true nature of the charge against him, the first and most universally recognized requirement of due process," *Smith v. O'Grady*. Where the record discloses that defense counsel did not purport to stipulate that respondent had the requisite intent or explain to him that his plea would be admission of that fact, and he made no factual statement or admission necessarily implying that he had such intent, it is impossible to conclude that his plea to the unexplained charge of second-degree murder was voluntary.

C

Affirmed.

North Carolina v. Alford

400 U.S. 25 (1970)

FACTS

Appellee Alford was indicted for the capital crime of first-degree murder. At that time North Carolina law provided for the penalty of life imprisonment when a plea of guilty was accepted to a first-degree murder charge; for the death penalty following a jury verdict of guilty, unless the jury recommended life imprisonment; and for a penalty of from two to 30 years' imprisonment for second-degree murder. Appellee's attorney, in the face of strong evidence of guilt, recommended a guilty plea, but left the decision to appellee. The prosecutor agreed to accept a plea of guilty to second-degree murder. The trial court heard damaging evidence from certain witnesses before accepting a plea. Appellee pleaded guilty, although disclaiming guilt, because of the threat of the death penalty, and was sentenced to 30 years' imprisonment. The Court of Appeals, on an appeal from a denial of a writ of habeas corpus, found that appellee's guilty plea was involuntary because it was motivated principally by fear of the death penalty.

I

Should the court accept a guilty plea even after the defendant continues to profess his innocence?

R

A court may accept a guilty plea if it is satisfied that a factual basis for the plea exists.

A

The trial judge did not commit constitutional error in accepting appellee's guilty plea. A guilty plea that represents a voluntary and intelligent choice among the alternatives available to a defendant, especially one represented by competent counsel, is not compelled within the meaning of the Fifth Amendment because it was entered to avoid the possibility of the death penalty. *Hudson v. United States*, which held that a federal court may impose a prison sentence after accepting a plea of *nolo contendere*, implicitly recognized that there is no constitutional bar to imposing a prison sentence upon an accused who is unwilling to admit guilt but who is willing to waive trial and accept the sentence. An accused may voluntarily, knowingly, and understandingly consent to the imposition of a prison sentence even though he is unwilling to admit participation in the crime, or even if his guilty plea contains a protestation of innocence, when, as here, he intelligently concludes that his interests require a guilty plea and the record strongly evidences guilt. The Fourteenth Amendment and the Bill of Rights do not prohibit the States from accepting pleas to lesser included offenses.

C

Reversed and remanded.

Bordenkircher v. Hayes

434 U.S. 357 (1978)

FACTS

The Defendant-Respondent, Paul Lewis Hayes, was indicted by a grand jury on a charge of uttering a forged instrument in the amount of $88.30, an offense then punishable by a term of 2 to 10 years in prison. After arraignment, Hayes, his retained counsel, and the Commonwealth's Attorney met in the presence of the Clerk of the Court to discuss a possible plea agreement. During these conferences the prosecutor offered to recommend a sentence of five years in prison if Hayes would plead guilty to the indictment. He also said that if Hayes did not plead guilty and "save the court the inconvenience and necessity of a trial," he would return to the grand jury to seek an indictment under the Kentucky Habitual Criminal Act, which would subject Hayes to a mandatory sentence of life imprisonment by reason of his two prior felony convictions. Hayes chose not to plead guilty, and the prosecutor did obtain an indictment charging him under the Habitual Criminal Act. It is not disputed that the recidivist charge was fully justified by the evidence, that the prosecutor was in possession of this evidence at the time of the original indictment, and that Hayes' refusal to plead guilty to the original charge was what led to his indictment under the habitual criminal statute. A jury found Hayes guilty on the principal charge of uttering a forged instrument and, in a separate proceeding, further found that he had twice before been convicted of felonies. As required by the habitual offender statute, he was sentenced to a life term in the penitentiary. The Kentucky Court of Appeals rejected Hayes' constitutional objections to the enhanced sentence, holding in an unpublished opinion that imprisonment for life with the possibility of parole was constitutionally permissible in light of the previous felonies of which Hayes had been convicted, and that the prosecutor's decision to indict him as a habitual offender was a legitimate use of available leverage in the plea-bargaining process. On Hayes' petition for a federal writ of habeas corpus, the United States District Court for the Eastern District of Kentucky agreed that there had been no constitutional violation in the sentence or the indictment procedure, and denied the writ. The Court of Appeals for the Sixth Circuit reversed the District Court's judgment. While recognizing "that plea bargaining now plays an important role in our criminal justice system," the appellate court thought that the prosecutor's conduct during the bargaining negotiations had violated the principles of *Blackledge v. Perry*, which "protect[ed] defendants from the vindictive exercise of a prosecutor's discretion." Accordingly, the court ordered that Hayes be discharged "except for his confinement under a lawful sentence imposed solely for the crime of uttering a forged instrument." We granted certiorari to consider a constitutional question of importance in the administration of criminal justice.

I Is the Due Process Clause of the Fourteenth Amendment violated when a state prosecutor carries out a threat made during plea negotiations to re-indict the accused on more serious charges if he does not plead guilty to the offense with which he was originally charged?

R The choice of which charges to bring rests in his discretion and his basing that choice on a desire to induce a guilty plea does not violate due process if the prosecutor has probable cause to support each charge.

Bordenkircher v. Hayes

434 U.S. 357 (1978)

A We hold that the Due Process Clause of the Fourteenth Amendment is not violated when a state prosecutor carries out a threat made during plea negotiations to have the accused re-indicted on more serious charges on which he is plainly subject to prosecution if he does not plead guilty to the offense with which he was originally charged. "The guilty plea and the often concomitant plea bargain are important components of this country's criminal justice system. Properly administered, they can benefit all concerned." When the defendant decided to plead not guilty, he knew the terms of the plea offer. The prosecution did not bring an additional and more serious charge without notice to the defendant. Rather, this situation is the same as if the prosecutor obtained in indictment on both the forgery and recidivist charges at the onset, and then offered to drop the recidivist charge as part of the plea bargain. The Court of Appeals essentially held that the substance of the plea offer itself violated due process. We disagree. Though to punish a person because he has done what the law allows (where he is unilaterally penalized for having exercised his right to attack his conviction) does violate due process (see *North Carolina v. Pearce*) we see no such evidence here. We see no element of punishment in the "give-and-take" of plea bargaining as the accused was free to accept or reject the prosecutor's offer. We accept as constitutionally legitimate the simple reality that the prosecutor's interest at the bargaining table is to persuade the defendant to forgo his right to plead not guilty, and in pursuing that course here the prosecutor did not exceed constitutional bounds.

C No. The choice of which charges to bring rests in his discretion and his basing that choice on a desire to induce a guilty plea does not violate due process if the prosecutor has probable cause to support each charge.

Santobello v. New York

404 U.S. 257 (1971)

FACTS

Defendant-Petitioner Santobello was originally charged with two felony counts. After negotiations with the prosecutor broke down, Defendant-Petitioner Santobello withdrew his previous not-guilty plea to the two felony counts and pleaded guilty to a lesser-included offense, the prosecutor having agreed to make no recommendation as to sentence. At petitioner's appearance for sentencing many months later a new prosecutor recommended the maximum sentence, which the judge (who stated that he was uninfluenced by that recommendation) imposed. Petitioner attempted unsuccessfully to withdraw his guilty plea, and his conviction was affirmed on appeal.

I

Are the promises that prosecutors make in plea agreements enforceable?

R

A prosecutor's promise is enforceable when the plea rests in any significant degree on the promise.

A

The disposition of charges after plea discussions is not only an essential part of the process but a highly desirable part for many reasons. It leads to the prompt and final disposition of most criminal cases; it decreases pretrial confinement pending trial; it protects the public from those accused persons who are prone to continue criminal conduct even while on pretrial release; and, by shortening the time between charge and disposition, it enhances the rehabilitative prospects of the guilty when they are ultimately imprisoned. However, all of these considerations presuppose fairness in securing agreement between an accused and a prosecutor. It is now clear, for example, that the accused pleading guilty must be counseled, absent a waiver. Federal Rule of Criminal Procedure 11, governing pleas in federal courts, now makes clear that the sentencing judge must develop, on the record, the factual basis for the plea, as, for example, by having the accused describe the conduct that gave rise to the charge. The plea must, of course, be voluntary and knowing and if it was induced by promises, the essence of those promises must in some way be made known. There is, of course, no absolute right to have a guilty plea accepted. A court may reject a plea in exercise of sound judicial discretion. This phase of the process of criminal justice, and the adjudicative element inherent in accepting a plea of guilty, must be attended by safeguards to insure the defendant what is reasonably due in the circumstances. Those circumstances will vary, but a constant factor is that when a plea rests in any significant degree on a promise or agreement of the prosecutor, so that it can be said to be part of the inducement or consideration, such promise must be fulfilled. On this record, petitioner "bargained" and negotiated for a particular plea in order to secure dismissal of more serious charges, but also on condition that no sentence recommendation would be made by the prosecutor. It is now conceded that the promise to abstain from a recommendation was made, and at this stage the prosecution is not in a good position to argue that its inadvertent breach of agreement is immaterial. The staff lawyers in a prosecutor's office have the burden of "letting the left hand know what the right hand is doing" or has done. That the breach of agreement was inadvertent does not lessen its impact. We need not reach the question whether the sentencing judge would or would not have been influenced had he known all the details of the negotiations for the plea. He stated that the prosecutor's recommendation did not influence him and we have no reason to doubt that. Nevertheless, we conclude that the interests of justice and appropriate recognition of the duties of the prosecution in relation to promises made in the negotiation of pleas of guilty will be best served by remanding the case to the state courts for further consideration. The ultimate relief to which petitioner is entitled we leave to the discretion of the state court, which is in a better position to decide whether the circumstances of this case require only that there be specific performance of the agreement on the plea, in which case petitioner should be re-sentenced by a different judge, or whether, in the view of the state court, the circumstances require granting the relief sought by petitioner, e. g., the opportunity to withdraw his plea of guilty. We emphasize that this is in no sense to question the fairness of the sentencing judge; the fault here rests on the prosecutor, not on the sentencing judge. Thus, we remand to the state courts to determine whether justice would be best served by requiring specific performance of the plea agreement by having a different judge re-sentence the defendant, or by granting defendant's request to withdraw his guilty plea.

C

Yes. A prosecutor's promise is enforceable when the plea rests in any significant degree on the promise. Vacated and remanded.

United States v. Brechner

99 F.3d 96 (1996)

FACTS

This is an appeal by the government from a sentence imposed by the United States District Court for the Eastern District of New York upon the defendant Milton Brechner in which the court departed downward by reason of the defendant's cooperation. Brechner was president of a company that manufactured stuffed toy animals for sale to carnivals. In January 1992, shortly after the government began investigating him, Brechner offered to plead guilty to four counts of income tax evasion. In exchange for his plea, the government agreed not to prosecute him. Brechner and the government entered into a written cooperation agreement which provided that if the United States Attorney's Office determined that Brechner had cooperated fully, provided substantial assistance, and otherwise complied with the terms of the agreement, the government would move for a downward departure on his sentence under §5K1.1 of the U.S. Sentencing Guidelines. Brechner went to considerable lengths to help the government obtain incriminating evidence against another person, but lied to prosecutors about the extent of his own criminal activities. At sentencing, the Assistant U.S. Attorney declined to move for a downward departure. Brechner moved for specific performance of the agreement. The district court found that the government's refusal was in bad faith and that the plea agreement entitled the defendant to the benefit of such a motion. Accordingly, on imposing sentence, the court departed downward from the level indicated by the Guidelines. On appeal, the government argues that Brechner's lies justified the prosecutor's refusal to move for a downward departure.

I

Is the prosecutor's office [i.e., the U.S. Attorney] bound by its promises pursuant to a cooperation agreement when the defendant does not fully comply with the terms of the agreement?

R

The U.S. Attorney is not bound by its promises pursuant to a cooperation agreement when the defendant does not fully comply with the terms of the agreement.

A

We agree that because Brechner breached his cooperation agreement in a way that damaged the case in which he was cooperating the government's refusal to make its promised motion was justified. We therefore vacate and remand for re-sentencing. The government entered into the agreement with Brechner in order to conduct an investigation of a bank officer. When the defendant was not truthful, he undermined the purpose of that investigation, even though he later corrected his misstatements. Thus, defendant's misstatements were material and the district court was correct when it held them to be "not trivial."

C

Reversed.

McMann v. Richardson

397 U.S. 759 (1970)

FACTS

This is a petition for certiorari to the U.S. Supreme Court which seeks reversal of three separate judgments of the Court of Appeals for the Second Circuit ordering hearings on petitions for habeas corpus filed by the respondents in this case. The three respondents now before the Supreme Court are Dash, Richardson, and Williams. All three defendant-prisoners claim that there pleas should be set aside because they were allegedly coerced. The Court of Appeals for the Second Circuit reversed in each case, sitting en banc and dividing six to three in Dash's case and disposing of Richardson's and Williams' cases in decisions by three-judge panels. In each case it was directed that a hearing be held on the petition for habeas corpus. It was the Court of Appeals' view that a plea of guilty is an effective waiver of pretrial irregularities only if the plea is voluntary and that a plea is not voluntary if it is the consequence of an involuntary confession. That the petitioner was represented by counsel and denied the existence of coercion or promises when tendering his plea does not foreclose a hearing on his petition for habeas corpus alleging matters outside the state court record.

I Whether and to what extent an otherwise valid guilty plea may be impeached in collateral proceedings by assertions or proof that the plea was motivated by a prior coerced confession?

R When a defendant's guilty plea is based on reasonably competent advice, it is an intelligent plea not open to collateral attack [an attack on the ground that defendant's counsel miscalculated the admissibility of the defendant's confession].

A The core of the Court of Appeals' holding is the proposition that if in a collateral proceeding a guilty plea is shown to have been triggered by a coerced confession - if there would have been no plea had there been no confession - the plea is vulnerable at least in cases coming from New York where the guilty plea was taken prior to *Jackson v. Denno*. We disagree.

A conviction after a plea of guilty normally rests on the defendant's own admission in open court that he committed the acts with which he is charged. That admission may not be compelled, and since the plea is also a waiver of trial, unless the applicable law provides otherwise, it must be an intelligent act "done with sufficient awareness of the relevant circumstances and likely consequences." The issue on which we differ with the Court of Appeals arises in those situations involving the counseled defendant who allegedly would put the State to its proof if there was a substantial enough chance of acquittal, who would do so except for a prior confession that might be offered against him, and who because of the confession decides to plead guilty to save himself the expense and agony of a trial and perhaps also to minimize the penalty that might be imposed. After conviction on such a plea, is a defendant entitled to a hearing, and to relief if his factual claims are accepted, when his petition for habeas corpus alleges that his confession was in fact coerced and that it motivated his plea? We think not if he alleges and proves no more than this.

We hold, therefore, that a defendant who alleges that he pleaded guilty because of a prior coerced confession is not, without more, entitled to a hearing on his petition for habeas corpus. Nor do we deem the situation substantially different where the defendant's plea was entered prior to *Jackson v. Denno*. At issue in that case was the constitutionality of the New York procedure for determining the voluntariness of a confession offered in evidence at a jury trial. This procedure, which would have been applicable to the respondents if they had gone to trial, required the trial judge, when the confession was offered and a prima facie case of voluntariness established, to submit the issue to the jury without himself finally resolving disputed issues of fact and determining whether or not the confession was voluntary. The Court held this procedure unconstitutional because it did not 'afford a reliable determination of the voluntariness of the confession offered in evidence at the trial, did not adequately protect Jackson's right to be free of a conviction based upon a coerced confession and therefore cannot withstand constitutional attack under the Due Process Clause of the Fourteenth Amendment.' In reaching that conclusion, the Court overruled *Stein v. New York,* which had approved the New York practice.

Whether a guilty plea was entered before or after *Jackson v. Denno*, the question of the validity of the plea remains the same: was the plea a voluntary and intelligent act of the defendant? As we have previously set out, a plea of guilty in a state court is not subject to collateral attack in a federal court on the ground that it was motivated by a coerced confession unless the defendant was incompetently advised by his attorney. For the respondents successfully to claim relief based on *Jackson v. Denno*, each must demonstrate gross error on the part of counsel when he recommended that the defendant plead guilty instead of going to trial and challenging the New York procedures for determining the admissibility of confessions. Such showing cannot be made for precisely this challenge was presented to the New York courts and to this Court in *Stein v. New York*, supra, and in 1953 this Court found no constitutional infirmity in the New York procedures for dealing with coerced-confession claims. Counsel for these respondents cannot be faulted for not anticipating *Jackson v. Denno* or for considering the New York procedures to be as valid as the four dissenters in that case thought them to be.

As we have previously indicated, in each case below the Court of Appeals ruled that a hearing was required to consider claims other than the claim that the plea of guilty rested on a coerced confession and was entered prior to *Jackson v. Denno*. With respect to these other claims, we now express no disagreement with the judgments of the Court of Appeals; but since our holding will require reassessment of the petitions for habeas corpus in the light of the standards expressed herein, the judgments of the Court of Appeals are vacated and the case is remanded to that court for further proceedings consistent with this opinion.

C

Judgment of the Court of Appeals is vacated.

Duncan v. Louisiana

391 U.S. 145 (1968)

FACTS

Appellant Gary Duncan was 19 years of age when tried. While driving on Highway 23 in Plaquemines Parish on October 18, 1966, he saw two younger cousins engaged in a conversation by the side of the road with four white boys. Knowing his cousins, Negroes who had recently transferred to a formerly all-white high school, had reported the occurrence of racial incidents at the school, Duncan stopped the car, got out, and approached the six boys. At trial the white boys and a white onlooker testified, as did appellant and his cousins. The testimony was in dispute on many points, but the witnesses agreed that appellant and the white boys spoke to each other, that appellant encouraged his cousins to break off the encounter and enter his car, and that appellant was about to enter the car himself for the purpose of driving away with his cousins. The whites testified that just before getting in the car appellant slapped Herman Landry, one of the white boys, on the elbow. The Negroes testified that appellant had not slapped Landry, but had merely touched him. The trial judge concluded that the State had proved beyond a reasonable doubt that Duncan had committed simple battery, was convicted of simple battery in the Twenty-fifth Judicial District Court of Louisiana. Under Louisiana law simple battery is a misdemeanor, punishable by a maximum of two years' imprisonment and a $300 fine. Appellant sought trial by jury, but because the Louisiana Constitution grants jury trials only in cases in which capital punishment or imprisonment at hard labor may be imposed, the trial judge denied the request. Appellant was convicted and sentenced to serve 60 days in the parish prison and pay a fine of $150. Appellant sought review in the Supreme Court of Louisiana, asserting that the denial of jury trial violated rights guaranteed to him by the United States Constitution. The Supreme Court, finding "[n]o error of law in the ruling complained of," denied appellant a writ of certiorari. Pursuant to 28 U.S.C. 1257 appellant sought review in this Court, alleging that the Sixth and Fourteenth Amendments to the United States Constitution secure the right to jury trial in state criminal prosecutions where a sentence as long as two years may be imposed. We noted probable jurisdiction, and set the case for oral argument with No. 52, *Bloom v. Illinois*.

I

Does the Fourteenth Amendment Due Process Clause extend to defendants in state criminal trials under the Sixth Amendment's guarantee of trial by jury?

R

The Fourteenth Amendment guarantees a right of jury trial in all criminal cases which, were they tried in a federal court, would come within the Sixth Amendment's guarantee of trial by jury.

A

Since trial by jury in criminal cases is fundamental to the American scheme of justice, the Fourteenth Amendment guarantees a right of jury trial in all criminal cases which, were they tried in a federal court, would come within the Sixth Amendment's guarantee of trial by jury. The penalty authorized for a particular crime is of major relevance in determining whether it is a serious one subject to the mandates of the Sixth Amendment, and it is sufficient here, without defining the boundary between petty offenses and serious crimes, to hold that a crime punishable by two years in prison is a serious crime and that appellant was entitled to a jury trial.

C

Reversed and remanded.

Taylor v. Louisiana

419 U.S. 522 (1975)

FACTS

Appellant, Billy J. Taylor, was indicted by the grand jury of St. Tammany Parish, in the Twenty-second Judicial District of Louisiana, for aggravated kidnapping. On April 12, 1972, appellant moved the trial court to quash the petit jury venire drawn for the special criminal term beginning with his trial the following day. Appellant alleged that women were systematically excluded from the venire and that he would therefore be deprived of what he claimed to be his federal constitutional right to "a fair trial by jury of a representative segment of the community . . ." The Twenty-second Judicial District comprises the parishes of St. Tammany and Washington. The appellee has stipulated that 53% of the persons eligible for jury service in these parishes were female, and that no more than 10% of the persons on the jury wheel in St. Tammany Parish were women. During the period from December 8, 1971, to November 3, 1972, 12 females were among the 1,800 persons drawn to fill petit jury venires (special panel from which the jury is selected) in St. Tammany Parish. It was also stipulated that the discrepancy between females eligible for jury service and those actually included in the venire was the result of the operation of the Louisiana Constitution. In the present case, a venire totaling 175 persons was drawn for jury service beginning April 13, 1972. There were no females on the venire. Appellant's motion to quash the venire was denied that same day. After being tried, convicted, and sentenced to death, appellant sought review in the Supreme Court of Louisiana, where he renewed his claim that the petit jury venire should have been quashed. The Supreme Court of Louisiana, recognizing that this claim drew into question the constitutionality of the provisions of the Louisiana Constitution and Code of Criminal Procedure dealing with the service of women on juries, squarely held, one justice dissenting, that these provisions were valid and not unconstitutional under federal law. Appellant appealed from that decision to this Court.

I

Is the Sixth Amendment violated when women are systematically excluded from such venires, panels or lists? Does the fulfillment of the Sixth Amendment's guarantee of an impartial jury trial in criminal prosecutions mandate the presence of a fair cross section of the community on venires, panels or lists from which petit juries are drawn?

R

When women are systematically excluded from the jury panel from which petit juries (special panel from which the jury is selected) are drawn, the fair-cross-section rule is violated.

A

Appellant had standing to make his constitutional claim, there being no rule that such a claim may be asserted only by defendants who are members of the group excluded from jury service. The requirement that a petit jury be selected from a representative cross section of the community, which is fundamental to the jury trial, guaranteed by the Sixth Amendment, is violated by the systematic exclusion of women from jury panels, which in the judicial district here involved amounted to 53% of the citizens eligible for jury service. No adequate justification was shown here for the challenged jury-selection provisions and the right to a jury selected from a fair cross section of the community cannot be overcome on merely rational grounds. It can no longer be held that women as a class may be excluded from jury service or given automatic exemptions based solely on sex if the consequence is that criminal jury venires are almost all male, and contrary implications of prior cases cannot be followed. Consistent with this court's previous holding that the exclusion of women from jury venires violated a statutory fair cross-section requirement, we hold here that the fair cross-section requirement of the Sixth Amendment is also violated by the systematic exclusion of women. Both sexes are not interchangeable; and a group made up of one is different from a group composed of both. Moreover, the systematic exclusion cannot be justified on the grounds that women serve a unique role in society, a role which would be hindered by jury service. And although we recognize that the States may grant exemptions in cases of hardship, they may not exclude all women by suggesting that we cannot spare them from their other responsibilities in society.

C When women are systematically excluded from the jury panel from which petit juries are drawn the fair-cross-section rule is violated. Reversed.

Ham v. South Carolina

409 U.S. 524 (1973)

FACTS

Petitioner, a civil rights worker, claims that the trial resulting in his drug conviction (which was affirmed by the South Carolina Supreme Court) was not fair because of the trial court's refusal to examine jurors on *voir dire* as to possible prejudice arising from the fact that petitioner is a Negro and that he wears a beard.

I

Does the trial court's refusal to make any inquiry of the jurors as to racial bias after petitioner's timely request deny petitioner a fair trial in violation of the Due Process Clause of the Fourteenth Amendment?

R

The trial court's refusal to make any inquiry of the jurors as to racial bias after petitioner's timely request therefore denied petitioner a fair trial in violation of the Due Process Clause of the Fourteenth Amendment..

A

The trial court's refusal to make any inquiry of the jurors as to racial bias after petitioner's timely request therefore denied petitioner a fair trial in violation of the Due Process Clause of the Fourteenth Amendment. Its refusal to inquire as to particular bias against beards, after it had make inquiries as to bias in general, was not constitutional error. The trial court's refusal to make any inquiry of the jurors as to racial bias after petitioner's timely request therefore denied petitioner a fair trial in violation of the Due Process Clause of the Fourteenth Amendment. Its refusal to inquire as to particular bias against beards, after it had make inquiries as to bias in general, was not constitutional error.

C

Reversed.

People v. Newton

Cal. Super.Ct (1968)

FACTS

Defendant Newton was the co-founder and Minister of Defense of the Black Panther Party. In 1967 he was charged with the murder of a white police officer in Oakland, California. The judge allowed extensive voir dire by defense counsel to ensure the jury was impartial. After the jury was empanelled, Newton was convicted of murder.

I

Must a prospective juror who harbors preconceived notions of a defendant's guilt and is unable to set aside those notions via consideration of the evidence be dismissed for cause?

R

A prospective juror who harbors preconceived notions of a defendant's guilt and is unable to set aside those notions via consideration of the evidence must be dismissed for cause.

A

A prospective juror who harbors preconceived notions of a defendant's guilt and is unable to set aside those notions via consideration of the evidence must be dismissed for cause. Even though the district attorney established that without further evidence the juror would vote not guilty as to the charges, the juror testified under oath that he believed Newton was guilty. Thus, the juror must be dismissed under such circumstances.

C

See above.

United States v. Salamone

800 F.2d 1216 (3rd Cir. 1986)

FACTS

Defendant-appellant Salamone was convicted of 6 firearms offenses whereupon the United States moved for detention of Salamone prior to imposition of sentence pursuant to 18 U.S.C. § 3143. On March 14, 1985, we held a hearing at which time Salamone was given an opportunity to establish by clear and convincing evidence that he was not likely to flee or pose a danger to the safety of any other person in the community. At the conclusion of the hearing we ruled that Salamone had not established that he was unlikely to flee pending sentence. We ordered Salamone detained. On April 15, 1985, we sentenced Salamone to 20 years and fined him $35,000.00. An appeal was taken to the 3rd Circuit Court of Appeals.

I

Did the trial court abuse its discretion when it dismissed potential jurors solely on the basis of the NRA membership?

R

A juror may be challenged based upon his/her membership in a particular group or affiliation; however, such a challenge may only be challenged only upon a factual showing that the juror negatively influences or prejudices the impartiality of the juror.

A

We reverse the judgment of the lower Court on the basis that prospective jurors affiliated with the National Rifle Association have been excluded on challenges for cause. A juror may be challenged based upon his/her membership in a particular group or affiliation; however, such a challenge may only be challenged only upon a factual showing that the juror negatively influences or prejudices the impartiality of the juror. We reject all of Salamone's other grounds for appeal.

C

The judgment is reversed.

Batson v. Kentucky

476 U.S. 79 (1986)

FACTS

Defendant Batson, a black man, was indicted burglary and receipt of stolen goods. During the criminal trial in a Kentucky state court of petitioner, a black man, the judge conducted *voir dire* examination of the jury venire and excused certain jurors for cause. The prosecutor then used his peremptory challenges to strike all four black persons on the venire, and a jury composed only of white persons was selected. Defense counsel moved to discharge the jury on the ground that the prosecutor's removal of the black veniremen violated petitioner's rights under the Sixth and Fourteenth Amendments to a jury drawn from a cross section of the community, and under the Fourteenth Amendment to equal protection of the laws. Without expressly ruling on petitioner's request for a hearing, the trial judge denied the motion, reasoning that the fair cross-section requirement applies only to selection of the venire and not to selection of the jury, and that the parties could use their peremptory challenges to "strike anyone they want to." The jury ultimately convicted petitioner. Affirming the conviction, the Kentucky Supreme Court observed that recently, in another case, it had relied on *Swain v. Alabama* and had held that a defendant alleging lack of a fair cross section must demonstrate systematic exclusion of a group of jurors from the venire.

I

Can a *prima facie* case of purposeful discrimination in violation of the Equal Protection Clause be established via the use of peremptory challenges in a single case to exclude veniremen solely on the basis of race?

R

A *prima facie* case of purposeful discrimination CAN be established via the use of peremptory challenges in a single case to exclude veniremen solely on the basis of race in violation of the Equal Protection Clause.

A

The principle announced in *Strauder v. West Virginia*, that a State denies a black defendant equal protection when it puts him on trial before a jury from which members of his race have been purposefully excluded, is reaffirmed. A defendant has no right to a petit jury composed in whole or in part of persons of his own race. However, the Equal Protection Clause guarantees the defendant that the State will not exclude members of his race from the jury venire on account of race, or on the false assumption that members of his race as a group are not qualified to serve as jurors. By denying a person participation in jury service on account of his race, the State also unconstitutionally discriminates against the excluded juror. Moreover, selection procedures that purposefully exclude black persons from juries undermine public confidence in the fairness of our system of justice. The same equal protection principles as are applied to determine whether there is discrimination in selecting the venire also govern the State's use of peremptory challenges to strike individual jurors from the petit jury. Although a prosecutor ordinarily is entitled to exercise peremptory challenges for any reason, as long as that reason is related to his view concerning the outcome of the case to be tried, the Equal Protection Clause forbids the prosecutor to challenge potential jurors solely on account of their race or on the assumption that black jurors as a group will be unable impartially to consider the State's case against a black defendant. The portion of *Swain v. Alabama*, supra, concerning the evidentiary burden placed on a defendant who claims that he has been denied equal protection through the State's discriminatory use of peremptory challenges is rejected. In Swain, it was held that a black defendant could make out a prima facie case of purposeful discrimination on proof that the peremptory challenge system as a whole was being perverted. Evidence offered by the defendant in Swain did not meet that standard because it did not demonstrate the circumstances under which prosecutors in the jurisdiction were responsible for striking black jurors beyond the facts of the defendant's case. This evidentiary formulation is inconsistent with equal protection standards subsequently developed in decisions relating to selection of the jury venire. A defendant may make a prima facie showing of purposeful racial discrimination in selection of the venire by relying solely on the facts concerning its selection in his case. A defendant may establish a prima facie case of purposeful discrimination solely on evidence concerning the prosecutor's exercise of peremptory challenges at the defendant's trial. The defendant first must show that he is a member of a cognizable racial group, and that the prosecutor has exercised peremptory challenges to remove from the venire members of the defendant's race. The defendant may also rely on the fact that peremptory challenges constitute a jury selection practice that permits those to discriminate who are of a mind to discriminate. Finally, the defendant must show that such facts and any other relevant circumstances raise an inference that the prosecutor used peremptory challenges to exclude the veniremen from the petit jury on account of their race. Once the defendant makes a *prima facie* showing, the burden shifts to the State to come forward with a race-neutral explanation for challenging the black jurors. The prosecutor may not rebut a prima facie showing by stating that he challenged the jurors on the assumption that they would be partial to the defendant because of their shared race or by affirming his good faith in individual selections. While the peremptory challenge occupies an important position in trial procedures, the above-stated principles will not undermine the contribution that the challenge generally makes to the administration of justice. Nor will application of such principles create serious administrative difficulties. Because the trial court here flatly rejected petitioner's objection to the prosecutor's removal of all black persons on the venire without requiring the prosecutor to explain his action, the case is remanded for further proceedings. If the trial court decides that the facts establish a prima facie case of purposeful discrimination and the prosecutor does not provide a race neutral explanation for his action, defendant's conviction must be reversed.

C

Yes. A *prima facie* case of purposeful discrimination can be established via the use of peremptory challenges in a single case to exclude veniremen solely on the basis of race in violation of the Equal Protection Clause. Reversed and remanded.

United States v. Dougherty

476 F.2d 1113 (D.C. Cir. 1972)

FACTS

Seven of the so-called "D.C. Nine," including defendant-appellant Dougherty, bring this joint appeal from conviction arising from their arrest in relation to their entry into the Washington office of the Dow Chemical Company, and the destruction of certain property therein caused by them. After a jury trial, all seven appellants were each convicted of two counts of malicious destruction and all appeal their conviction on the grounds that 1) the trial judge erroneously refused to instruct the jury of its right to acquit the defendants without regard to the law and the evidence; and 2) the judge also refused to permit the appellants to argue that issue to the jury.

I

Must a trial judge inform the jury that they may, at their own discretion, wholly disregard the law and the evidence and acquit a defendant in a criminal trial?

R

While a jury has the power to acquit a defendant and discount the instructions on the law given by the trial judge, however, the judge need not expressly tell them so and may additionally instruct the jury that they are required to follow the instruction of the court on all matters of law.

A

On the basis of defendants' first contention we reverse and remand for new trial. To provide an appropriate mandate governing the new trial, we consider the second and third contentions, and conclude that these cannot be accepted. While juries have long enjoyed an unreviewable and unreversible power to acquit a defendant in disregard of the instructions on the law given by the trial judge, the judge may instruct the jury that they are required to follow the instructions of the court on all matters of law. Historically, as distrust for judges appointed and removed by the king receded, there came an increasing acceptance that under a republic the protection of citizens lay not in recognizing the right of each jury to make its own law, but in following democratic processes for changing the law. The right of jury nullification is put forward in the name of liberty and democracy, but its explicit avowal risks the ultimate logic of anarchy. The danger of the excess rigidity may now occasionally exist, but it is not as great as the danger of removing the boundaries of constraint provided by the announced rules. "To encourage individuals to make their determinations as to which laws they will obey and which they will permit themselves as a matter of conscience to disobey is to invite chaos." Moreover, to compel a juror to assume the burdens of the legislator or judge, as is implicit in the doctrine of nullification, is to put untoward strains on the jury system. To tell him [the juror] *expressly* of the nullification option is to inform him, in effect, that it is he who fashions the rule also condemns. That is an overwhelming responsibility, an extreme burden for the juror to take on.

C

Reversed and remanded.

United States v. Thomas

116 F.3d 606 (2nd Cir. 1997)

FACTS

This is an appeal from judgments of conviction on federal narcotics charges following jury trial in the United States District Court for the Northern District of New York. The defendants challenge, *inter alia*, the district court's decision to dismiss one of the jurors [Juror No. 5] during the course of jury deliberations pursuant to Federal Rule of Criminal Procedure 23(b). They urge that the district court erred in finding that the juror was unwilling to follow the court's instructions on the law.

I

Did the court err in disqualifying a black juror in a defendant's drug trial when some evidence suggested that his views were based on the sufficiency of the government's evidence?

R

When the evidence discloses any possibility that a juror's views come from the sufficiency of the government's evidence, that juror must not be disqualified.

A

On appeal, defendants argue, chiefly, that the district court abused its discretion when it ordered the dismissal of one of the jurors pursuant to Rule 23(b) during the course of jury deliberations. The court based its decision to remove the juror, in large part, on a finding that the juror was purposefully disregarding the court's instructions on the law--in effect, that the juror intended to acquit the defendants regardless of the evidence of their guilt. We hold that a juror's purposeful unwillingness to apply the law, including stated intentions to (in effect) "nullify" on the basis of racial, cultural or political affinities with the defendants, is a proper basis for removal of a juror from a venire or from a petit jury in the course of trial, and constitutes "just cause" for dismissal of the juror from a deliberating jury under Rule 23(b). We also reaffirm, however, the indispensability of secrecy to the proper functioning of the jury system and conclude that, where a deliberating juror is alleged to be engaging in "nullification," the principle of secrecy in jury deliberations, coupled with the need to protect against the dismissal of a juror based on his doubts about the guilt of a criminal defendant, requires that the juror be removed only where the record evidence leaves no doubt that the juror was in fact engaged in deliberate misconduct - that he was not simply unpersuaded by the Government's case against the defendants. We hold that, in the instant case, the district court erred in relying, as the primary basis for a deliberating juror's removal, on a finding that the juror refused to follow the law as instructed by the court, where the court's interviews with members of the jury raised the possibility that the juror was in fact following the court's instructions, but was simply unpersuaded by the prosecution's case. Accordingly, we conclude that, in the particular circumstances presented here, the court erred in dismissing the juror under Rule 23(b), and we vacate the judgments of the district court and remand for a new trial.

For the reasons stated above, we conclude that: (1) The district court properly determined that a juror's purposeful disregard of the law as set forth in the court's instruction may constitute "just cause" for that juror's removal under Rule 23(b); (2) A court must not, however, remove a juror for an alleged refusal to follow the law as instructed unless the record leaves no doubt that the juror was in fact engaged in deliberate misconduct - that he was not simply unpersuaded by the Government's case against the defendants; and (3) The court in the instant case thus erred by dismissing Juror No. 5, and permitting the jury of eleven to continue its deliberations, based largely on Juror No. 5's alleged refusal to follow the court's instructions on the law, where the record evidence raises the possibility that the juror was attempting to follow the law as instructed, but that he simply remained unpersuaded of the defendants' guilt.

C

Reversed and remanded.

Maryland v. Craig

497 U.S. 836 (1990)

FACTS

Respondent Craig was tried in a Maryland court on several charges related to her alleged sexual abuse of a six-year-old child. Before the trial began, the State sought to invoke a state statutory procedure permitting a judge to receive, by one-way closed circuit television, the testimony of an alleged child abuse victim upon determining that the child's courtroom testimony would result in the child's suffering serious emotional distress such that he or she could not reasonably communicate. If the procedure is invoked, the child, prosecutor, and defense counsel withdraw to another room, where the child is examined and cross-examined; the judge, jury, and defendant remain in the courtroom, where the testimony is displayed. Although the child cannot see the defendant, the defendant remains in electronic communication with counsel, and objections may be made and ruled on as if the witness were in the courtroom. The court rejected Craig's objection that the procedure's use violates the Confrontation Clause of the Sixth Amendment, ruling that Craig retained the essence of the right to confrontation. Based on expert testimony, the court also found that the alleged victim and other allegedly abused children who were witnesses would suffer serious emotional distress if they were required to testify in the courtroom, such that each would be unable to communicate. Finding that the children were competent to testify, the court permitted testimony under the procedure, and Craig was convicted. The State Court of Special Appeals affirmed, but the State Court of Appeals reversed. Although it rejected Craig's argument that the Clause requires in all cases a face-to-face courtroom encounter between the accused and accusers, it found that the State's showing was insufficient to reach the high threshold required by *Coy v. Iowa,* before the procedure could be invoked. The court held that the procedure usually cannot be invoked unless the child initially is questioned in the defendant's presence, and that, before using the one-way television procedure, the trial court must determine whether a child would suffer severe emotional distress if he or she were to testify by two-way television.

I Must a child witness in a child abuse case to testify against a defendant at trial face-to-face in court or may he/she do so outside the defendant's presence [by a one-way closed circuit TV] without implicating the Sixth Amendment's Confrontation Clause?

R The Confrontation Clause does not guarantee criminal defendants an absolute right to a face-to-face meeting with the witnesses against them at trial.

A The Confrontation Clause does not guarantee criminal defendants an absolute right to a face-to-face meeting with the witnesses against them at trial. The Clause's central purpose, to ensure the reliability of the evidence against a defendant by subjecting it to rigorous testing in an adversary proceeding before the trier of fact, is served by the combined effects of the elements of confrontation: physical presence, oath, cross-examination, and observation of demeanor by the trier of fact. Although face-to-face confrontation forms the core of the Clause's values, it is not an indispensable element of the confrontation right. If it were, the Clause would abrogate virtually every hearsay exception, a result long rejected as unintended and too extreme. Accordingly, the Clause must be interpreted in a manner sensitive to its purpose and to the necessities of trial and the adversary process. Nonetheless, the right to confront accusatory witnesses may be satisfied absent a physical, face-to-face confrontation at trial only where denial of such confrontation is necessary to further an important public policy, and only where the testimony's reliability is otherwise assured. Maryland's interest in protecting child witnesses from the trauma of testifying in a child abuse case is sufficiently important to justify the use of its special procedure, provided that the State makes an adequate showing of necessity in an individual case. The Court of Appeals erred to the extent that it may have rested its conclusion that the trial court did not make the requisite necessity finding on the lower court's failure to observe the children's behavior in the defendant's presence and its failure to explore less restrictive alternatives to the one-way television procedure. While such evidentiary requirements could strengthen the grounds for the use of protective measures, only a case-specific necessity finding is required. This Court will not establish, as a matter of federal constitutional law, such categorical evidentiary prerequisites for the use of the one-way procedure.

C Vacated and remanded.

Oregon v. Kennedy

456 U.S. 667 (1982)

FACTS

Defendant Kennedy was charged him with the theft of an Oriental rug. During Defendant-Respondent Kennedy's trial for theft in an Oregon state court, the State's expert witness testified as to the value and identity of the property involved. On cross-examination, he acknowledged that he had once filed an unrelated criminal complaint against respondent, but explained that no action had been taken on his complaint. On redirect examination, the court sustained a series of objections to the prosecutor's questions seeking to establish the reasons why the witness had filed a complaint against respondent. After eliciting from the witness that he had never done business with respondent, the prosecutor asked: "Is that because he is a crook?" The trial court then granted respondent's motion for a mistrial. On retrial, the court rejected respondent's contention that the Double Jeopardy Clause of the Fifth Amendment, as made applicable to the States by the Fourteenth Amendment, barred further prosecution, finding that "it was not the intention of the prosecutor in this case to cause a mistrial." Respondent was convicted, but the Oregon Court of Appeals reversed, sustaining the double jeopardy claim because the prosecutorial misconduct that had occasioned the mistrial, even if not intended to cause a mistrial, amounted to "overreaching."

I When the conduct which gave rise to the motion was intended to provoke the defendant into moving for a mistrial, may a defendant who has successfully moved for a mistrial invoke the bar of double jeopardy in a second effort to try him?

R When the conduct giving rise to the successful motion for a mistrial was intended to provoke the defendant into moving for a mistrial, a defendant who has successfully moved for a mistrial may invoke the bar of double jeopardy in a second effort to try him.

A There is no merit to respondent's contentions that the Court of Appeals' decision was based upon an adequate and independent state ground, or that in the alternative the case should be remanded in order that the court may clarify the grounds upon which its judgment rested. A fair reading of the opinion below shows that the court rested its decision solely on federal law. Where a defendant in a criminal trial successfully moves for a mistrial, he may invoke the bar of double jeopardy in a second effort to try him only if the conduct giving rise to the successful motion for a mistrial was prosecutorial or judicial conduct intended to provoke the defendant into moving for a mistrial. A more general test of "overreaching" is rejected because it offers virtually no standards for its application and because such a rule may not aid defendants as a class. By contrast, a standard that examines the prosecutor's intent is a manageable standard to apply. Our opinion does not lay down a flat rule that when a defendant in a criminal trial successfully moves for mistrial, he may not therefore invoke the bar of double jeopardy against a second trial. We point out, however, that the circumstances under which such a defendant may invoke the bar of double jeopardy in a second effort to try him are limited to those cases in which the conduct giving rise to the successful motion for mistrial was intended to provoke the defendant into moving for a mistrial. Since the courts below both agreed that the prosecutor did not intend her conduct to provoke respondent into moving for a mistrial, that is the end of the matter for purposes of the Double Jeopardy Clause.

C

Yes. When the conduct giving rise to the successful motion for a mistrial was intended to provoke the defendant into moving for a mistrial, a defendant who has successfully moved for a mistrial may invoke the bar of double jeopardy in a second effort to try him.

Idaho v. Wright

497 U.S. 805 (1990)

FACTS

Respondent Wright was charged under Idaho law with two counts of lewd conduct with a minor, specifically her 5 ½ - and 2 ½ - year-old daughters. At the trial, it was agreed that the younger daughter was not "capable of communicating to the jury." However, the court admitted, under Idaho's residual hearsay exception, certain statements she had made to a pediatrician having extensive experience in child abuse cases. The doctor testified that she had reluctantly answered questions about her own abuse, but had spontaneously volunteered information about her sister's abuse. Wright was convicted on both counts, but appealed only from the conviction involving the younger child. The State Supreme Court reversed, finding that the admission of the doctor's testimony under the residual hearsay exception violated Wright's rights under the Confrontation Clause. The court noted that the child's statements did not fall within a traditional hearsay exception and lacked "particularized guarantees of trustworthiness" because the doctor had conducted the interview without procedural safeguards: he failed to videotape the interview, asked leading questions, and had a preconceived idea of what the child should be disclosing. This error, the court found, was not harmless beyond a reasonable doubt.

I

Are incriminating statements, which are admissible under an exception to the hearsay rule, also admissible under the Confrontation Clause?

R

Incriminating statements admissible under an exception to the hearsay rule are not admissible under the Confrontation Clause unless the prosecution produces, or demonstrates the unavailability of, the declarant whose statement it wishes to use and unless the statement bears adequate indicia of reliability.

A

The admission of the child's hearsay statements violated Wright's Confrontation Clause rights. Incriminating statements admissible under an exception to the hearsay rule are not admissible under the Confrontation Clause unless the prosecution produces, or demonstrates the unavailability of, the declarant whose statement it wishes to use and unless the statement bears adequate indicia of reliability. The reliability requirement can be met where the statement either falls within a firmly rooted hearsay exception or is supported by a showing of "particularized guarantees of trustworthiness," *Ohio v. Roberts*. Although it is presumed here that the child was unavailable within the meaning of the Clause, the evidence will be barred unless the reliability requirement is met.

C

Affirmed.

Cruz v. New York

481 U.S. 186 (1987)

FACTS

Under *Bruton v. United States*, a defendant is deprived of his rights under the Confrontation Clause of the Sixth Amendment when his codefendant's incriminating confession is introduced at their joint trial, even if the jury is instructed to consider that confession only against the codefendant. Here, at petitioner's and his brother's joint trial for the felony murder of a gas station attendant, the court allowed the State, over petitioner's objection, to introduce the brother's videotaped confession that he had killed the attendant who had just shot petitioner. The brother did not himself testify, and the court warned the jury that his confession was not to be used against petitioner. The State also called a witness who testified about a conversation with petitioner which recited essentially the same facts as the brother's confession. The New York Court of Appeals affirmed petitioner's conviction, adopting the reasoning of the plurality opinion in *Parker v. Randolph*, that *Bruton* did not require the brother's confession to be excluded because petitioner had himself confessed and his confession "interlocked" with his brother's.

I Is the Sixth Amendment's Confrontation Clause violated when the government introduces evidence of a non-testifying co-defendant's interlocked confession?

R Where a non-testifying codefendant's confession facially incriminating the defendant is not directly admissible against the defendant, the Confrontation Clause bars its admission at their joint trial, even if the jury is instructed not to consider it against the defendant, and even if the defendant's own confession is admitted against him.

A Where a non-testifying codefendant's confession facially incriminating the defendant is not directly admissible against the defendant, the Confrontation Clause bars its admission at their joint trial, even if the jury is instructed not to consider it against the defendant, and even if the defendant's own confession is admitted against him. The Parker plurality's view that *Bruton* is inapplicable to cases involving interlocking confessions is rejected in favor of JUSTICE BLACKMUN's view in Parker that, although introduction of the defendant's own interlocking confession cannot cure the Confrontation Clause violation caused by introduction of the non-testifying codefendant's confession, it might, in some cases, render that violation harmless. The Parker plurality's view is predicated on the erroneous theory that, when the defendant has himself confessed, introduction of the codefendant's confession will seldom, if ever, be of the "devastating" character required by *Bruton* to prove a Confrontation Clause violation. Although *Bruton* did consider "devastating" effect, it did so in the context of justification for excluding the entire category of codefendant confessions that implicate the defendant, and not as a factor whose existence must be assessed on a case-by-case basis. The assumption [481 U.S. 186, 187] that an interlocking confession precludes devastation is rendered untenable by the infinite variability of inculpatory statements and their likely effect on juries. In fact, "interlocking" bears an inverse relationship to devastation, since a codefendant's confession that corroborates the defendant's alleged confession significantly harms the defendant's case, whereas one that is positively incompatible gives credence to the defendant's assertion that his own alleged confession was nonexistent or false. The "interlocking" nature of a codefendant's confession pertains not to its harmfulness but to its reliability, which, although relevant to whether the confession should be admitted as evidence against the defendant, is irrelevant to the questions whether the jury is likely to obey the instruction to disregard it or whether the jury's failure to do so is likely to be inconsequential. Although a codefendant's interlocking confession incriminating the defendant may not be admitted at trial, the defendant's own confession may be considered in assessing whether his codefendant's statements are supported by sufficient "indicia of reliability" to be directly admissible against him (assuming the codefendant's "unavailability") despite the lack of opportunity for cross-examination, and may be considered on appeal in assessing whether any Confrontation Clause violation was harmless.

C

Reversed and remanded.

Gray v. Maryland

523 U.S. 185 (1998)

FACTS

Anthony Bell confessed to the police that he, Defendant-Petitioner Gray, and another man participated in the beating that caused Stacy Williams' death. After the third man died, a Maryland grand jury indicted Bell and Gray for murder, and the State tried them jointly. When the trial judge permitted the State to introduce a redacted version of Bell's confession, the detective who read it to the jury substituted the words "deleted" or "deletion" whenever the name of Gray or the third participant appeared. Immediately after that reading, however, the detective answered affirmatively when the prosecutor asked, "after Bell gave you that information, you subsequently were able to arrest . . . Gray; is that correct?" The State also introduced a written copy of the confession with the two names omitted, leaving in their place blanks separated by commas. The judge instructed the jury that the confession could be used as evidence only against Bell, not Gray. The jury convicted both defendants. Maryland's intermediate appellate court held that *Bruton v. United States* prohibited use of the confession and set aside Gray's conviction. Maryland's highest court disagreed and reinstated that conviction. This appeal followed.

I

Is a co-defendant's confession admissible at a joint trial where it implicates a non-confessing defendant?

R

As applied under *Bruton v. United States,* certain incriminating extrajudicial statements of a co-defendant naming another co-defendant, when considered as a class, are so prejudicial that limiting instructions are inadequate.

A

The confession here at issue, which substituted blanks and the word "delete" for Gray's proper name, falls within the class of statements to which *Bruton's* protective rule applies. *Bruton* also involved two defendants tried jointly for the same crime, with the confession of one them incriminating both himself and the other. This Court held that, despite a limiting instruction that the jury should consider the confession as evidence only against the confessing co-defendant, the introduction of such a confession at a joint trial violates the non-confessing defendant's Sixth Amendment right to cross-examine witnesses. The Court explained that this situation, in which the powerfully incriminating extrajudicial statements of a codefendant are deliberately spread before the jury in a joint trial, is one of the contexts in which the risk that the jury will not, or cannot, follow limiting instructions is so great, and the consequences of failure so devastating to the defendant, that the introduction of the evidence cannot be allowed. *Bruton's* scope was limited by *Richardson v. Marsh*, in which the Court held that the Confrontation Clause is not violated by the admission of a non-testifying codefendant's confession with a proper limiting instruction when the confession is redacted to eliminate not only that defendant's name, but any reference to his or her existence. Unlike Richardson's redacted confession, the confession here refers directly to Gray's "existence." Redactions that simply replace a name with an obvious blank space or a word such as "deleted" or a symbol or other similarly obvious indications of alteration leave statements that, considered as a class, so closely resemble

Bruton's unredacted statements as to warrant the same legal results. For one thing, a jury will often react similarly to an unredacted confession and a confession redacted as here, for it will realize that the confession refers specifically to the defendant, even when the State does not blatantly link the defendant to the deleted name, as it did below by asking the detective whether Gray was arrested on the basis of information in Bell's confession. For another thing, the obvious deletion may well call the jurors' attention specially to the removed name. By encouraging the jury to speculate about the reference, the redaction may overemphasize the importance of the confession's accusation-once the jurors work out the reference. Finally, *Bruton's* protected statements and statements redacted to leave a blank or some other similarly obvious alteration function the same way grammatically: They point directly to, and accuse, the non-confessing codefendant. Although Richardson placed outside *Bruton's* scope statements that incriminate inferentially and the jury must use inference to connect Bell's statements with Gray, Richardson does not control the result here. Inference pure and simple cannot make the critical difference. If it did, then *Richardson* would also place outside *Bruton's* scope confessions that use, e.g., nicknames and unique descriptions, whereas this Court has assumed that such identifiers fall inside *Bruton's* protection, see *Harrington v. California.* Thus, *Richardson* must depend in significant part upon the kind of, not the simple fact of, inference. *Richardson's* inferences involved statements that did not refer directly to the defendant himself, but became incriminating "only when linked with evidence introduced later at trial." In contrast, the inferences here involve statements that, despite redaction, obviously refer directly to someone, often obviously to Gray, and involve inferences that a jury ordinarily could make immediately, even were the confession the very first item introduced at trial. Richardson 's policy reasons for its conclusion-that application of *Bruton's* rule would force prosecutors to abandon use either of the confession or of a joint trial in instances where adequate redaction would "not [be] possible," and would lead to those same results, or provoke mistrials, because of the difficulty of predicting, before introduction of all the evidence, whether *Bruton's* barred use of a particular confession that incriminated "by connection," are inapplicable in the circumstances here.

C No. As applied under *Bruton v. United States,* certain incriminating extrajudicial statements of a co-defendant naming another co-defendant, when considered as a class, are so prejudicial that limiting instructions are inadequate. Reversed.

United States v. Burr

25 Fed. Cas. 30 (D.Va. 1807)

FACTS

Defendant Burr subpoenaed a document from the President of the United States [Jefferson]. The document was a letter from General Wilkinson to Jefferson relating to the defendant and contained the President's response. Burr claimed the letter was material to his defense on charges of treason.

I Does the Sixth Amendment right to compel the attendance of a witness at trial permit a defendant to direct a subpoena dues tecum [a subpoena ordering the witness to appear and bring specific documents or records] to the President of the United States?

R The Sixth Amendment right to compel the attendance of a witness at trial does permit a defendant to direct a subpoena to the President of the United States.

A The Sixth Amendment right to compel the attendance of a witness at trial does permit a defendant to direct a subpoena to the President of the United States. It provides the defendant with a compulsory process for obtaining a witness for his/her defense and includes the right to compel the witness to produce the requested records or documents.

C See above.

Taylor v. Illinois

484 U.S. 400 (1988)

FACTS

Well in advance of Defendant-Petitioner Taylor's state-court trial for attempted murder, the prosecutor filed a discovery motion requesting a list of defense witnesses. Petitioner's answer failed to list one Wormley, as did his amended answer, submitted and accepted on the first day of trial, identifying two witnesses who were never called to testify. On the second day of trial, after the prosecution's two principal witnesses had completed their testimony, petitioner's counsel made an oral motion to further amend the discovery answer to include Wormley. Counsel explained that Wormley had probably seen the entire incident that led to the indictment and that, although petitioner had told counsel about Wormley earlier, counsel had been unable to locate Wormley. At a subsequent *voir dire* examination, Wormley testified that he had not been a witness to the incident itself but had earlier seen the victim and his brother carrying guns and threatening petitioner and that he just happened to run into petitioner and warned him to watch out. On cross-examination, Wormley acknowledged that he had first met petitioner over two years after the incident in question and that defense counsel had visited him at his home during the week before the trial began. As a sanction for the failure to identify Wormley in the discovery answer, the trial judge refused to allow Wormley to testify before the jury. The judge explained that petitioner's counsel had committed a blatant and willful violation of the discovery rules and that the judge doubted the veracity of Wormley's testimony. The Illinois Appellate Court affirmed petitioner's conviction. Defendant-Petitioner petitioned the Supreme Court for certiorari.

I Does a discovery sanction order that precludes the testimony of a defense witness violate a criminal defendant's Sixth Amendment right to obtain the testimony of favorable witnesses?

R The Sixth Amendment does not function as an absolutely bar in prohibiting a court from ordering the preclusion of defense evidence as a sanction for violation of a discovery rule.

A The Compulsory Process Clause of the Sixth Amendment may, in an appropriate case, be violated by the imposition of a discovery sanction that entirely excludes the testimony of a material defense witness. That is, we hold that the Sixth Amendment does not absolutely bar a court from ordering the preclusion of defense evidence as a sanction for violation of the discovery rule. The Clause is not merely a guarantee that the accused shall have the power to subpoena witnesses, but confers on the accused the fundamental right to present witnesses in his own defense. However, the Compulsory Process Clause does not create an absolute bar to preclusion of the testimony of a defense witness as a sanction for violating a discovery rule. Although a trial court may not ignore the fundamental character of the defendant's right to offer the testimony of witnesses in his favor, the mere invocation of that right cannot automatically and invariably outweigh countervailing public interests. If discovery violations are willful and motivated by a desire to obtain a tactical advantage or to conceal a plan to present fabricated testimony, it would be entirely appropriate to exclude the witnesses' testimony regardless of whether other, less drastic sanctions might be available, adequate, and merited. The exclusion of Wormley's testimony did not constitute constitutional error. The fact that the *voir dire* examination of Wormley may have adequately protected the prosecution from prejudice resulting from surprise does not render the imposition of the preclusion sanction unnecessarily harsh. The record raises strong inferences that petitioner's counsel was deliberately seeking a tactical advantage in failing to list Wormley as a witness and that "witnesses [were] being found that really weren't there." Thus, the case fits into the category of willful misconduct for which the severe sanction of preclusion is justified in order to protect the integrity of the judicial process. It is not unfair to hold petitioner responsible for his lawyer's misconduct. The lawyer necessarily has full authority to manage the conduct of the trial, and the client must accept the consequences of the lawyer's trial decisions.

C No. The Sixth Amendment does not function as an absolutely bar in prohibiting a court from ordering the preclusion of defense evidence as a sanction for violation of a discovery rule. Affirmed.

Griffin v. California

380 U.S. 609 (1965)

FACTS

Defendant-Petitioner Griffin was convicted of murder in the first degree after a jury trial in a California court. He did not testify at the trial on the issue of guilt, though he did testify at the separate trial on the issue of penalty. The trial court instructed the jury on the issue of guilt, stating that a defendant has a constitutional right not to testify but that the jury could hold Griffin's failure to testify against him if it believed that he had relevant facts within his knowledge. It added, however, that no such inference could be drawn as to evidence respecting which he had no knowledge. It stated that failure of a defendant to deny or explain the evidence of which he had knowledge does not create a presumption of guilt nor by itself warrant an inference of guilt nor relieve the prosecution of any of its burden of proof. Petitioner had been seen with the deceased the evening of her death, the evidence placing him with her in the alley where her body was found. The prosecutor made much of the failure of petitioner to testify. The death penalty was imposed and the California Supreme Court affirmed. The case is here on a writ of certiorari which we granted to consider whether comment on the failure to testify violated the Self-Incrimination Clause of the Fifth Amendment which we made applicable to the States by the 14th Amendment in *Malloy v. Hogan*, decided after the Supreme Court of California had affirmed the present conviction.

I

Is the defendant's Fifth Amendment right against self-incrimination violated by a comment directing attention to a defendant's decision not to testify at trial?

R

The prosecution and the court are prohibited from commenting on defendant's decision not to testify at trial by the Fifth Amendment's protection against self-incrimination.

A

We hold that any comment to the jury by a prosecutor in a state criminal trial upon a defendant's failure to testify violates the Self-Incrimination Clause of the Fifth Amendment of the Federal Constitution as made applicable to the States by the 14th Amendment. When a prosecutor comments upon a defendant's refusal to testify, the he punishes the defendant for invoking a constitutional privilege. We are not persuaded by the State's argument that the jury would have been just as likely to draw negative inferences from the defendant's refusal to testify even if the prosecutor were not allowed to draw attention to it. Accordingly, we hold that the Fifth Amendment forbids the prosecution from commenting on the accused's silence and forbids instructions by the court that such silence is evidence of guilt.

C

Yes. The prosecution and the court are prohibited from commenting upon a defendant's decision not to testify at trial by the Fifth Amendment's protection against self-incrimination. The decision of the California Supreme Court is reversed.

United States v. Thomas

116 F.3d 606 (2nd Cir. 1997)

FACTS

This is an appeal from judgments of conviction on federal narcotics charges following jury trial in the United States District Court for the Northern District of New York. The defendants challenge, *inter alia*, the district court's decision to dismiss one of the jurors [Juror No. 5] during the course of jury deliberations pursuant to Federal Rule of Criminal Procedure 23(b). They urge that the district court erred in finding that the juror was unwilling to follow the court's instructions on the law.

I Did the court err in disqualifying a black juror in a defendant's drug trial when some evidence suggested that his views were based on the sufficiency of the government's evidence?

R When the evidence discloses any possibility that a juror's views come from the sufficiency of the government's evidence, that juror must not be disqualified.

A On appeal, defendants argue, chiefly, that the district court abused its discretion when it ordered the dismissal of one of the jurors pursuant to Rule 23(b) during the course of jury deliberations. The court based its decision to remove the juror, in large part, on a finding that the juror was purposefully disregarding the court's instructions on the law--in effect, that the juror intended to acquit the defendants regardless of the evidence of their guilt. We hold that a juror's purposeful unwillingness to apply the law, including stated intentions to (in effect) "nullify" on the basis of racial, cultural or political affinities with the defendants, is a proper basis for removal of a juror from a venire or from a petit jury in the course of trial, and constitutes "just cause" for dismissal of the juror from a deliberating jury under Rule 23(b). We also reaffirm, however, the indispensability of secrecy to the proper functioning of the jury system and conclude that, where a deliberating juror is alleged to be engaging in "nullification," the principle of secrecy in jury deliberations, coupled with the need to protect against the dismissal of a juror based on his doubts about the guilt of a criminal defendant, requires that the juror be removed only where the record evidence leaves no doubt that the juror was in fact engaged in deliberate misconduct - that he was not simply unpersuaded by the Government's case against the defendants. We hold that, in the instant case, the district court erred in relying, as the primary basis for a deliberating juror's removal, on a finding that the juror refused to follow the law as instructed by the court, where the court's interviews with members of the jury raised the possibility that the juror was in fact following the court's instructions, but was simply unpersuaded by the prosecution's case. Accordingly, we conclude that, in the particular circumstances presented here, the court erred in dismissing the juror under Rule 23(b), and we vacate the judgments of the district court and remand for a new trial.

For the reasons stated above, we conclude that: (1) The district court properly determined that a juror's purposeful disregard of the law as set forth in the court's instruction may constitute "just cause" for that juror's removal under Rule 23(b); (2) A court must not, however, remove a juror for an alleged refusal to follow the law as instructed unless the record leaves no doubt that the juror was in fact engaged in deliberate misconduct - that he was not simply unpersuaded by the Government's case against the defendants; and (3) The court in the instant case thus erred by dismissing Juror No. 5, and permitting the jury of eleven to continue its deliberations, based largely on Juror No. 5's alleged refusal to follow the court's instructions on the law, where the record evidence raises the possibility that the juror was attempting to follow the law as instructed, but that he simply remained unpersuaded of the defendants' guilt.

C

Reversed and remanded.

Williams v. New York

337 U.S. 241 (1949)

FACTS

Defendant Williams was tried and convicted of first-degree murder. A jury in a New York state court found appellant guilty of murder in the first degree. The judge openly expressed belief in defendant's guilt and referred to 30 other burglaries in the same vicinity for which defendant was believed to be responsible. Defendant's attorneys did not challenge any of the judge's statements or ask for an opportunity to refute or discredit the allegations. The jury recommended life imprisonment, but the trial judge imposed sentence of death. In giving his reasons for imposing the death sentence the judge discussed in open court the evidence upon which the jury had convicted stating that this evidence had been considered in the light of additional information obtained through the court's Probation Department, and through other sources. Consideration of this additional information was pursuant to §482 of New York Criminal Code which provides that before rendering judgment or pronouncing sentence, the court shall cause the defendant's previous criminal record to be submitted to it, including any reports that may have been made as a result of a mental, psychiatric or physical examination of such person, and may seek any information that will aid the court in determining the proper treatment of such defendant. The Court of Appeals of New York affirmed the conviction and sentence over the contention that as construed and applied the controlling penal statutes are in violation of the due process clause of the Fourteenth Amendment of the Constitution of the United States in that the sentence of death was based upon information supplied by witnesses with whom the accused had not been confronted and as to whom he had no opportunity for cross-examination or rebuttal.

I

For the purposes of sentencing, may a judge properly consider out-of-court information that would have been inadmissible against a defendant at trial without violating Due process?

R

A judge may properly consider out-of-court information that would have been inadmissible against a defendant at trial for purposes of sentencing without violating Due process.

A

In determining whether a defendant shall receive a one year minimum or a twenty year maximum sentence, we do not think the Federal Constitution restricts the view of the sentencing judge to the information received in open court. The Due Process clause should not be treated as a device for freezing the evidential procedure of sentencing in the mold of trial procedure. To do so would hinder, if not preclude, all courts-state and federal-from making progressive efforts to improve the administration of criminal justice. It is urged, however, that we should draw a constitutional distinction as to the procedure for obtaining information where the death sentence is imposed. We cannot accept the contention. Leaving a sentencing judge free to avail himself of out-of-court information in making such a fateful choice of sentences does secure to him a broad discretionary power, one susceptible of abuse. But in considering whether a rigid constitutional barrier should be created, it must be remembered that there is possibility of abuse wherever a judge must choose between life imprisonment and death. And it is con- ceded that no federal constitutional objection would have been possible if the judge here had sentenced appellant to death because appellant's trial manner impressed the judge that appellant was a bad risk for society, or if the judge had sentenced him to death giving no reason at all. We cannot say that the due-process clause renders a sentence void merely because a judge gets additional out-of-court information to assist him in the exercise of this awesome power of imposing the death sentence. The sentencing judge must possess the most extensive and detailed information possible concerning the defendant's life and characteristics to impose a sentence that is appropriate under the circumstances. It would be reckless to deny judges the opportunity to obtain the pertinent information necessary to impose an adequate sentence by restricting them only to the information given in open court and subject to cross examination. Appellant was found guilty after a fairly conducted trial. His sentence followed a hearing conducted by the judge. Upon the judge's inquiry as to why sentence should not be imposed, the defendant made statements. His counsel made extended arguments. The case went to the highest court in the state, and that court had power to reverse for abuse of discretion or legal error in the imposition of the sentence. That court affirmed. We therefore hold that appellant was not denied due process of law.

C

Yes. A judge may properly consider out-of-court information that would have been inadmissible against a defendant at trial for purposes of sentencing without violating Due process. Affirmed.

McMillan v. Pennsylvania

477 U.S. 79 (1986)

FACTS

Defendant McMillan and three other defendants whose cases were consolidated with McMillan's were convicted of felonies. Pennsylvania's Mandatory Minimum Sentencing Act (Act) provides that anyone convicted of certain enumerated felonies is subject to a mandatory minimum sentence of five years imprisonment if the sentencing judge, upon considering the evidence introduced at the trial and any additional evidence offered by either the defendant or the Commonwealth at the sentencing hearing, finds, by a preponderance of the evidence, that the defendant "visibly possessed a firearm" during the commission of the offense. The Act, which also provides that visible possession shall not be an element of the crime, operates to divest the judge of discretion to impose any sentence of less than five years for the underlying felony, but does not authorize a sentence in excess of that otherwise allowed for the offense. Each of the petitioners was convicted of one of the Act's enumerated felonies, and in each case the Commonwealth gave notice that at sentencing it would seek to proceed under the Act. However, each of the sentencing judges found the Act unconstitutional and imposed a lesser sentence than that required by the Act. The Pennsylvania Supreme Court consolidated the Commonwealth's appeals, vacated petitioners' sentences, and remanded for sentencing pursuant to the Act. The court held that the Act was consistent with due process, rejecting petitioners' principal argument that visible possession of a firearm was an element of the crimes for which they were sentenced and thus must be proved beyond a reasonable doubt under *In re Winship* and *Mullaney v. Wilbur*. Defendant-petitioner and the three other defendants (petitioners) appealed that decision to the U.S. Supreme Court, which granted certiorari.

I Does the application of a "preponderance of the evidence" standard to factors taken into consideration at sentencing satisfy Due Process?

R The application of a "preponderance of the evidence" standard to factors taken into consideration at sentencing satisfies Due Process.

A A State may properly treat visible possession of a firearm as a sentencing consideration rather than an element of a particular offense that must be proved beyond a reasonable doubt. This case is controlled by *Patterson v. New York* (rejected a claim that whenever a State links the "severity of punishment" to the "presence or absence of an identified fact," the State must prove that fact beyond a reasonable doubt). While there are constitutional limits beyond which the States may not go in this regard, the applicability of the reasonable-doubt standard is usually dependent on how a State defines the offense that is charged in any given case. Here, the Pennsylvania Legislature has made visible possession of a firearm a sentencing factor that comes into play only after the defendant has been found guilty of one of the enumerated crimes beyond a reasonable doubt, and the constitutional limits to a State's power are not exceeded by the Act, which only raises the minimum sentence that may be imposed and neither alters the maximum sentence nor creates a separate offense calling for a separate penalty. There is no merit to petitioners' contention that even though States may treat visible possession of a firearm as a sentencing consideration rather than an element of a particular offense, due process nonetheless requires that visible possession be proved by at least clear and convincing evidence. The preponderance standard satisfies due process. Sentencing courts have traditionally heard evidence and found facts without any prescribed burden of proof at all. Nothing in Pennsylvania's scheme warrants "constitutionalizing" burdens of proof at sentencing. Nor is there merit to petitioners' claim that the Act denies them their Sixth Amendment right to a trial by jury. There is no Sixth Amendment right to jury sentencing, even where the sentence turns on specific findings of fact. The Pennsylvania legislature did not change the definition of any existing offense. It simply took one factor that has always been considered by sentencing courts to bear on punishment, the instrumentality used in committing a violent felony, and dictated the precise weight to be given that factor if the instrumentality is a firearm.

C

Yes. The application of a "preponderance of the evidence" standard to factors taken into consideration at sentencing satisfies Due Process. Affirmed.

Apprendi v. New Jersey

530 U.S. 466 (2000)

FACTS

Petitioner Apprendi fired several shots into the home of an African-American family and made a statement, which he later retracted, that he did not want the family in his neighborhood because of their race. He was charged under New Jersey law with, *inter alia,* second-degree possession of a firearm for an unlawful purpose, which carries a prison term of 5 to 10 years. The count did not refer to the State's hate crime statute, which provides for an enhanced sentence if a trial judge finds, by a preponderance of the evidence, that the defendant committed the crime with a purpose to intimidate a person or group because of race. After Apprendi pleaded guilty, the prosecutor filed a motion to enhance the sentence. The court found by a preponderance of the evidence that the shooting was racially motivated and sentenced Apprendi to a 12-year term on the firearms count. In upholding the sentence, the appeals court rejected Apprendi's claim that the Due Process Clause requires that a bias finding be proved to a jury beyond a reasonable doubt. The State Supreme Court affirmed.

I

If the judge finds by a preponderance of the evidence that the crime was racially motivated, may a sentencing statute allow for sentences greater than the ordinary term?

R

Facts that support an increase in a crime's maximum penalty beyond its ordinary prescribed range MUST be (1) charged in the indictment; (2) submitted to the jury; and (3) proven beyond a reasonable doubt.

A

The Constitution requires that any fact that increases the penalty for a crime beyond the prescribed statutory maximum, other than the fact of a prior conviction, must be submitted to a jury and proved beyond a reasonable doubt. The answer to the narrow constitutional question presented, whether Apprendi's sentence was permissible, given that it exceeds the 10-year maximum for the offense charged, was foreshadowed by the holding in *Jones* v. *United States.* That is, with regard to federal law, the Fifth Amendment's Due Process Clause and the Sixth Amendment's notice and jury trial guarantees require that any fact other than prior conviction that increases the maximum penalty for a crime must be charged in an indictment, submitted to a jury, and proved beyond a reasonable doubt. The Fourteenth Amendment commands the same answer when a state statute is involved. The Fourteenth Amendment right to due process and the Sixth Amendment right to trial by jury, taken together, entitle a criminal defendant to a jury determination that he is guilty of every element of the crime with which he is charged, beyond a reasonable doubt. The historical foundation for these principles extends down centuries into the common law. While judges in this country have long exercised discretion in sentencing, such discretion is bound by the range of sentencing options prescribed by the legislature. The historic inseparability of verdict and judgment and the consistent limitation on judges' discretion highlight the novelty of a scheme that removes the jury from the determination of a fact that exposes the defendant to a penalty exceeding the maximum he could receive if punished according to the facts reflected in the jury verdict alone. *McMillan* v. *Pennsylvania* was the first case in which the Court used "sentencing factor" to refer to a fact that was not found by the jury but could affect the sentence imposed by the judge. In finding that the scheme at issue there did not run afoul of *Winship*'s strictures, this Court did not budge from the position that (1) constitutional limits exist to States' authority to define away facts necessary to constitute a criminal offense and (2) a state scheme that keeps from the jury facts exposing defendants to greater or additional punishment may raise serious constitutional concerns, in which the Court upheld a federal law allowing a judge to impose an enhanced sentence based on prior convictions not alleged in the indictment--represents at best an exceptional departure from the historic practice. In light of the constitutional rule expressed here, New Jersey's practice cannot stand. It allows a jury to convict a defendant of a second-degree offense on its finding beyond a reasonable doubt and then allows a judge to impose punishment identical to that New Jersey provides for first-degree crimes on his finding, by a preponderance of the evidence, that the defendant's purpose was to intimidate his victim based on the victim's particular characteristic. The State's argument that the biased purpose finding is not an "element" of a distinct hate crime offense but a "sentencing factor" of motive is nothing more than a disagreement with the rule applied in this case. Beyond this, the argument cannot succeed on its own terms. It does not matter how the required finding is labeled, but whether it exposes the defendant to a greater punishment than that authorized by the jury's verdict, as does the sentencing "enhancement" here. The degree of culpability the legislature associates with factually distinct conduct has significant implications both for a defendant's liberty and for the heightened stigma associated with an offense the legislature has selected as worthy of greater punishment. That the State placed the enhancer within the criminal code's sentencing provisions does not mean that it is not an essential element of the offense.

C

No. Facts that support an increase in a crime's maximum penalty beyond its ordinary prescribed range must be (1) charged in the indictment; (2) submitted to the jury; and (3) proven beyond a reasonable doubt.

North Carolina v. Peace

395 U.S. 711 (1969)

FACTS

In each of these cases the respondent was convicted of a crime and sentenced to a prison term; the original conviction was set aside in a post-conviction proceeding for constitutional error several years later; and on retrial the respondent was again convicted and sentenced. In No. 413, the sentence, when added to the time respondent had served, amounted to a longer total sentence than that originally imposed; and in No. 418, respondent received a longer sentence, with no credit being given for the time already served. In neither case was any justification given for imposition of the longer sentence. Respondents sought habeas corpus relief in the District Courts, which in each instance held the longer sentence on retrial unconstitutional. The Courts of Appeals affirmed.

Specifically, in No. 413, the respondent Pearce was convicted in a North Carolina court upon a charge of assault with intent to commit rape. The trial judge sentenced him to prison for a term of 12 to 15 years. Several years later he initiated a state post-conviction proceeding which culminated in the reversal of his conviction by the Supreme Court of North Carolina, upon the ground that an involuntary confession had unconstitutionally been admitted in evidence against him. He was retried, convicted, and sentenced by the trial judge to an eight-year prison term, which, when added to the time Pearce had already spent in prison, the parties agree amounted to a longer total sentence than that originally imposed. The conviction and sentence were affirmed on appeal. Pearce then began this habeas corpus proceeding in the United States District Court for the Eastern District of North Carolina. That court held, upon the authority of a then very recent Fourth Circuit decision, *Patton v. North Carolina,* that the longer sentence imposed upon retrial was "unconstitutional and void." Upon the failure of the state court to re-sentence Pearce within 60 days, the federal court ordered his release. This order was affirmed by the United States Court of Appeals and we granted certiorari.

In No. 418 the respondent Rice pleaded guilty in an Alabama trial court to four separate charges of second-degree burglary. He was sentenced to prison terms aggregating 10 years. Two and one-half years later the judgments were set aside in a state *coram nobis* proceeding, upon the ground that Rice had not been accorded his constitutional right to counsel. He was retried upon three of the charges, convicted, and sentenced to prison terms aggregating 25 years. No credit was given for the time he had spent in prison on the original judgments. He then brought this habeas corpus proceeding in the United States District Court for the Middle District of Alabama, alleging that the state trial court had acted unconstitutionally in failing to give him credit for the time he had already served in prison, and in imposing grossly harsher sentences upon retrial. United States District Judge Frank M. Johnson, Jr., agreed with both contentions. While stating that he did "not believe that it is constitutionally impermissible to impose a harsher sentence upon retrial if there is recorded in the court record some legal justification for it," Judge Johnson found that Rice had been denied due process of law, because "[u]nder the evidence in this case, the conclusion is inescapable that the State of Alabama is punishing petitioner Rice for his having exercised his post-conviction right of review and for having the original sentences declared unconstitutional." The judgment of the District Court was affirmed by the United States Court of Appeals and the U.S. Supreme Court granted certiorari.

North Carolina v. Peace

395 U.S. 711 (1969)

I When at the behest of the defendant a criminal conviction has been set aside and a new trial ordered, to what extent does the Constitution limit the imposition of a harsher sentence after conviction upon retrial?

R After having successfully attacked his original conviction, a defendant may be given a harsher sentence on re-conviction if there is n judicial vindictiveness present.

A The problem before us involves two related but analytically separate issues. One concerns the constitutional limitations upon the imposition of a more severe punishment after conviction for the same offense upon retrial. The other is the more limited question whether, in computing the new sentence, the Constitution requires that credit must be given for that part of the original sentence already served. The second question is not presented in *Pearce*, for in North Carolina it appears to be the law that a defendant must be given full credit for all time served under the previous sentence. In any event, Pearce was given such credit. Alabama law, however, seems to reflect a different view. And respondent Rice, upon being re-sentenced, was given no credit at all for the two and one-half years he had already spent in prison.

The basic Fifth Amendment guarantee against double jeopardy, which is enforceable against the States by the Fourteenth Amendment, *Benton v. Maryland*, is violated when punishment already exacted for an offense is not fully "credited" in imposing a new sentence for the same offense. There is no absolute constitutional bar to imposing a more severe sentence on reconviction. The guarantee against double jeopardy does not restrict the length of sentence upon re-conviction; the power to impose whatever sentence is legally authorized being a corollary of the well-established power to retry a defendant whose conviction has been set aside for an error in the previous proceeding. Imposition of a more severe sentence upon retrial does not violate the Equal Protection Clause of the Fourteenth Amendment, since there is no invidious "classification" of those successfully seeking new trials. Due process of law requires that vindictiveness against a defendant for having successfully attacked his first conviction must play no part in the sentence he receives after a new trial and that a defendant be freed of any apprehension of retaliatory motivation on the part of the sentencing judge. Accordingly, the reasons for imposition after retrial of a more severe sentence must affirmatively appear in the record and must be based on objective information concerning the defendant's identifiable conduct after the original sentencing proceeding.

C Affirmed

Mistretta v. United States

488 U.S. 361 (1989)

FACTS

Because the existing indeterminate sentencing system resulted in serious disparities among the sentences imposed by federal judges upon similarly situated offenders and in uncertainty as to an offender's actual date of release by Executive Branch parole officials, Congress passed the Sentencing Reform Act of 1984 (Act), which, inter alia, created the United States Sentencing Commission as an independent body in the Judicial Branch with power to promulgate binding sentencing guidelines establishing a range of determinate sentences for all categories of federal offenses and defendants according to specific and detailed factors. The District Court upheld the constitutionality of the Commission's resulting Guidelines against claims by petitioner Mistretta, who was under indictment on three counts centering in a cocaine sale, that the Commission was constituted in violation of the separation-of-powers principle, and that Congress had delegated excessive authority to the Commission to structure the Guidelines. Mistretta had pleaded guilty to a conspiracy-to-distribute count, was sentenced under the Guidelines to 18 months' imprisonment and other penalties, and filed a notice of appeal. This Court granted his petition and that of the United States for certiorari before judgment in the Court of Appeals in order to consider the Guidelines' constitutionality.

I

Are the sentencing guidelines constitutional?

R

The Sentencing Guidelines are constitutional, since Congress neither (1) delegated excessive legislative power to the Commission nor (2) violated the separation-of-powers principle by placing the Commission in the Judicial Branch, by requiring federal judges to serve on the Commission and to share their authority with non-judges, or by empowering the President to appoint Commission members and to remove them for cause.

A

The Sentencing Guidelines are constitutional, since Congress neither (1) delegated excessive legislative power to the Commission nor (2) violated the separation-of-powers principle by placing the Commission in the Judicial Branch, by requiring federal judges to serve on the Commission and to share their authority with non-judges, or by empowering the President to appoint Commission members and to remove them for cause. The Constitution's structural protections do not prohibit Congress from delegating to an expert body within the Judicial Branch the intricate task of formulating sentencing guidelines consistent with such significant statutory direction as is present here, nor from calling upon the accumulated wisdom and experience of the Judicial Branch in creating policy on a matter uniquely within the ken of judges.

C

Affirmed.

United States v. Harrington

947 F.2d 956 (D.C. Cir. 1991)

FACTS

The district court departed downward from the sentencing range indicated by the U.S. Sentencing Guidelines when sentencing defendant Harrington for narcotics offenses. The defendant's potential for rehabilitation from drug addiction was a mitigating circumstance, the judge held, <u>not</u> adequately considered by the Sentencing Commission in promulgating the guidelines. The government appealed.

I Must the defendant's potential for rehabilitation from drug addiction be considered a mitigating circumstance in determining whether he is eligible for a reduced sentence?

R Rigid sentencing guidelines often produce harsh results that a patently unfair because they fail to take into account individual circumstances.

A Rigid sentencing guidelines often produce harsh results that a patently unfair because they fail to take into account individual circumstances.

C Vacated and remanded

United States v. Dunnigan

507 U.S. 87 (1993)

FACTS

At respondent's federal trial for conspiracy to distribute cocaine, the Government's case in chief consisted of five witnesses who took part in, or observed, her cocaine trafficking. As the sole witness in her own defense, respondent denied the witnesses' inculpatory statements and claimed she had never possessed or distributed cocaine. In rebuttal, the Government called an additional witness and recalled one of its earlier witnesses, both of whom testified that respondent sold crack cocaine to them. Respondent was convicted and sentenced pursuant to the United States Sentencing Guidelines. Finding that she had committed perjury, the District Court enhanced her sentence, which is required under 3C1.1 of the Guidelines when a "defendant willfully impeded or obstructed, or attempted to impede or obstruct the administration of justice during the investigation or prosecution of the instant offense." In reversing the sentence, the Court of Appeals found that a 3C1.1 enhancement based on a defendant's alleged perjury would be unconstitutional. It also distinguished the precedent of *United States v. Grayson* - in which this Court upheld a sentence increase stemming from an accused's false testimony at trial - on the grounds that 3C1.1's goal is punishment for obstruction of justice, rather than rehabilitation, and that, in contravention of the admonition in *Grayson*, 3C1.1 is applied in a wooden or reflex fashion to enhance the sentences of all defendants whose testimony is deemed false.

I Can the court increase a defendant's sentence if it finds that the defendant committed perjury at trial?

R Upon a proper determination that the accused has committed perjury at trial, a court may enhance the accused's sentence under 3C1.1.

A Upon a proper determination that the accused has committed perjury at trial, a court may enhance the accused's sentence under 3C1.1. The parties agree, and the commentary to 3C1.1 is explicit, that the phrase "impede or obstruct the administration of justice" includes perjury. Perjury is committed when a witness testifying under oath or affirmation gives false testimony concerning a material matter with the willful intent to provide false testimony. Because a defendant can testify at trial and be convicted, yet not have committed perjury - for example, the accused may give inaccurate testimony as a result of confusion, mistake, or faulty memory or give truthful testimony that a jury finds insufficient to excuse criminal liability or prove lack of intent - not every testifying defendant who is convicted qualifies for a 3C1.1 enhancement. If a defendant objects to such an enhancement resulting from her trial testimony, a district court must review the evidence and make independent findings necessary to establish that the defendant committed perjury. While a court should address each element of the alleged perjury in a clear and distinct finding, its enhancement decision is sufficient where, as here, it makes a determination of an obstruction or impediment of justice that encompasses all of the factual predicates for a perjury finding. An enhanced sentence for the willful presentation of false testimony does not undermine the right to testify. The concern that a court will enhance a sentence as a matter of course whenever the accused takes the stand and is found guilty is dispelled by the requirement that a district court make findings to support all the elements of a perjury violation in a specific case. Any risk from a district court's incorrect perjury findings is inherent in a system which insists on the value of testimony under oath. A 3C1.1 enhancement is also more than a mere surrogate for a separate and subsequent perjury prosecution. It furthers legitimate sentencing goals relating to the principal crime, including retribution and incapacitation. The enhancement may not serve the additional goal of rehabilitation, which was the justification for enhancement in Grayson, but rehabilitation is not the only permissible justification for increasing a sentence based on perjury. Finally, the enhancement under 3C1.1 is far from automatic - when contested, the elements of perjury must be found by the district court with specificity - and the fact that the enhancement stems from a congressional mandate, rather than from a court's discretionary judgment, cannot be grounds for its invalidation.

C

Reversed.

Koon v. United States

518 U.S. 81 (1996)

FACTS

After petitioners, Los Angeles police officers, were acquitted on state charges of assault and excessive use of force in the beating of a suspect during an arrest, they were convicted under 18 U. S. C. Section(s) 242 of violating the victim's constitutional rights under color of law. Although the applicable United States Sentencing Guideline, 1992 USSG Section(s) 2H1.4, indicated that they should be imprisoned for 70 to 87 months, the District Court granted them two downward departures from that range. The first was based on the victim's misconduct, which contributed significantly to provoking the offense. The second was based on a combination of four factors: (1) that petitioners were unusually susceptible to abuse in prison; (2) that petitioners would lose their jobs and be precluded from employment in law enforcement; (3) that petitioners had been subject to successive state and federal prosecutions; and (4) that petitioners posed a low risk of recidivism. The sentencing range after the departures was 30 to 37 months, and the court sentenced each petitioner to 30 months. The Ninth Circuit reviewed the departure decisions de novo and rejected all of them.

I Did the district court abuse its discretion in departing downward when sentencing the defendants?

R An appellate should review district court's sentencing departure under the abuse of discretion standard, not *de novo*.

A An appellate court should not review de novo a decision to depart from the Guideline sentencing range, but instead should ask whether the sentencing court abused its discretion. Although the Sentencing Reform Act of 1984 requires that a district court impose a sentence within the applicable Guideline range in an ordinary case, 18 U. S. C. Section(s) 3553(a), it does not eliminate all of the district court's traditional sentencing discretion. Rather, it allows a departure from the range if the court finds ``there exists an aggravating or mitigating circumstance of a kind, to a degree, not adequately taken into consideration" by the Sentencing Commission in formulating the Guidelines, Section(s) 3553(b). Although Section(s) 3742 established a limited appellate review of sentencing decisions, Section(s) 3742(e)(4)'s direction to "give due deference to the district court's application of the guidelines to the facts" demonstrates that the Act was not intended to vest in appellate courts wide-ranging authority over district court sentencing decisions. Because the Court of Appeals erred in rejecting certain of the downward departure factors relied upon by the District Judge, the foregoing principles require reversal of the appellate court's rulings in significant part. Victim misconduct is an encouraged basis for departure under USSG Section(s) 5K2.10, and the District Court did not abuse its discretion in basing a departure on it. The court's analysis of this departure factor showed a correct understanding in applying Section(s) 2H1.4, the Guideline applicable to 18 U. S. C. Section(s) 242, both as a mechanical matter and in interpreting its heartland. This Court rejects the Government's contention that some of the four considerations underlying the District Court's second downward departure are impermissible departure factors under all circumstances. For a court to conclude that a factor must never be considered would be to usurp the policy-making authority that Congress vested in the Commission, and 18 U. S. C. Section(s) 3553(a)(2) does not compel such a result. The low likelihood of petitioners' recidivism was also an inappropriate ground for departure, since the Commission specifically addressed this factor in formulating the sentencing range for petitioners' criminal history category. However, the District Court did not abuse its discretion in relying upon susceptibility to abuse in prison and the burdens of successive prosecutions. The District Court's finding that the case is unusual due to petitioners exceptional susceptibility to abuse in prison is just the sort of determination that must be accorded deference on appeal. Moreover, although consideration of petitioners' successive prosecutions could be incongruous with the dual responsibilities of citizenship in our federal system, this Court cannot conclude the District Court abused its discretion by considering that factor. Where a reviewing court concludes that a district court based a departure on both valid and invalid factors, a remand is required unless the reviewing court determines that the district court would have imposed the same sentence absent reliance on the invalid factors. Because the District Court here stated that none of four factors standing alone would justify its second departure, it is not evident that the court would have imposed the same sentence had it relied only on susceptibility to abuse and the hardship of successive prosecutions. The Court of Appeals should therefore remand the case to the District Court.

C

Affirmed in part, reversed in part and remanded.

Fong Foo v. United States

369 U.S. 141 (1962)

FACTS

The petitioners, a corporation and two of its employees, were brought to trial before a jury in a federal district court upon an indictment charging a conspiracy and the substantive offense of concealing material facts in a matter within the jurisdiction of an agency of the United States, in violation of 18 U.S.C. 371 and 1001. After seven days of what promised to be a long and complicated trial, three government witnesses had appeared and a fourth was in the process of testifying. At that point the district judge directed the jury to return verdicts of acquittal as to all the defendants, and a formal judgment of acquittal was subsequently entered. The record shows that the district judge's action was based upon one or both of two grounds: supposed improper conduct on the part of the Assistant United States Attorney who was prosecuting the case, and a supposed lack of credibility in the testimony of the witnesses for the prosecution who had testified up to that point. The Government filed a petition for a writ of mandamus in the Court of Appeals for the First Circuit, praying that the judgment of acquittal be vacated and the case reassigned for trial. The court granted the petition, upon the ground that under the circumstances revealed by the record the trial court was without power to direct the judgment in question.

I If a judgment of acquittal is based on an erroneous foundation, may it be set aside?

R A judgment of acquittal, even if based on an erroneous foundation, may not be set aside.

A The judgment of the Court of Appeals was contrary to the guaranty of the Fifth Amendment against double jeopardy. In holding that the District Court was without power to direct acquittals under the circumstances disclosed by the record, the Court of Appeals relied primarily upon two decisions of this Court, *Ex parte United States* and *Ex parte United States*. In the first of these cases it was held that a district judge had no power to suspend a mandatory prison sentence, and that a writ of mandamus would lie to require the judge to vacate his erroneous order of suspension. In the second case the Court issued a writ of mandamus ordering a district judge to issue a bench warrant which he had refused to do, in the purported exercise of his discretion, for a person under an indictment returned by a properly constituted grand jury. Neither of those decisions involved the guaranty of the Fifth Amendment that no person shall "be subject for the same offense to be twice put in jeopardy of life or limb." That constitutional provision is at the very root of the present case, and we cannot but conclude that the guaranty was violated when the Court of Appeals set aside the judgment of acquittal and directed that the petitioners be tried again for the same offense. The petitioners were tried under a valid indictment in a federal court which had jurisdiction over them and over the subject matter. The trial did not terminate prior to the entry of judgment. It terminated with the entry of a final judgment of acquittal as to each petitioner. The Court of Appeals thought, not without reason, that the acquittal was based upon an egregiously erroneous foundation.

C Reversed.

Ashe v. Swenson

397 U.S. 436 (1970)

FACTS

Sometime in the early hours of the morning of January 10, 1960, six men were engaged in a poker game in the basement of the home of John Gladson in Missouri. Suddenly three or four masked men, armed with a shotgun and pistols, broke into the basement and robbed each of the poker players of money and various articles of personal property. The robbers-and it has never been clear whether there were three or four of them-then fled in a car belonging to one of the victims of the robbery. Shortly thereafter the stolen car was discovered in a field, and later that morning three men were arrested by a state trooper while they were walking on a highway not far from where the abandoned car had been found. The petitioner was arrested by another officer some distance away. The four were subsequently charged with seven separate offenses-the armed robbery of each of the six poker players and the theft of the car. In May 1960 the petitioner went to trial on the charge of robbing Donald Knight, one of the participants in the poker game. The proof that an armed robbery had occurred and that personal property had been taken from Knight as well as from each of the others was unassailable. Defense counsel made no attempt to question their testimony regarding the holdup itself or their claims as to their losses. Knight testified without contradiction that the robbers had stolen from him his watch, $250 in cash, and about $500 in checks. The defense offered no testimony and waived final argument. The trial judge instructed the jury that if it found that the petitioner was one of the participants in the armed robbery, the theft of 'any money' from Knight would sustain a conviction. He also instructed the jury that if the petitioner was one of the robbers, he was guilty under the law even if he had not personally robbed Knight. The jury found the petitioner not guilty due to insufficient evidence. Six weeks later the petitioner was brought to trial again, this time for the robbery of another participant in the poker game, a man named Roberts. The petitioner filed a motion to dismiss, based on his previous acquittal. The motion was overruled, and the second trial began. The witnesses were for the most part the same, though this time their testimony was substantially stronger on the issue of the petitioner's identity. The case went to the jury on instructions virtually identical to those given at the first trial. This time the jury found the petitioner guilty, and he was sentenced to a 35-year term in the state penitentiary. The Supreme Court of Missouri affirmed the conviction, holding that the plea of former jeopardy must be denied. A collateral attack upon the conviction in the state courts five years later was also unsuccessful. The petitioner then brought the present habeas corpus proceeding in the United States District Court for the Western District of Missouri, claiming that the second prosecution had violated his right not to be twice put in jeopardy. Considering itself bound by this court's decision in *Hoag v. New Jersey*, the District Court denied the writ, although apparently finding merit in the petitioner's claim. The Court of Appeals for the Eighth Circuit affirmed, also upon the authority of *Hoag*. We granted certiorari to consider the important constitutional question this case presents.

I

After an issue of ultimate fact was determined in a previous trial resulting in an acquittal, can a defendant be tried for a related offense?

Ashe v. Swenson

397 U.S. 436 (1970)

R The same issue cannot be re-litigated between the same parties in any future proceeding after an issue of ultimate fact has been finally determined.

A In *Benton v. Maryland*, the Court held that the Fifth Amendment guarantee against double jeopardy is enforceable against the States through the Fourteenth Amendment. The question in this case is whether the State of Missouri violated that guarantee when it prosecuted the petitioner a second time for armed robbery in the circumstances here presented. The ultimate question to be determined, then, in the light of *Benton* is whether this established rule of federal law is embodied in the Fifth Amendment guarantee against double jeopardy. We do not hesitate to hold that it is. For whatever else that constitutional guarantee may embrace it surely protects a man who has been acquitted from having to 'run the gantlet' a second time. The question is not whether Missouri could validly charge the petitioner with six separate offenses for the robbery of the six poker players. It is not whether he could have received a total of six punishments if he had been convicted in a single trial of robbing the six victims. It is simply whether, after a jury determined by its verdict that the petitioner was not one of the robbers, the State could constitutionally hale him before a new jury to litigate that issue again. After the first jury had acquitted the petitioner of robbing Knight, Missouri could certainly not have brought him to trial again upon that charge. Once a jury had determined upon conflicting testimony that there was at least a reasonable doubt that the petitioner was one of the robbers, the State could not present the same or different identification evidence in a second prosecution for the robbery of Knight in the hope that a different jury might find that evidence more convincing. The situation is constitutionally no different here, even though the second trial related to another victim of the same robbery. For the name of the victim, in the circumstances of this case, had no bearing whatever upon the issue of whether the petitioner was one of the robbers. In this case the State in its brief has frankly conceded that following the petitioner's acquittal, it treated the first trial as no more than a dry run for the second prosecution: No doubt the prosecutor felt the state had a provable case on the first charge and, when he lost, he did what every good attorney would do-he refined his presentation in light of the turn of events at the first trial. But this is precisely what the constitutional guarantee forbids.

C No. The same issue cannot be re-litigated between the same parties in any future proceeding after an issue of ultimate fact has been finally determined.

Downum v. United States

372 U.S. 734 (1963)

FACTS

In a Federal District Court, petitioner was indicted on six counts for federal offenses. When his case was called for trial, both sides announced they were ready. A jury was selected and sworn and instructed to return at 2 p. m. When it did so, the prosecution asked that the jury be discharged because a key witness on two counts was not present. Petitioner moved that those two counts be dismissed for want of prosecution and that the trial continue on the remaining counts. That motion was denied, and the judge discharged the jury over petitioner's objection. Two days later, the case was called again; a second jury was impaneled; and petitioner pleaded former jeopardy.

I Does double jeopardy apply to bar the impaneling of a second jury and new trial if an impaneled jury in the first trial was discharged because the prosecution's witness was unavailable to testify?

R Double jeopardy does apply to bar the impaneling of a second jury and new trial if an impaneled jury in the first trial was discharged because the prosecution's witness was unavailable to testify.

A In the circumstances of this case, that plea should have been sustained. The jury first selected to try petitioner and sworn was discharged because a prosecution witness had not been served with a summons and because no other arrangements had been made to assure his presence. That witness was essential only for two of the six counts concerning petitioner. Yet the prosecution opposed petitioner's motion to dismiss those two counts and to proceed with a trial on the other four counts - a motion the court denied. Here, as in *Wade v. Hunter*, we refuse to say that the absence of witnesses "can never justify discontinuance of a trial." Each case must turn on its facts. On this record, however, we think what was said in *Cornero v. United States,* states the governing principle. There, a trial was first continued because prosecution witnesses were not present, and when they had not been found at the time the case was again called, the jury was discharged. A plea of double jeopardy was sustained when a second jury was selected. That view, which has some support in the authorities is in our view the correct one. We resolve any doubt "in favor of the liberty of the citizen, rather than exercise what would be an unlimited, uncertain, and arbitrary judicial discretion." This means that the judgment below must be and is reversed.

C Reversed.

Illinois v. Somerville

410 U.S. 458 (1973)

FACTS

Defendant Somerville was indicted for theft. Defendant-Respondent was brought to trial under an indictment which, it developed before any evidence was presented, contained a defect that under Illinois law could not be cured by amendment and that on appeal could be asserted to overturn any judgment of conviction. The trial judge declared a mistrial over respondent's objection, following which respondent was re-indicted, tried, and convicted. He thereafter petitioned for habeas corpus, which was ultimately granted on the ground that, jeopardy having attached when the jury was initially impaneled and sworn, the second trial constituted double jeopardy.

I

Is the State prevented from subsequently trying the defendant under a valid indictment by a prior mistrial granted over a defendant's objection, because of a defective indictment?

R

Where there is a "manifest necessity" for the mistrial or it is otherwise required by the "ends of public justice," a declaration of mistrial over defendant's objection does not preclude a second trial.

A

We hold that under the circumstances of this case, the trial judge's action in declaring a mistrial was a rational determination designed to implement a legitimate state policy, with no suggestion that the policy was manipulated to respondent's prejudice. Here, the delay to the defendant was minimal. The mistrial was the only way under Illinois law that the defect in the indictment could be cured. We cannot say that the decision was not required by "manifest necessity" or the "ends of public justice." Of course, the decision to afford a trial after jeopardy has attached should not be taken lightly. The defendant has an interest in being tried by the first jury impaneled. But here, when the declaration of a mistrial implements a reasonable state policy and a verdict would have likely been upset, the defendant's interest in proceeding to a verdict is outweighed by the legitimate demand for public justice. Thus, the declaration of a mistrial is required by "manifest necessity" and the "ends of public justice," and the Double Jeopardy Clause of the Fifth Amendment as made applicable to the States by the 14th Amendment did not bar the respondent's retrial.

C

No. Where there is a "manifest necessity" for the mistrial or it is otherwise required by the "ends of public justice," a declaration of mistrial over defendant's objection does not preclude a second trial. Defendant's conviction is sustained.

Blockburger v. United States

284 U.S. 299 (1932)

FACTS

The petitioner was charged with violating provisions of the Harrison Narcotic Act. The indictment contained five counts. The court sentenced petitioner to five years' imprisonment and a fine of $2,000 upon each count, the terms of imprisonment to run consecutively; and this judgment was affirmed on appeal. The principal contentions here made by petitioner are as follows: (1) That, upon the facts, the two sales charged in the second and third counts as having been made to the same person constitute a single offense; and (2) that the sale charged in the third count as having been made not from the original stamped package, and the same sale charged in the fifth count as having been made not in pursuance of a written order of the purchaser, constitute but one offense, for which only a single penalty lawfully may be imposed.

I Did the defendant's two illegal drug sales to the same purchaser over a short period of time constitute a continuing offense for which only one penalty could be imposed?

R The defendant's two illegal drug sales to the same purchaser over a short period of time do not constitute a continuing offense for which only one penalty could be imposed.

A The sales charged in the second and third counts, although made to the same person, were distinct and separate sales made at different times. It appears from the evidence that, shortly after delivery of the drug which was the subject of the first sale, the purchaser paid for an additional quantity, which was delivered the next day. But the first sale had been consummated, and the payment for the additional drug, however closely following, was the initiation of a separate and distinct sale completed by its delivery. Section 1 of the Narcotic Act creates the offense of selling any of the forbidden drugs except in or from the original stamped package; and section 2 creates the offense of selling any of such drugs not in pursuance of a written order of the person to whom the drug is sold. Thus, upon the face of the statute, two distinct offenses are created. Here there was but one sale, and the question is whether, both sections being violated by the same act, the accused committed two offenses or only one. Each of the offenses created requires proof of a different element. The applicable rule is that, where the same act or transaction constitutes a violation of two distinct statutory provisions, the test to be applied to determine whether there are two offenses or only one is whether each provision requires proof of an additional fact which the other does not. It is not necessary to discuss the additional assignments of error in respect of cross-examination, admission of testimony, statements made by the district attorney to the jury claimed to be prejudicial, and instructions of the court. These matters were properly disposed of by the court below. The plain meaning of the provision is that each offense is subject to the penalty prescribed; and, if that be too harsh, the remedy must be afforded by act of Congress, not by judicial legislation under the guise of construction. Under the circumstances, so far as disclosed, it is true that the imposition of the full penalty of fine and imprisonment upon each count seems unduly severe; but there may have been other facts and circumstances before the trial court properly influencing the extent of the punishment. In any event, the matter was one for that court, with whose judgment there is no warrant for interference on our part.

C

Judgment affirmed.

Brown v. Ohio

432 U.S. 161 (1977)

FACTS

On November 29, 1973, the petitioner, Nathaniel Brown, stole a 1965 Chevrolet from a parking lot in East Cleveland, Ohio. Nine days later, on December 8, 1973, Brown was caught driving the car in Wickliffe, Ohio. The Wickliffe police charged him with "joyriding." Brown pleaded guilty to this charge and was sentenced to 30 days in jail and a $100 fine. Upon his release from jail on January 8, 1974, Brown was returned to East Cleveland to face further charges, and on February 5 he was indicted by the Cuyahoga County grand jury. The indictment was in two counts, the first charging the theft of the car "on or about the 29th day of November 1973," in violation of Ohio Rev. Code and the second charging joyriding on the same date in violation of 4549.04 (D). On March 18, 1974, at a pretrial hearing in the Cuyahoga County Court of Common Pleas, Brown pleaded guilty to the auto theft charge on the understanding that the court would consider his claim of former jeopardy on a motion to withdraw the plea. Upon submission of the motion, the court overruled Brown's double jeopardy objections. The court sentenced Brown to six months in jail but suspended the sentence and placed Brown on probation for one year. The Ohio Court of Appeals affirmed. It held that under Ohio law the misdemeanor of joyriding was included in the felony of auto theft. The Ohio Supreme Court denied leave to appeal. The U.S. Supreme Court granted certiorari to consider Brown's double jeopardy claim.

I

Does the Double Jeopardy Clause of the Fifth Amendment bar prosecution and punishment for the crime of stealing an automobile following prosecution and punishment for the lesser included offense of operating the same vehicle without the owner's consent?

R

The Double Jeopardy Clause of the Fifth Amendment precludes prosecution and punishment for the crime of stealing an automobile following prosecution and punishment for the lesser included offense of operating the same vehicle without the owner's consent.

A

The Double Jeopardy Clause of the Fifth Amendment, applied to the States through the Fourteenth, held to bar prosecution and punishment for the crime of stealing an automobile following prosecution and punishment for the lesser included offense of operating the same vehicle without the owner's consent. "[W]here the same act or transaction constitutes a violation of two distinct statutory provisions, the test to be applied to determine whether there are two offenses or only one, is whether each provision requires proof of a fact which the other does not," *Blockburger v. United* States. In line with that test, the Double Jeopardy Clause generally forbids successive prosecution and cumulative punishment for a greater and lesser included offense. Here, though the Ohio Court of Appeals properly held that under state law joyriding (taking or operating a vehicle without the owner's consent) and auto theft (joyriding with the intent permanently to deprive the owner of possession) constitute "the same statutory offense" within the meaning of the Double Jeopardy Clause, it erroneously concluded that petitioner could be convicted of both crimes because the charges against him had focused on different parts of the 9-day interval between petitioner's taking of the car and his apprehension. There was still only one offense under Ohio law, and the specification of different dates in the two charges against petitioner cannot alter the fact that he was twice placed in jeopardy for the same offense in violation of the Fifth and Fourteenth Amendments.

C Reversed.

Harris v. Oklahoma

433 U.S. 682 (1977)

FACTS

A clerk in a Tulsa, Okla., grocery store was shot and killed by a companion of petitioner in the course of a robbery of the store by the two men. Petitioner was convicted of felony-murder in Oklahoma State court. The opinion of the Oklahoma Court of Criminal Appeals in this case states that "[i]n a felony murder case, the proof of the underlying felony [here robbery with firearms] is needed to prove the intent necessary for a felony murder conviction." Petitioner nevertheless was thereafter brought to trial and convicted on a separate information charging the robbery with firearms, after denial of his motion to dismiss on the ground that this prosecution violated the Double Jeopardy Clause of the Fifth Amendment because he had been already convicted of the offense in the felony-murder trial. The Oklahoma Court of Criminal Appeals affirmed.

I

Where petitioner had been convicted of felony-murder based on his companion's killing of a victim during the course of an armed robbery, does the Double Jeopardy Clause of the Fifth Amendment barred a separate prosecution of petitioner for the lesser crime of robbery with firearms?

R

Where petitioner had been convicted of felony-murder based on his companion's killing of a victim during the course of an armed robbery, the Double Jeopardy Clause of the Fifth Amendment barred a separate prosecution of petitioner for the lesser crime of robbery with firearms, since conviction of the greater crime of murder could not be had without conviction of the lesser crime.

A

Where petitioner had been convicted of felony-murder based on his companion's killing of a victim during the course of an armed robbery, the Double Jeopardy Clause of the Fifth Amendment barred a separate prosecution of petitioner for the lesser crime of robbery with firearms, since conviction of the greater crime of murder could not be had without conviction of the lesser crime. When, as here, conviction of a greater crime, murder, cannot be had without conviction of the lesser crime, robbery with firearms, the Double Jeopardy Clause bars prosecution for the lesser crime after conviction of the greater one. "[A] person [who] has been tried and convicted for a crime which has various incidents included in it, . . . cannot be a second time tried for one of those incidents without being twice put in jeopardy for the same offence," *In re Nielsen*. The motion for leave to proceed in *forma pauperis* is granted, the petition for writ of certiorari is granted, and the judgment of the Court of Criminal Appeals is reversed.

C

Reversed.

Missouri v. Hunter

459 U.S. 359 (1983)

FACTS

A Missouri statute provides that any person who commits any felony under the laws of the State through the use of a dangerous or deadly weapon is also guilty of the crime of armed criminal action punishable by imprisonment for not less than three years, which punishment shall be in addition to any punishment provided by law for the felony. Another Missouri statute provides that any person convicted of the felony of first-degree robbery by means of a dangerous and deadly weapon shall be punished by imprisonment for not less than five years. Respondent, as the result of a robbery of a supermarket in which he used a revolver, was convicted in a Missouri state court of both first-degree robbery and armed criminal action and pursuant to the statutes was sentenced to concurrent prison terms of 10 years for robbery and 15 years for armed criminal action. The Missouri Court of Appeals reversed respondent's conviction and sentence for armed criminal action on the ground that his sentence for both robbery and armed criminal action violated the protection against multiple punishments for the same offense provided by the Double Jeopardy Clause of the Fifth Amendment as made applicable to the states by the Fourteenth Amendment. The court construed the robbery and armed criminal action statutes as defining the "same offense" under the *Blockburger* test [i.e., where the same act or transaction constitutes a violation of two distinct statutes, the test for determining whether there are two offenses or only one, is whether each statute requires proof of a fact which the other does not].

I

Does the Double Jeopardy Clause prohibit a cumulative punishment when cumulative sentences imposed in a single trial?

R

With respect to cumulative sentences imposed in a single trial, a cumulative punishment may be imposed under statute in a single trial with violating the Double Jeopardy Clause.

A

Respondent's conviction and sentence for both armed criminal action and first-degree robbery in a single trial did not violate the Double Jeopardy Clause. With respect to cumulative sentences imposed in a single trial, the Double Jeopardy Clause does no more than prevent the sentencing court from prescribing greater punishment than the legislature intended. Simply because two criminal statutes may be construed to proscribe the same conduct under *Blockburger* does not mean that the Double Jeopardy Clause precludes the imposition, in a single trial, of cumulative punishments. Thus, where, as here, a legislature specifically authorizes cumulative punishment under two statutes, regardless of whether those statutes proscribe the "same" conduct under *Blockburger*, a court's task of statutory construction is at an end and the prosecution may seek and the trial court or jury may impose cumulative punishment under such statutes in a single trial.

C

Vacated and remanded.

Bartkus v. Illinois

359 U.S. 121 (1959)

FACTS

Petitioner was tried and acquitted in a Federal District Court for violation of 18 U.S.C. 2113, which makes it a crime to rob a federally insured bank. On substantially the same evidence, he was later tried and convicted in an Illinois State Court for violation of an Illinois robbery statute.

I

Does the Fifth Amendment's Double Jeopardy Clause bar the prosecution of a defendant in a state court after he had been acquitted of the same charges in federal court [issue of the "separate sovereigns"]?

R

The Fifth Amendment's Double Jeopardy Clause does not bar the prosecution of a defendant in a state court after he had been acquitted of the same charges in federal court.

A

The cooperation of federal law enforcement officers with Illinois officials did not violate the Double Jeopardy Clause of the Fifth Amendment. The Fourteenth Amendment does not impliedly extend the first eight amendments to the States. The Illinois prosecution for violation of its own penal law after a prior acquittal for a federal offense, on substantially the same evidence, did not violate the Due Process Clause of the Fourteenth Amendment. Since the new prosecution was by Illinois, and not by the Federal Government, the claim of unconstitutionality must rest upon the Due Process Clause of the Fourteenth Amendment. Prior cases in this Court relating to successive state and federal prosecutions have been concerned with the Fifth Amendment and the scope of its proscription of second prosecutions by the Federal Government, not with the Fourteenth Amendment's effect on state action. We have held from the beginning and uniformly that the Due Process Clause of the Fourteenth Amendment does not apply to the States any of the provisions of the first eight amendments as such. The relevant historical materials have been canvassed by this Court and by legal scholars. These materials demonstrate conclusively that Congress and the members of the legislatures of the ratifying States did not contemplate that the Fourteenth Amendment was a short-hand incorporation of the first eight amendments making them applicable as explicit restrictions upon the States.

C

Affirmed.

Jackson v. Virginia

443 U.S. 307 (1979)

FACTS

Petitioner was convicted of first-degree murder after a bench trial in a Virginia court, and his motion and petition in the state courts to set aside the conviction on the ground that there was insufficient evidence of premeditation, a necessary element of first-degree murder, were denied. He then brought a habeas corpus proceeding in Federal District Court, which, applying the "no evidence" standard of *Thompson v. Louisville* found the record devoid of evidence of premeditation and granted the writ. Applying the same criterion, the Court of Appeals reversed, holding that there was some evidence that petitioner had intended to kill the victim.

I

Is the "no evidence" standard the proper standard to be used in a federal habeas corpus proceeding when a claim is made that the defendant had been convicted in state court upon insufficient evidence?

R

The critical inquiry on review of the sufficiency of the evidence to support a criminal conviction is a determination as to whether the record evidence could reasonably support a finding of guilt beyond a reasonable doubt.

A

A federal habeas corpus court must consider not whether there was any evidence to support a state-court conviction, but whether there was sufficient evidence to justify a rational trier of fact to find guilt beyond a reasonable doubt. *In re Winship* presupposes as an essential of the due process guaranteed by the Fourteenth Amendment that no person shall be made to suffer the onus of a criminal conviction except upon sufficient proof - defined as evidence necessary to convince a trier of fact beyond a reasonable doubt of the existence of every element of the offense. After *In re Winship*, the critical inquiry on review of the sufficiency of the evidence to support a criminal conviction must be not simply to determine whether the jury was properly instructed on reasonable doubt, but to determine whether the record evidence could reasonably support a finding of guilt beyond a reasonable doubt. The relevant question is whether after viewing the evidence in the light most favorable to the prosecution, any rational trier of fact could have found the essential elements of the crime beyond a reasonable doubt. The Thompson "no evidence" rule is simply inadequate to protect against misapplications of the constitutional standard of reasonable doubt. In a challenge to a state conviction brought under 28 U.S.C. 2254, which requires a federal court to entertain a state prisoner's claim that he is being held in "custody in violation of the Constitution or laws or treaties of the United States," the applicant is entitled to habeas corpus relief if it is found that upon the evidence adduced at the trial no rational trier of fact could have found proof of guilt beyond a reasonable doubt. A review of the record in this case in the light most favorable to the prosecution shows that a rational factfinder could have found petitioner guilty beyond a reasonable doubt.

C

Affirmed.

Arizona v. Fulminante

489 U.S. 279 (1991)

FACTS

After respondent Fulminante's 11-year-old stepdaughter was murdered in Arizona, he left the State, was convicted of an unrelated federal crime, and was incarcerated in a federal prison in New York. There he was befriended by Anthony Sarivola, a fellow inmate who was a paid informant for the Federal Bureau of Investigation and was masquerading as an organized crime figure. When Sarivola told Fulminante that he knew Fulminante was getting tough treatment from other inmates because of a rumor that he was a child murderer, and offered him protection in exchange for the truth, Fulminante admitted that he had killed the girl and provided details about the crime. After Fulminante was released from prison, he also confessed to Sarivola's wife, whom he had never met before. Subsequently, he was indicted in Arizona for first-degree murder. The trial court denied his motion to suppress, inter alia, the confession to Sarivola, rejecting his contention that it was coerced, and thus barred by the Fifth and Fourteenth Amendments. He was convicted and sentenced to death. The State Supreme Court held that the confession was coerced and that this Court's precedent precluded the use of harmless error analysis in such a case. It remanded the case for a new trial without the use of the confession.

I

Should the harmless error test be applied in cases which involve the admission of a coerced confession?

R

The harmless error test should be applied in cases which involve the admission of a coerced confession.

A

The State Supreme Court properly concluded that Fulminante's confession was coerced. The court applied the appropriate test, totality of the circumstances, to determine the confession's voluntariness, and plainly found that Fulminante was motivated to confess by a fear of physical violence, absent protection from his friend Sarivola. The court's finding, permissible on this record, that there was a credible threat of physical violence is sufficient to support a finding of coercion. Under harmless error analysis, which the Court has determined applies to the admission of coerced confessions, the State has failed to meet its burden of establishing, beyond a reasonable doubt, that the admission of Fulminante's confession to Sarivola was harmless. THE CHIEF JUSTICE delivered the opinion of the Court with respect to Part II, concluding that the harmless error rule adopted in *Chapman v. California*, is applicable to the admission of involuntary confessions. The admission of such a confession is a "trial error," which occurs during a case's presentation to the trier of fact, and may therefore be quantitatively assessed in the context of other evidence presented in order to determine whether its admission is harmless beyond a reasonable doubt.

C

Judgment affirmed.

Teague v. Lane

489 U.S. 288 (1989)

FACTS

Petitioner Teague, a black man, was convicted in an Illinois state court of attempted murder and other offenses by an all-white jury. During jury selection, the prosecutor used all 10 of his peremptory challenges to exclude blacks. Petitioner twice unsuccessfully moved for a mistrial, arguing that he was "entitled to a jury of his peers." The prosecutor defended the challenges by stating that he was trying to achieve a balance of men and women on the jury. After an unsuccessful state-court appeal, in which he argued that the prosecutor's use of peremptory challenges denied him the right to be tried by a jury that was representative of the community, petitioner filed a habeas corpus petition in Federal District Court, repeating his fair cross section claim. He further argued that the opinions of several Justices concurring in, or dissenting from, the denial of certiorari in *McCray v. New York*, had invited a reexamination of *Swain v. Alabama*, as to what a defendant must show to establish a *prima facie* case of discrimination with respect to a peremptory challenge system. He also argued, for the first time that under *Swain,* a prosecutor could be questioned about his use of peremptory challenges once he volunteered an explanation. The District Court held that it was bound by Swain and Circuit precedent and denied relief. A panel of the Court of Appeals agreed with petitioner that the Sixth Amendment's fair cross section requirement that applied to a jury venire also applied to a petit jury, and held that he had made out a *prima facie* case of discrimination. But the Court of Appeals voted to rehear the case en banc and postponed rehearing until after this Court's decision in *Batson v. Kentucky*. Ultimately, Batson was decided and overruled that portion of Swain setting forth the evidentiary showing necessary to make out a prima facie case of racial discrimination under the Equal Protection Clause of the 14th Amendment with respect to a peremptory challenge system. Batson held that a defendant can establish such a case by showing that he is a "member of a cognizable racial group," that the prosecutor exercised "peremptory challenges to remove from the venire members of the defendant's race," and that these "facts and any other relevant circumstances raise an inference that the prosecutor used that practice to exclude the veniremen from the petit jury on account of their race." The Court of Appeals then held that petitioner could not benefit from the *Batson* rule because, in the meantime, *Allen v. Hardy* had held that *Batson* could not be applied retroactively to cases on collateral review. The Court of Appeals also held that petitioner's claim was procedurally barred and meritless, and that the fair cross section requirement was limited to the jury venire.

I Should the Sixth Amendment's fair cross section requirement extend to the petit jury (the ordinary jury for the trial of a civil or criminal action)?

R New rules of criminal procedure are not applicable to cases which have become final before the new rules are announced, unless an exception applies.

Teague v. Lane

489 U.S. 288 (1989)

A

Allen v. Hardy prevented petitioner from benefiting from the rule announced in Batson, since his conviction became final before Batson was decided. The opinions filed in McCray - which involved the question whether the Constitution prohibits the use of peremptory challenges to exclude members of a particular group from the jury, based on the prosecutor's assumption that they would be biased in favor of other members of the same group - did not destroy *Swain's* precedential effect, as petitioner urges they did, since a denial of certiorari imports no expression of opinion on the merits of the case, and, concomitantly, opinions accompanying such denial cannot have the same effect as decisions on the merits. Petitioner is procedurally barred from raising the claim that he has established a violation of the Equal Protection Clause under *Swain* and that *Swain* did not preclude an examination of the prosecutor's stated reasons for his peremptory challenges to determine the legitimacy of his motive. Since petitioner did not raise the Swain claim at trial or on direct appeal, he forfeited review of the claim in collateral proceedings in the state courts. Under *Wainwright v. Sykes*, he is barred from raising the claim in a federal habeas corpus proceeding, since he made no attempt to show cause for his default and the Illinois Appellate Court, contrary to his contention, did not address the *Swain* claim.

C

New rules of criminal procedure are not applicable to cases which have become final before the new rules are announced, unless an exception applies.

Wainwright v. Sykes

433 U.S. 72 (1977)

FACTS

During Defendant-Respondent Sykes's trial for murder, inculpatory (imputing blame) statements made by him to police officers were admitted into evidence. No challenge was made on the grounds that the respondent had not understood the warnings read to him pursuant to *Miranda v. Arizona*, nor did the trial judge *sua sponte* question their admissibility or hold a fact finding hearing. Respondent, who was convicted, did not challenge the admissibility of the statements on appeal, though later he did so, unavailingly, in a motion to vacate the conviction and in state habeas corpus petitions. He then brought this federal habeas corpus action under 28 U.S.C. §2254, asserting the inadmissibility of his statements by reason of his lack of understanding of the *Miranda* warnings. The District Court ruled that under *Jackson v. Denno*, respondent had a right to a hearing in the state court on the voluntariness of the statements, and that he had not lost that right by failing to assert his claim at trial or on appeal. The Court of Appeals agreed that respondent was entitled to a *Jackson v. Denno* hearing and ruled that respondent's failure to comply with Florida's procedural "contemporaneous objection rule" (which, except as specified, requires a defendant to make a motion to suppress evidence prior to trial) would not bar review of the suppression claim unless the right to object was deliberately bypassed for tactical reasons.

I

Should a petitioner for habeas corpus relief be barred from review when he defaulted under a state procedure, absent a showing of good cause?

R

A respondent's failure to make timely objection under the Florida contemporaneous-objection rule to the admission of his inculpatory statements, absent a showing of cause for the noncompliance and some showing of actual prejudice, bars federal habeas corpus review of his *Miranda* claim.

A

Respondent's failure to make timely objection under the Florida contemporaneous-objection rule to the admission of his inculpatory statements, absent a showing of cause for the noncompliance and some showing of actual prejudice, bars federal habeas corpus review of his *Miranda* claim. Florida's rule in unmistakable terms and with specified exceptions requires that motions to suppress be raised before trial. There is no constitutional requirement in *Jackson v. Denno*, or later cases that there be a voluntariness hearing absent some contemporaneous challenge to the use of a confession. The sweeping language set forth in *Fay v. Noia*, which would render a State's contemporaneous objection rule ineffective to bar review of underlying federal claims in federal habeas corpus proceedings absent a "knowing waiver" or a "deliberate bypass" of the right to so object, is rejected as according too little respect to the state contemporaneous objection rule. Such a rule enables the record to be made with respect to a constitutional claim when witnesses' recollections are freshest; enables the trial judge who observed the demeanor of witnesses to make the factual determinations necessary for properly deciding the federal question; and may, by forcing a trial court decision on the merits of federal constitutional contentions, contribute to the finality of criminal litigation.

Conversely, the rule of *Fay v. Noia* may encourage defense lawyers to take their chances on a verdict of not guilty in a state trial court, intending to raise their constitutional claims in a federal habeas corpus court if their initial gamble fails, and detracts from the perception of the trial of a criminal case as a decisive and portentous event. Adoption of the "cause" and "prejudice" test of Francis, while giving greater respect than did Fay to the operation of state contemporaneous-objection rules, affords an adequate guarantee that federal habeas corpus courts will not be barred from hearing claims involving an actual miscarriage of justice. The procedural history of this case and the evidence as presented at trial indicate that there exist here neither "cause" nor "prejudice" as is necessary to support federal habeas corpus review of the underlying constitutional contention.

C

Yes. Respondent's failure to make timely objection under the Florida contemporaneous-objection rule to the admission of his incriminating statements, absent a showing of cause for the noncompliance and some showing of actual prejudice, bars federal habeas corpus review of his *Miranda* claim.

Smith v. Murray

477 U.S. 527 (1986)

FACTS

Prior to petitioner's trial in a Virginia state court for murder of a woman, he was examined by a psychiatrist appointed by the court at the request of his counsel. During the examination, the psychiatrist asked petitioner both about the murder and prior incidents of deviant sexual conduct, and petitioner stated that he once tore the clothes off a girl on a school bus before deciding not to rape her. Following a jury trial, petitioner was convicted. At the sentencing phase, the prosecution called the psychiatrist to the stand, and, over the defense's objection, he described the incident on the school bus. After further evidence was presented both for the prosecution and petitioner, the jury recommended the death sentence. On appeal to the Supreme Court of Virginia, petitioner raised a number of claims but did not assign any error concerning the admission of the psychiatrist's testimony, his counsel later explaining at a post-conviction hearing that he had decided not to pursue that claim after determining that Virginia case law would not support his position at the time. The Supreme Court affirmed the conviction and sentence, not addressing any issues concerning the prosecution's use of the psychiatric testimony because under a rule of the court only errors assigned by the appellant would be considered. After exhausting state remedies, petitioner sought a writ of habeas corpus in Federal District Court, which denied the petition. The Court of Appeals affirmed.

I

Should a habeas corpus petition be dismissed when the underlying constitutional claim was not first raised in a state proceeding on direct appeal?

R

A habeas corpus petition should be dismissed when the underlying constitutional claim was not first raised in a state proceeding on direct appeal in the absence of "cause" or "prejudice."

A

Petitioner forfeited his underlying constitutional claim as to the admission of the psychiatrist's testimony by failing to press it before the Supreme Court of Virginia on direct appeal. Petitioner has not carried his burden of showing cause for his noncompliance with Virginia's rules of procedure. A deliberate, tactical decision not to pursue a particular claim is the very antithesis of the kind of circumstance that would warrant excusing a defendant's failure to adhere to a State's rules for the fair and orderly disposition of its criminal cases. Here, counsel's decision not to press the claim in question was not an error of such magnitude that it rendered his performance constitutionally deficient under the test of *Strickland v. Washington.* Nor can petitioner rely on the novelty of the claim as "cause" for noncompliance with Virginia's rules, where it appears that various forms of such a claim had been percolating in the lower courts for years at the time of petitioner's original appeal. It is clear on the record that application of the "cause and prejudice" test will not result in a "fundamental miscarriage of justice," where the alleged constitutional error neither precluded the development of true facts nor resulted in the admission of false ones. Thus, even assuming that, as a legal matter, the psychiatrist's testimony should not have been presented to the jury, its admission did not pervert the jury's deliberations concerning the ultimate question of whether in fact petitioner constituted a continuing threat to society.

C

Affirmed.